The MOST DANGEROUS SUPERSTITION

Larken Rose

TABLE OF CONTENTS

This book, and other works by Larken Rose, are available at **www.LarkenRose.com**

DEDICATION

This book is dedicated to two people:
the first person who, because of reading this book,
disobeys an order to harm someone else, and
the person who, as a result, is not harmed.

What you read in this book will, in all likelihood, go directly against what you have been taught by your parents and your teachers, what you have been told by the churches, the media and the government, and much of what you, your family and your friends have always believed. Nonetheless, it is the truth, as you will see if you allow yourself to consider the issue objectively. Not only is it the truth, it also may be the most important truth you will ever hear.

More and more people are discovering this truth, but to do so, it is necessary to look past many preconceived assumptions and deeply ingrained superstitions, to set aside one's life-long indoctrination, and to examine some new ideas fairly and honestly. If you do this, you will experience a dramatic change in how you view the world. It will almost certainly feel uncomfortable at first, but in the long run it will be well worth the effort. And if enough people choose to see this truth, and embrace it, not only will it drastically change the way those people see the world; it will drastically change the world itself, for the better.

But if such a simple truth could change the world, wouldn't we all already know about it, and wouldn't we have put it into practice long ago? If humans were purely a race of thinking, objective beings, yes. But history shows that most human beings would literally rather die than objectively reconsider the belief systems they were brought up in. The average man who reads in the newspaper about war, oppression and injustice will wonder why such pain and suffering exists, and will wish for it to end. However, if it is suggested to him that his *own* beliefs are contributing to the misery, he will almost certainly dismiss such a suggestion without a second thought, and may even attack the one making the suggestion.

So, reader, if your beliefs and superstitions — many of which you did not choose for yourself, but merely inherited as unquestioned "hand-me-down" beliefs — matter to you more than truth and justice, then please stop reading now and give this book to someone else. If, on the other hand, you are willing to question some of your long-held, preconceived notions if doing so might reduce the suffering of others, then read this book. And *then* give it to someone else.

Part I

The Most Dangerous Superstition

✴ ## *Starting with the Punch Line*

How many millions have gazed upon the brutal horrors of history, with its countless examples of man's inhumanity to man, and wondered aloud how such things could happen? The truth is, most people wouldn't want to know how it happens, because they themselves are religiously attached to the very belief that makes it possible. The vast majority of suffering and injustice in the world, today and spanning back thousands of years, can be directly attributed to a single *idea*. It is not greed or hatred, or any of the other emotions or ideas that are usually blamed for the evils of society. Instead, most of the violence, theft, assault and murder in the world is the result of a mere *superstition* — a belief which, though almost universally held, runs contrary to all evidence and reason (though, of course, those who hold the belief do not see it that way). The "punch line" of this book is easy to express, albeit difficult for most people to accept, or even to calmly and rationally contemplate:

The belief in "authority," which includes all belief in "government," is irrational and self-contradictory; it is contrary to civilization and morality, and constitutes the most dangerous, destructive superstition that has ever existed. Rather than being a force for order and justice, the belief in "authority" is the arch-enemy of humanity.

2

Of course, nearly everyone is raised to believe the exact opposite: that obedience to "authority" is a virtue (at least in most cases), that respecting and complying with the "laws" of "government" is what makes us civilized, and that disrespect for "authority" leads only to chaos and violence. In fact, people have been so thoroughly trained to associate obedience with "being good" that attacking the concept of "authority" will sound, to most people, like suggesting that there is no such thing as right and wrong, no need to abide by any standards of behavior, no need to have any morals at all. That is *not* what is being advocated here—quite the opposite.

Indeed, the reason the myth of "authority" needs to be demolished is precisely because there *is* such a thing as right and wrong, it *does* matter how people treat each other, and people *should* always strive to live moral lives. Despite the constant authoritarian propaganda claiming otherwise, having respect for "authority" and having respect for humanity are mutually exclusive and diametrically opposed. The reason to have no respect for the myth of "authority" is so that we *can* have respect for humanity and justice.

There is a harsh contrast between what we are taught is the purpose of "authority" (to create a peaceful, civilized society) and the real-world *results* of "authority" in action. Flip through any history book and you will see that most of the injustice and destruction that has occurred throughout the world was not the result of people "breaking the law," but rather the result of people *obeying* and *enforcing* the "laws" of various "governments." The evils that have been committed in spite of "authority" are trivial compared to the evils that have been committed *in the name* of "authority."

Nevertheless, children are still taught that peace and justice come from authoritarian control and that, despite the flagrant evils committed by authoritarian regimes around the world throughout history, they are still morally obligated to respect and obey the current "government" of their own country. They are taught that "doing as you're told" is synonymous with being a good person, and that "playing by the rules" is synonymous with doing the right thing. On the contrary, being a moral person requires taking on the personal responsibility of judging right from wrong and following one's own conscience, the opposite of respecting and obeying "authority."

The reason it is so important that people understand this fact is that the primary danger posed by the myth of "authority" is to be found *not* in the minds of the controllers in "government" but in the minds of those *being controlled*. One nasty individual who loves to dominate others is a trivial threat to humanity unless a lot of other people view such domination as legitimate because it is achieved via the "laws" of "government." The twisted mind of Adolf Hitler, by itself, posed little or no threat to humanity. It was the millions of people who viewed Hitler as "authority," and thus felt obligated to obey his commands and carry out his orders, who actually caused the damage done by the Third Reich. In other words, the problem is not that *evil* people believe in "authority"; the problem is that basically *good* people believe in "authority," and as a result, end up advocating and even committing acts of aggression, injustice and oppression, even murder.

The average statist (one who believes in "government"), while lamenting all the ways in which "authority" has been used as a tool for evil, even in his own country, will still insist that it is possible for "government" to be a force for good, and will still imagine that "authority" can and must provide the path to peace and justice.

People falsely assume that many of the useful and legitimate things that benefit human society require the existence of "government." It is good, for example, for people to organize for mutual defense, to work together to achieve common goals, to find ways to cooperate and get along peacefully, to come up with agreements and plans that better allow human beings to exist and thrive in a mutually beneficial and non-violent state of civilization. But that is *not* what "government" is. Despite the fact that "governments" always claim to be acting on behalf of the people and the common good, the truth is that "government," by its very nature, is always in direct opposition to the interests of mankind. "Authority" is not a noble idea that some-times goes wrong, nor is it a basically valid concept that is sometimes corrupted. From top to bottom, from start to finish, the very *concept* of "authority" itself is anti-human and horribly destructive.

Of course, most people will find such an assertion hard to swallow. Isn't government an essential part of human society? Isn't it the mechanism by which civilization is made possible, because it forces us imperfect humans to behave in an orderly, peaceful manner? Isn't the enacting of common rules and laws what allows us to get along, to settle disputes in a civilized manner, and to trade and otherwise interact in a fair, non-violent way? Haven't we always heard that if not for the "rule of law" and a common respect for "authority," we would be no better than a bunch of stupid, violent beasts, living in a state of perpetual conflict and chaos?

Yes, we have been told that. And no, none of it is true. But trying to disentangle our minds from age-old lies, trying to distill the truth out of a jungle of deeply entrenched falsehoods, can be exceedingly difficult, not to mention uncomfortable.

Overview

In the following pages the reader will be taken through several stages, in order to fully understand why the belief in "authority" truly is the most dangerous superstition in the history of the world. First, the concept of "authority" will be distilled down to its most basic essence, so it can be defined and examined objectively.

In Part II, it will be shown that *the concept itself* is fatally flawed, that the underlying premise of all "government" is utterly incompatible with logic and morality. In fact, it will be shown that "government" is a purely *religious* belief—a faith-based acceptance of a superhuman, mythological entity that has never existed and will never exist. (The reader is not expected to accept such a startling claim without ample evidence and sound reasoning, which will be provided.)

In Part III, it will be shown why the belief in "authority," including all belief in "government," is horrendously dangerous and destructive. Specifically, it will be shown how the belief in "authority" dramatically impacts both the *perceptions* and the *actions* of various categories of people, leading literally billions of otherwise good, peaceful people to condone or commit acts of violent, immoral aggression. In fact, everyone who believes in "government" does this, though the vast majority do not realize it, and would vehemently deny it.

Finally, in Part IV, the reader will be given a glimpse into what life *without* the belief in "authority" could look like. Contrary to the usual assumption that an absence of "government" would mean chaos and destruction, it will be shown that when the myth of "authority" is abandoned, much will change, but much will also stay the same. It will be shown why, rather than the belief in "government" being conducive to and necessary for a peaceful society, as nearly everyone has been taught, the belief is by far the biggest *obstacle* to mutually beneficial organization, cooperation, and peaceful coexistence. In short, it will be shown why true civilization can and will exist only after the myth of "authority" has been eradicated.

From early childhood we are taught to submit to the will of "authority," to obey the edicts of those who, in one way or another, have acquired positions of power and control. From the beginning, the goodness of a child is graded, whether explicitly or implicitly, first by how well he obeys his parents, then by how well he obeys his teachers, and then by how well he obeys the "laws" of "government." Whether implied or stated, society is saturated with the message that obedience is a virtue, and that the good people are the ones who do what "authority" tells them to do. As a result of that message, the concepts of morality and obedience have become so muddled in most people's minds that any attack on the notion of "authority" will, to most people, feel like an attack on morality itself. Any suggestion that "government" is inherently illegitimate will sound like suggesting that everyone should behave as uncaring, vicious animals, living life by the code of survival of the fittest.

The trouble is that the average person's belief system rests upon a hodgepodge of vague, often contradictory, concepts and assumptions. Terms such as morality and crime, law and legislation, leaders and citizens, are often used by people who have never rationally examined such concepts. To understand the nature of "authority" and "government," we must begin by precisely defining what those terms mean.

What is this thing we call "government"? It is an organization that tells people what to do. But that alone does not provide a complete definition, because all sorts of other individuals and organizations that we do not call "government" also tell people what to do. "Government," however, does not simply suggest or request; it commands. Then again, advertisers and preachers could also be said to give commands, but they are not considered "government." Unlike the "commands" of preachers and advertisers, the commands of "government" are backed by the threat of punishment, the use of force against those who do not comply. But even that does not give us a complete definition, because street thugs and bullies also enforce their commands, but no one refers to them as "government."

The distinguishing feature of "government" is that it is thought to have the moral *right* to give and enforce commands. Its commands are called "laws," and disobeying its commands is called "crime." In short, the defining factor which makes something "government" is the perceived legitimacy and righteousness of the power and control it exerts over others--in other words, its "authority."

"Authority" can be summed up as *the right to rule*. It is not merely the *ability* to forcibly control others, which to some extent nearly everyone possesses. It is the supposed moral *right* to forcibly control others. What distinguishes a street gang from "government" is how they are perceived by the people they control. The trespasses, robbery, extortion, assault and murder committed by common thugs are perceived by almost everyone as being immoral, unjustified, and criminal. Their victims may comply with their demands, but not out of any feeling of moral obligation to obey, merely out of fear. If the intended victims of the street gang thought they could resist without any danger to themselves, they would do so, without the slightest feeling of guilt. They do not perceive the street thug to be any sort of legitimate, rightful ruler; they do not imagine him to be "authority." The loot the thug collects is not referred to as "taxes," and his threats are not called "laws."

The commands issued by those who wear the label of "government," on the other hand, are perceived very differently by most of those at whom the commands are aimed. Most people perceive the power and control which the "lawmakers" in "government" exert over everyone else to be valid and legitimate, "legal" and good. Most who comply with such commands by "obeying the law," and who surrender their money by "paying taxes," do not do so merely out of fear of punishment if they disobey, but also out of a feeling of *duty* to obey. No one takes pride in being robbed by a street gang, but many wear the label of "law-abiding taxpayer" as a badge of honor. This is due entirely to how the obedient perceive the ones giving them commands. If the controllers are perceived as "authority," then by definition they are seen as having the moral right to give such commands, which in turn implies a moral obligation on the part of the people to obey those commands. To label oneself a "law-abiding taxpayer" is to *brag* about one's loyal obedience to "government."

In the past, some churches have claimed the right to punish heretics and other sinners, but in the Western world today, the concept of "authority" is almost always linked to "government." In fact, in this day and age, each term implies the other: "authority" supposedly derives from the decrees ("laws") of "government," and "government" is the organization imagined to have the right to rule, i.e., "authority."

It is essential to differentiate between a command being justified based upon the *situation* and being justified based upon *who gave* the command. Only the latter is the type of "authority" being addressed in this book, though the term is occasionally used in another sense which tends to muddle this distinction. When, for example, someone asserts that he had the "authority" to stop a mugger to get an old lady's purse back, or says he had the "authority" to chase trespassers off his property, he is not claiming to possesses any special rights that others do not possess. He is simply saying that he believes that certain *situations* justify giving orders or using force.

In contrast, the concept of "government" is about *certain people* having some special right to rule. And that idea, the notion that some people — as a result of elections or other political rituals, for example — have the moral right to control others, in situations where most people would not, is the concept being addressed here. Only those in "government" are thought to have the right to enact "laws"; only they are thought to have the right to impose "taxes"; only they are thought to have the right to wage wars, to regulate certain matters, to grant licenses for various activities, and so on. When "the belief in authority" is discussed in this book, that is the meaning being referred to: the idea that some people have the moral right to forcibly control others, and that, consequently, those others have the moral obligation to obey.

It should be stressed that "authority" is always in the eye of the beholder. If the one being controlled believes that the one controlling him has the right to do so, then the one being controlled sees the controller as "authority." If the one being controlled does not perceive the control to be legitimate, then the controller is not viewed as "authority" but is seen simply as a bully or a thug. The tentacles of the belief in "authority" reach into every aspect of human life, but the common denominator is always the *perceived legitimacy* of the control it exerts over others. Every "law" and "tax" (federal, state and local), every election and campaign, every license and permit, every political debate and movement — in short, everything having to do with "government," from a trivial town ordinance to a "world war" — rests entirely upon the idea that some people have acquired the moral right — in one way or another, to one degree or another — to rule over others.

The issue here is not just the misuse of "authority" or an argument about "good government" versus "bad government," but an examination of the fundamental, underlying concept of "authority." Whether an "authority" is seen as absolute or as having conditions or limits upon it may have a bearing on how much damage that "authority" does, but it has no bearing on whether the underlying concept is rational. The U.S. Constitution, for example, is imagined to have created an "authority" which, at least in theory, had a severely restricted right to rule. Nonetheless, it still sought to create an "authority" with the right to do things (e.g., "tax" and "regulate") which the average citizen has no right to do on his own. Though it pretended to give the right to rule only over certain specific matters, it still claimed to bestow some "authority" upon a ruling class, and as such, is just as much a target of the following criticism of "authority" as the "authority" of a supreme dictator would be.

(The term "authority" is sometimes used in ways that have nothing to do with the topic of this book. For example, one who is an expert in some field is often referred to as an "authority." Likewise, some relationships resemble "authority" but do not involve any right to rule. The employer-employee relationship is often viewed as if there is a "boss" and an "underling." However, no matter how domineering or over-bearing an employer may be, he cannot conscript workers, or imprison them for disobedience. The only power he really has is the power to terminate the arrange-ment by firing the employee. And the employee has the same power, because he can quit. The same is true of other relationships that may resemble "authority," such as a craftsman and his apprentice, a martial arts sensei and his pupil, or a trainer and the athlete he trains. Such scenarios involve arrangements based upon mutual, voluntary agreement, in which either side is free to opt out of the arrangement. Such a relationship, where one person voluntarily allows another to direct his actions in the hopes that he will benefit from the other's knowledge or skill, is not the type of "authority" that is the subject of this book.)

No Such Thing ✹

Most people believe that "government" is necessary, though they also acknowledge that "authority" often leads to corruption and abuse. They know that "government" can be inefficient, unfair, unreasonable and oppressive, but they still believe that "authority" can be a force for good. What they fail to realize is that the problem is not just that "government" produces inferior results, or that "authority" is often abused. The problem is that the *concept itself* is utterly irrational and self-contradictory. It is nothing but a superstition, devoid of any logical or evidentiary support, which people hold only as a result of constant cult-like indoctrination designed to hide the logical absurdity of the concept. It is not a matter of degree, or how it is used; the truth is that "authority" *does not and cannot exist at all*, and failure to recognize that fact has led billions of people to believe things and do things that are horrendously destructive. There can be no such thing as good "authority" — in fact, there is no such thing as "authority" *at all*. As strange as that may sound, it can easily be proven.

In short, <u>government does not exist</u>. It never has and it never will. The politicians are real, the soldiers and police who enforce the politicians' will are real, the buildings they inhabit are real, the weapons they wield are very real, but their supposed "authority" is not. And without that "authority," without the *right* to do what they do, they are nothing but a gang of thugs. The term "government" implies *legitimacy* — it means the exercise of "authority" over a certain people or place. The way people speak of those in power, calling their commands "laws," referring to disobedience to them as a "crime," and so on, implies the right of "government" to rule, and a corresponding obligation on the part of its subjects to obey. Without the *right* to rule ("authority"), there is no reason to call the entity "government," and all of the politicians and their mercenaries become utterly indistinguishable from a giant organized crime syndicate, their "laws" no more valid than the threats of muggers and carjackers. And that, in reality, is what every "government" is: an illegitimate gang of thugs, thieves and murderers, masquerading as a rightful ruling body.

(The reason the terms "government" and "authority" appear inside quotation marks throughout this book is because there is never a legitimate right to rule, so government and authority never actually exist. In this book such terms refer only to the people and gangs erroneously *imagined* to have the right to rule.)

All mainstream political discussion — all debate about what should be "legal" and "illegal," who should be put into power, what "national policy" should be, how "government" should handle various issues — all of it is utterly irrational and a complete waste of time, as it is all based upon the false premise that one person can have the right to rule another, that "authority" can even exist. The entire debate about how "authority" should be used, and what "government" should do, is exactly as useful as debating how Santa Claus should handle Christmas. But it is infinitely more dangerous. On the bright side, removing that danger — the biggest threat that humanity has ever faced, in fact — does not require changing the fundamental nature of man, or converting all hatred to love, or performing any other drastic alteration to the state of the universe. Instead, it requires only that people recognize and then let go of one particular superstition, one irrational lie that almost everyone has been taught to believe. In one sense, most of the world's problems could be solved overnight if everyone did something akin to giving up the belief in Santa Claus.

Any idea or proposed solution to a problem that depends upon the existence of "government," and that includes absolutely everything within the realm of politics, is inherently invalid. To use an analogy, two people could engage in a useful, rational discussion about whether nuclear power or hydroelectric dams are the better way to produce electricity for their town. But if someone suggested that a better option would be to generate electricity using magic pixie dust, his comments would be and should be dismissed as ridiculous, because real problems cannot be solved by mythical entities. Yet almost all modern discussion of societal problems is nothing but an argument about which type of magic pixie dust will save humanity. All political discussion rests upon an unquestioned but false assumption, which everyone takes on faith simply because they see and hear everyone else repeating the myth: the notion that there can be such a thing as legitimate "government."

The problem with popular misconceptions is just that: they are popular. When any belief—even the most ridiculous, illogical belief—is held by most people, it will not feel unreasonable to the believers. Continuing in the belief will feel easy and safe, while questioning it will be uncomfortable and very difficult, if not impossible. Even abundant evidence of the horrendously destructive power of the myth of "authority," on a nearly incomprehensible level and stretching back for thousands of years, has not been enough to make more than a handful of people even begin to question the fundamental concept. And so, believing themselves to be enlightened and wise, human beings continue to stumble into one colossal disaster after another, as a result of their inability to shake off *the most dangerous superstition*: the belief in "authority."

Offshoots of the Superstition ✸

There is a large collection of terminology that grows out of the concept of "authority." What all such terms have in common is that they imply a certain legitimacy to one group of people forcibly controlling another group. Here are just a few examples:

"Government": As mentioned before, "government" is simply the term for the organization or group of people imagined to possess the right to rule. Many other terms, describing parts of "government" (such as "president," "congressman," "judge," and "legislature") reinforce the supposed legitimacy of the ruling class.

"Law": The terms "law" and "legislation" have very different connotations from the words "threat" and "command." The difference, again, depends upon whether the ones issuing and imposing such "laws" are imagined to have the *right* to do so. If a street gang issues commands to everyone in its neighborhood, no one calls such commands "laws." But if "government" issues commands through the "legislative" process, nearly everyone calls them "laws." In truth, every authoritarian "law" is a command backed by the threat of retaliation against those who do not comply. Whether it is a "law" against committing murder or against building a deck without a building permit, it is neither a suggestion nor a request, but a command, backed by the threat of violence, whether in the form of forced confiscation of property (i.e., fines) or the kidnapping of a human being (i.e., imprisonment). What might be called "extortion" if done by the average citizen is called "taxation" when done by people who are imagined to have the right to rule. What would normally be seen as harassment, assault, kidnapping, and other offenses are seen as "regulation" and "law enforcement" when carried out by those claiming to represent "authority."

Of course, using the term "law" to describe the inherent properties of the universe, such as the *laws* of physics and mathematics, has nothing to do with the concept of "authority." Furthermore, there is another concept, called "natural law," which is very different from statutory "law" (i.e., "legislation"). The concept of natural law is that there are standards of right and wrong intrinsic to humanity that do not depend upon any human "authority," and that in fact supersede all human "authority." Though that concept was the topic of many discussions in the not-too-distant past, it is rare to hear Americans using the term "law" in such a context today, and that concept is not what is meant by "law" in this book.

"Crime": A derivative of the concept of "law" is the concept of "crime." The phrase "committing a crime" obviously has a negative connotation. The notion that "breaking the law" is morally wrong implies that the command being disobeyed is inherently legitimate, based solely upon who gave the command. If a street gang tells a store owner, "Give us half of your profits or we will hurt you," no one would consider the store owner a "criminal" if he resisted such extortion. But if the same demand is made by those wearing the label of "government," with the demand being called "law" and "taxes," then that very same store owner would be viewed, by almost everyone, as a "criminal" if he refused to comply.

The terms "crime" and "criminal" do not, by themselves, even hint at *what* "law" is being disobeyed. It is a "crime" to slowly drive through a red light at an empty intersection, and it is a "crime" to murder one's neighbors. A hundred years ago it was a "crime" to teach a slave to read; in 1940s Germany it was a "crime" to hide Jews from the SS. In Pennsylvania, it is a "crime" to sleep in or on top of a refrigerator outside. Literally, committing a "crime" means disobeying the commands of politicians, and a "criminal" is anyone who does so. Again, such terms have an obviously negative connotation. Most people do not want to be called a "criminal," and they mean it as an insult if they call someone else a "criminal." Again, this implies that the "authority" issuing and enforcing the "laws" has the *right* to do so.

"Lawmakers": There is a strange paradox involved in the concept of "lawmakers," in that they are perceived to have the right to give commands, impose "taxes," regulate behavior, and otherwise coercively control people, but only if they do so via the "legislative" process. The people in "government" legislatures are seen as having the right to rule, but *only* if they exert their supposed "authority" by way of certain accepted political rituals. When they do, the "lawmakers" are then imagined to have the exclusive right to give commands and hire people to enforce them—a right no other individuals possess. To put it another way, the general public honestly imagines that morality is *different* for "lawmakers" than it is for everyone else. Demanding money under threat of violence is immoral theft when most people do it, but is seen as "taxation" when politicians do it. Bossing people around and forcibly controlling their actions is seen as harassment, intimidation and assault when most people do it, but is seen as "regulation" and "law enforcement" when politicians do it. They are called "lawmakers," rather than "threat-makers," because their commands—if done via certain "legislative" procedures—are seen as inherently legitimate. In other words, they are seen as "authority," and obedience to their legislative commands is seen as a moral imperative.

"Law Enforcement": One of the most common examples of "authority," which many people see on a daily basis, wears the label of "police" or "law enforcement." The behavior of "law enforcers," and the way they are regarded and treated by others, shows quite plainly that they are viewed *not* simply as people, but as representatives of the entity called "authority," to which very different standards of morality are believed to apply.

Suppose, for example, someone was driving a car without wearing a seat belt. If another average citizen noticed that, and forced the driver to stop and demanded a large sum of money from him, the driver would be outraged. It would be viewed as extortion, harassment, and possibly assault and kidnapping. But when one claiming to act on behalf of "government" does the exact same thing, by flashing his lights (and chasing the person down if he doesn't stop) and then issuing a "ticket," such actions are viewed by most as being perfectly legitimate.

In a very real sense, the people who wear badges and uniforms are not viewed as mere people by everyone else. They are viewed as the arm of an abstract thing called "authority." As a result, the properness of "police officer" behavior and the righteousness of their actions are measured by a far different standard than is the behavior of everyone else. They are judged by how well they enforce "the law" rather than by whether their individual actions conform to the normal standards of right and wrong that apply to everyone else. The difference is voiced by the "law enforcers" themselves, who often defend their actions by saying things such as "I don't make the law, I just enforce it." Clearly, they expect to be judged only by how faithfully they carry out the will of the "lawmakers," rather than by whether they behave like civilized, rational human beings.

"Countries" and "Nations": The concepts of "law" and "crime" are obvious offshoots of the concepts of "government" and "authority," but many other words in the English language are either changed by the belief in "authority" or exist entirely because of that belief. A "country" or "nation," for example, is a purely political concept. The line around a "country" is, by definition, the line defining the area over which one particular "authority" claims the right to rule, which distinguishes that location from the areas over which *other* "authorities" claim the right to rule.

Geographical locations are, of course, very real, but the term "country" does not refer only to a place. It always refers to a political "jurisdiction" (another term stemming from the belief in "authority"). When people speak of loving their country, they are rarely capable of even defining what that means, but ultimately, the only thing the word "country" can mean is not the place, or the people, or any abstract principle or concept, but merely the turf a certain gang claims the right to rule. In light of that fact, the concept of loving one's country is a rather strange idea; it expresses little more than a psychological attachment to the other subjects who are controlled by the same ruling class — which is not at all what most people envision when they feel national loyalty and patriotism. People may feel love for a certain culture, or a certain location and the people who live there, or to some philosophical ideal, and mistake that for love of country, but ultimately, a "country" is simply the area that a particular "government" claims the right to rule. That is what defines the borders, and it is those borders which define the "country."

Attempting to Rationalize the Irrational ✸

People who consider themselves educated, open-minded and progressive do not want to think of themselves as the slaves of a master, or even the subjects of a ruling class. Because of this, much rationalizing and obfuscating has been done in an attempt to deny the fundamental nature of "government" as a ruling class. A lot of verbal gymnastics, misleading terminology and mythology have been manufactured to try to obscure the true relationship between "governments" and their subjects. This mythology is taught to children as "civics," even though most of it is completely illogical and flies in the face of all evidence. The following covers a few of the popular types of propaganda used to obfuscate the nature of "authority."

The Myth of Consent ✸

In the modern world, slavery is almost universally condemned. But the relationship of a perceived "authority" to his subject is very much the relationship of a slave master (owner) to a slave (property). Not wanting to admit that, and not wanting to condone what amounts to slavery, those who believe in "authority" are trained to memorize and repeat blatantly inaccurate rhetoric designed to hide the true nature of the situation. One example of this is the phrase "consent of the governed."

There are two basic ways in which people can interact: by mutual agreement, or by one person using threats or violence to force his will upon another. The first can be labeled "consent" — both sides willingly and voluntarily agreeing to what is to be done. The second can be labeled "governing" — one person controlling another. Since these two — consent and governing — are opposites, the concept of "consent of the governed" is a contradiction. If there is mutual consent, it is not "government"; if there is governing, there is no consent. Some will claim that a majority, or the people as a whole, have given their consent to be ruled, even if many individuals have not. But such an argument turns the concept of consent on its head. No one, individually or as a group, can give consent for something to be done to someone *else*. That is simply not what "consent" means. It defies logic to say, "I give *my* consent for *you* to be robbed." Yet that is the basis of the cult of "democracy": the notion that a majority can give consent on behalf of a minority. That is not "consent of the governed"; it is forcible control of the governed, with the "consent" of a third party.

Even if someone were silly enough to actually tell someone else, "I agree to let you forcibly control me," the moment the controller must force the "controllee" to do something, there is obviously no longer "consent." Prior to that moment, there is no "governing" — only voluntary cooperation. Expressing the concept more precisely exposes its inherent schizophrenia: "I agree to let you force things upon me, whether I agree to them or not."

But in reality, no one ever agrees to let those in "government" do whatever they want. So, in order to fabricate "consent" where there is none, believers in "authority" add another, even more bizarre, step to the mythology: the notion of "implied consent." The claim is that, by merely living in a town, or a state, or a country, one is "agreeing" to abide by whatever rules happen to be issued by the people who claim to have the right to rule that town, state, or country. The idea is that if someone does not like the rules, he is free to leave the town, state, or country altogether, and if he chooses not to leave, that constitutes giving his consent to be controlled by the rulers of that jurisdiction.

Though it is constantly parroted as gospel, the idea defies common sense. It makes no more sense than a carjacker stopping a driver on a Sunday and telling him, "By driving a car in this neighborhood on Sunday, you are *agreeing* to give me your car." One person obviously cannot decide what counts as someone else "agreeing" to something. An agreement is when two or more people communicate a mutual willingness to enter into some arrangement. Simply being born somewhere is not agreeing to anything, nor is living in one's own house when some king or politician has declared it to be within the realm he rules. It is one thing for someone to say, "If you want to ride in my car, you may not smoke," or "You can come into my house only if you take your shoes off." It is quite another to try to tell other people what they can do on their own property. Whoever has the right to make the rules for a particular place is, by definition, the owner of that place. That is the basis of the idea of private property: that there can be an "owner" who has the exclusive right to decide what is done with and on that property. The owner of a house has the right to keep others out of it and, by extension, the right to tell visitors what they can and cannot do as long as they are in the house.

And that sheds some light on the underlying assumption behind the idea of implied consent. To tell someone that his only valid choices are either to leave the "country" or to abide by whatever commands the politicians issue logically implies that everything in the "country" is the property of the politicians. If a person can spend year after year paying for his home, or even building it himself, and his choices are still to either obey the politicians or get out, that means that his house *and* the time and effort he invested in the house are the property of the politicians. And for one person's time and effort to rightfully belong to another is the definition of slavery. That is exactly what the "implied consent" theory means: that every "country" is a huge slave plantation, and that everything and everyone there is the property of the politicians. And, of course, the master does not need the consent of his slave.

Believers in "government" never explain how it is that a few politicians could have acquired the right to unilaterally claim exclusive ownership of thousands of square miles of land, where other people were already living, as their territory, to rule and exploit as they see fit. It would be no different from a lunatic saying, "I hereby declare North America to be my rightful domain, so anyone living here has to do whatever I say. If you don't like it, you can leave."

There is also a practical problem with the "obey or get out" attitude, which is that getting out would only relocate the individual to some *other* giant slave plantation, a different "country." The end result is that everyone on earth is a slave, with the only choice being *which* master to live under. This completely rules out actual freedom. More to the point, that is not what "consent" means.

The belief that politicians own everything is demonstrated even more dramatically in the concept of immigration "laws." The idea that a human being needs permission from politicians to set foot anywhere in an entire country — the notion that it can be a "crime" for someone to step across an invisible line, from one authoritarian jurisdiction into another — implies that the entire country is the property of the ruling class. If a citizen is not allowed to hire an "illegal alien," is not allowed to trade with him, is not even allowed to invite an "illegal" into his own home, then that individual citizen owns nothing, and the politicians own everything.

Not only is the theory of "implied consent" logically flawed, but it also obviously does not describe reality. Any "government" that had the consent of its subjects would not need, and would not have, "law" *enforcers*. Enforcement happens only if someone does not consent to something. Anyone with their eyes open can see that "government," on a regular basis, does things to a lot of people against their will. To be aware of the myriad of tax collectors, beat cops, inspectors and regulators, border guards, narcotics agents, prosecutors, judges, soldiers, and all the other mercenaries of the state, and to still claim that "government" does what it does with the *consent* of the "governed," is utterly ridiculous. Each individual, if he is at all honest with himself, knows that those in power do not care whether he consents to abide by their "laws." The politicians' orders will be carried out, by brute force if necessary, with or without any individual's consent.

✳ *More Mythology*

In addition to the myth of "the consent of the governed," other political sayings and dogmatic rhetoric are often repeated, despite being completely inaccurate. For example, in the United States the people are taught — and faithfully repeat — such ideas as "We *are* the government" and "The government works for us" and "The government *represents* us." Such aphorisms are blatantly and obviously untrue, despite the fact that they are constantly parroted by rulers and subjects alike.

One of the most bizarre and delusional (but very common) claims is that "We, the people, *are* the government." Schoolchildren are taught to repeat this absurdity, even though everyone is fully aware that the politicians issue commands and demands, and everyone else either complies or is punished. In the United States there is a ruling class and a subject class, and the differences between them are many and obvious. One group commands, the other obeys. One group demands huge sums of money, the other group pays. One group tells the other group where they can live, where they can work, what they can eat, what they can drink, what they can drive, who they can work for, what work they can do, and so on. One group takes and spends trillions of dollars of what the other group earns. One group consists entirely of economic parasites, while the efforts of the other group produce all the wealth.

In this system, it is patently obvious who commands and who obeys. The people are not the "government," by any stretch of the imagination, and it requires profound denial to believe otherwise. But other myths are also used to try to make that lie sound rational. For example, it is also claimed that "the government works for us; it is our servant." Again, such a statement does not even remotely match the obvious reality of the situation; it is little more than a cult mantra, a delusion intentionally programmed into the populace in order to twist their view of reality. And most people never even question it. Most never wonder, If "government" works for us, if it is our employee, why does it decide how much we pay it? Why does our "employee" decide what it will do for us? Why does our "employee" tell us how to live our lives? Why does our "employee" demand our obedience for whatever arbitrary commands it issues, sending armed enforcers after us if we disobey? It is impossible for "government" to *ever* be the servant, because of what "government" is. To put it in simple, personal terms, if someone can boss you around and take your money, he is not your servant; and if he *cannot* do those things, he is not "government." However limited, "government" is the organization thought to have the right to forcibly control the behavior of its subjects via "laws," rendering the popularly accepted rhetoric about "public servants" completely ridiculous. To imagine that a *ruler* could ever be the *servant* of those over whom he rules is patently absurd. Yet that impossibility is spouted as indisputable gospel in "civics" classes.

An even more prevalent lie, used to try to hide the master-slave relationship between "government" and the public, is the notion of "representative government." The claim is that the people, by electing certain individuals into positions of power, are "choosing their leaders," and that those in office are merely representing the will of the people. Again, not only does this claim not at all match reality, but the underlying abstract theory is inherently flawed as well.

In the real world, so-called "representative governments" are constantly doing things their subjects do not want them to do: increasing "taxes," engaging in warmongering, selling off power and influence to whoever gives them the most money, and so on. Every taxpayer can easily think of examples of things funded with his money that he objects to, whether it be handouts to huge corporations, handouts to certain individuals, government actions that infringe on individual rights, or just the overall wasteful, corrupt, inefficient bureaucratic machine of "government." There is no one who can honestly say that "government" does everything that he wants, and nothing that he does not want.

Even in theory, the concept of "representative government" is inherently flawed, because "government" cannot possibly represent the people as a whole unless everyone wants exactly the same thing. Because different people want "government" to do different things, "government" will always be going against the will of at least some of the people. Even if a "government" did exactly what a majority of its subjects wanted (which never actually happens), it would not be serving the people as a whole; it would be forcibly victimizing smaller groups on behalf of larger groups.

Furthermore, one who represents someone else cannot have *more* rights than the one he represents. For example, if one person has no right to break into his neighbor's house and steal his valuables, then he also has no right to designate a representative to do that for him. To represent someone is to act on his behalf, and a true representative can only do what the person he represents has the right to do. But in the case of "government," the people whom the politicians claim to represent have no right to do *anything* that politicians do: impose "taxes," enact "laws," etc. Average citizens have no right to forcibly control the choices of their neighbors, tell them how to live their lives, and punish them if they disobey. So when a "government" does such things, it is not representing anyone or anything but itself.

Interestingly, even those who talk about "representative government" refuse to accept any personal responsibility for actions taken by those for whom they voted. If their candidate of choice enacts a harmful "law," or raises "taxes," or wages war, the voters never feel the same guilt or shame they would feel if they themselves had personally done such things, or had hired or instructed someone else to do such things. This fact demonstrates that even the most enthusiastic voters do not actually believe the rhetoric about "representative government," and do not view politicians as their representatives. The terminology does not match reality, and the only purpose of the rhetoric is to obfuscate the fact that the relationship between every "government" and its subjects is the same as the relationship between a master and a slave. One master may whip his slaves less severely than another; one master may allow his slaves to keep more of what they produce; one master may take better care of his slaves—but none of that changes the basic, underlying nature of the master-slave relationship. The one with the right to rule is the master; the one with the obligation to obey is the slave. And that is true even when people choose to describe the situation using inaccurate rhetoric and deceptive euphemisms, such as "representative government," "consent of the governed," and "will of the people."

The entire notion of "a government of the people, by the people, and for the people," while it makes nice feel-good political rhetoric, is a logical impossibility. A ruling class cannot serve or represent those it rules any more than a slave owner can serve or represent his slaves. The only way he could do so is by ceasing to be a slave owner, by freeing his slaves. Likewise, the only way a ruling class could become a servant of the people is by *ceasing to be* a ruling class, by relinquishing all of its power. "Government" cannot serve the people unless it ceases to be "government."

Another example of irrational statist doctrine is the concept of the "rule of law." The idea is that rule by mere *men* is bad, because it serves those with a malicious lust for power, while the "rule of law," as the theory goes, is all about objective, reasonable rules being imposed upon humanity equally. A moment's thought reveals the absurdity of this myth. Despite the fact that "the law" is often spoken of as some holy, infallible set of rules spontaneously flowing from the nature of the universe, in reality "the law" is simply a collection of commands issued and enforced by the *people* in "government." There would be a difference between "rule of law" and "rule of men" only if the so-called "laws" were written by something *other* than men.

The Secret Ingredient　✳

In their attempts to justify the existence of a ruling class ("government"), statists often describe perfectly reasonable, legitimate, useful things, and then proclaim them to be "government." They may argue, "Once people cooperate to form an organized system of mutual defense, that's government." Or they may claim, "When people collectively decide the way things like roads and commerce and property rights will work in their town, that's government." Or they may say, "When people pool their resources, to do things collectively rather than each individual having to do everything for himself, that is government." None of those statements are true.

Such assertions are intended to make "government" sound like a natural, legitimate, and useful part of human society. But all of them completely miss the fundamental nature of "government." "Government" is not organization, cooperation, or mutual agreement. Countless groups and organizations—supermarkets, football teams, car companies, archery clubs, etc.—engage in cooperative, mutually beneficial collective actions, but they are not called "government," because they are not imagined to have the right to rule. And that is the secret ingredient that makes something "authority": the supposed *right* to forcibly control others.

"Governments" do not just evolve out of supermarkets or football teams, nor do they evolve out of people preparing and providing for their mutual defense. There is a fundamental difference between "How can we effectively defend ourselves?" and "I have the right to rule you!" Contrary to what civics textbooks may claim, "governments" are not the result of either economics or basic human interaction. They do not just happen as a result of people being civilized and organized. They are entirely the product of the myth that "someone has to be in charge." Without the superstition of "authority," no amount of cooperation or organization would ever become "government." It requires a drastic change in public perception for a *service provider*, whether the service is food, shelter, information, protection, or anything else, to transform into a rightful *ruler*. A system of organization cannot magically become "government" any more than a security guard can magically become a king.

And that fact relates to another claim of statists: that doing away with "government" would simply result in violent gangs gaining power, which would, in turn, become a new "government." But violent conquest does not naturally become "government" any more than peaceful cooperation does. Unless the new gang is imagined to have the *right* to rule, it will not be seen as "government." In fact, the ability to control modern populations—especially armed populations—depends entirely upon the perceived *legitimacy* of the would-be controllers. Today, to rule any population of significant size by brute force alone would require an enormous amount of resources (weapons, spies, mercenaries, etc.), so much so that it would be nearly impossible. The specter of a gang of ruthless thugs taking over a country may make for an entertaining movie, but it cannot actually happen in a country equipped with even basic communications and firearms. The only way to control a large population today is for the would-be ruler to first convince the people that he has the moral *right* to exert control over them; he can acquire dominion only if he can first hammer the myth of "authority" into his intended victims' heads, thereby convincing his victims that he is a legitimate and proper "government." And if he can accomplish that, very little actual force will be required for him to acquire and maintain power. But if his regime ever loses legitimacy in the eyes of his victims, or if he never achieves it to begin with, brute force alone will not provide him with any lasting power.

In short, neither gangs nor cooperatives can ever become "government" unless the people believe that someone has the right to rule them. Likewise, once the people as a whole free themselves from the myth of "authority," they will not need any revolution to be free; "government" will simply cease to exist, because the only place it has ever existed is in the minds of those who believe in the superstition of "authority." Again, the politicians, and the mercenaries who carry out their threats, are very real, but without perceived *legitimacy*, they are recognized as a gang of power-happy thugs, not a "government."

It should also be mentioned that some have claimed (including Thomas Jefferson, in the Declaration of Independence) that it is possible, and desirable, to have a "government" which does nothing except protect the rights of individuals. But an organization which did only that would not be "government." Every individual has the right to defend himself and others against attackers. To exercise that right, even through a very organized, large-scale operation, would not be "government" any more than organized, large-scale food production constitutes "government." For something to be "government," it must, by definition, do something that average people do not have the right to do. A "government" with the same rights as everyone else is not a "government" any more than the average man on the street is "government."

The Excuse of Necessity   ✳

The excuse that statists (people who believe in "government") often resort to in the end is that humanity *requires* "government," that society needs rulers, that someone has to be in charge, or there would be constant chaos and bloody mayhem. But necessity, whether real or imagined, cannot make a mythical entity real. A right to rule is not going to come into existence just because we supposedly "need" it in order to have a peaceful society. No one would argue that Santa Claus must be real because we need him in order for Christmas to work. If "authority" does not and cannot exist, as will be proven below, saying that we "need" it is not only pointless but obviously untrue. We cannot conjure something into existence by sheer willpower. If you jump out of a plane without a parachute, your "need" for a parachute is not going to make one materialize. By the same token, if it is impossible for one person to acquire the right to rule over another, and impossible for one person to acquire the obligation to subjugate himself to another (as proven below), then claiming that such things "need" to happen is an empty argument.

Part II

Disproving the Myth

Letting Go of the Myth ✱

A growing number of people now believe that "government" is not necessary and that human society would, on a practical level, work a lot better without it. Others argue that regardless of which "works" better, society without a coercive state is the only moral choice, as it is the only choice that does not support the initiation of violence against innocent people. While such arguments are both valid and worthwhile, there is actually a more fundamental point that renders such discussions moot: "authority," whether moral or not, and whether it "works" or not, cannot exist. And this is not merely a statement of what *should* be, it is a description of what *is*. If "authority" cannot exist—as will be logically proven below—any debate about whether we "need" it, or how well it works on a practical level, is pointless.

Accordingly, the point of this book is not that "government" should be abolished, but that "government"—meaning a *legitimate* ruling class having "authority"—*does not and cannot exist*, and that the failure to recognize this fact has led to immeasurable suffering and injustice. Even most of those who recognize "government" as a huge threat to humanity speak of doing away with it, as if it actually exists. They speak as if there is a choice between having "government" and not having "government." There is not. "Government" is a logical impossibility. The problem is not actually "government," but the *belief* in "government." By analogy, one who realizes that Santa Claus is not real does not start a crusade to abolish Santa, or to evict him from the North Pole. He simply stops believing in him. The difference is that the belief in Santa Claus does little harm, while the belief in the mythical beast called "authority" has led to unimaginable pain and suffering, oppression and injustice.

The message here is not that we should try to create a world without "authority"; instead, the message is that it would behoove human beings to accept the fact that a world without "authority" is *all that has ever existed*, and that mankind would be far better off, and people would behave in a far more rational, moral and civilized manner, if that fact were widely understood.

✳ *Why the Myth Is Tempting*

Before demonstrating that "authority" cannot exist, brief mention should be made of why anyone would *want* such a thing to exist. It is obvious why those who seek dominion over others want "government" to exist: it gives them an easy, allegedly legitimate mechanism through which they can forcibly control others. But why would anyone else—why would those being *controlled*—want it to exist?

The mindset of statists usually starts with a reasonable concern, but ends with an insane "solution." The average person who looks out at the world, knowing there are billions of human beings out there, many of whom are stupid or hostile, naturally wants some sort of assurance that he will be protected from all the negligent and malicious things others may do. Most believers in "government" openly describe that as the reason "government" is needed: because people cannot be trusted, because it is in man's nature to steal, fight, etc. Statists often assert that without a controlling authority, without "government" making and enforcing the rules of society on everyone, every dispute would end in bloodshed, there would be little or no cooperation, trade would all but cease, it would be "every man for himself," and humanity would degrade into a caveman or "Mad Max" type of existence.

The debate between statism and anarchism (or voluntaryism) is often incorrectly assumed to be a question of whether people are inherently good and trustworthy and therefore need no controllers, or are inherently bad and untrustworthy and therefore need "government" to control them. In truth, whether humans are all good, all bad, or something in between, the belief in "authority" is still an irrational superstition. But the most popular excuse for "government"—that people are bad and need to be controlled—inadvertently exposes the lunacy inherent in all statism.

If human beings are so careless, stupid and malicious that they cannot be trusted to do the right thing on their own, how would the situation be improved by taking a *subset* of those very same careless, stupid and malicious human beings and giving them societal *permission* to forcibly control all the others? Why would anyone think that rearranging and reorganizing a group of dangerous beasts would make them civilized? The answer hints at the mythological nature of the belief in "authority." It is not merely a different arrangement of human beings that authoritarians seek, but the involvement of some *superhuman* entity, with rights that human beings do not have, and with *virtues* that human beings do not have, which can be used to keep all the untrustworthy humans in line. To say that human beings are so flawed that they need to be controlled—a common refrain among statists—implies that something *other* than human beings needs to do the controlling. But no matter how hard you study "government," you will find that it is always run entirely by *people*. Saying that "government" is necessary because *people* are untrustworthy is as irrational as saying that if someone is being attacked by a swarm of bees, the solution is to create an authoritarian hierarchy *among the bees*, assigning some of the bees the duty of preventing the *other* bees from doing harm. However dangerous the bees may be, such a "solution" is ridiculous.

What the believers really want out of "government" is a huge, unstoppable power that will be used for good. But there is no magic trick, political or otherwise, capable of guaranteeing that justice will occur, that the "good guys" will win or that the innocent will be protected and cared for. The giant, superhuman, magical savior that statists insist is needed to save humanity from itself *does not exist*. On this planet, at least, human beings are the top—there is nothing above them to control them and make them behave properly, and hallucinating such a superhuman entity does not make it real, nor does it help the situation.

The Religion of "Government"

"Government" is neither a scientific concept nor a rational sociological construct; nor is it a logical, practical method of human organization and cooperation. The belief in "government" is not based on reason; it is based on faith. In truth, the belief in "government" is a religion, made up of a set of dogmatic teachings, irrational doctrines which fly in the face of both evidence and logic, and which are methodically memorized and repeated by the faithful. Like other religions, the gospel of "government" describes a superhuman, supernatural entity, above mere mortals, which issues commandments to the peasantry, for whom unquestioning obedience is a moral imperative. Disobeying to the commandments ("breaking the law") is viewed as a sin, and the faithful delight in the punishment of the infidels and sinners ("criminals"), while at the same time taking great pride in their own loyalty and humble subservience to their god (as "law-abiding taxpayers"). And while the mortals may humbly beg their lord for favors, and for permission to do certain things, it is considered blasphemous and outrageous for one of the lowly peasants to imagine himself to be fit to decide which of the "government" god's "laws" he should follow and which it is okay for him to ignore. Their mantra is, "You can work to try to change the law, but as long as it's the law, we all have to follow it!"

The religious nature of the belief in "authority" is put on display for all to see whenever people solemnly stand, with their hands upon their hearts, and religiously proclaim their undying faith in, and loyalty to, a flag and a "government" (the "republic"). It rarely occurs to those who recite the Pledge of Allegiance, while feeling deep pride, that what they are actually doing is swearing allegiance to a system of subjugation and authoritarian control. In short, they are promising to do as they are told, and behave as loyal subjects to their masters. Aside from the patently inaccurate phrase at the end about "liberty and justice for all," the entire Pledge is about subservience to the "government" which claims to represent the collective, as if that in itself is some great and noble goal. The Pledge, and the mentality and emotions it is intended to stir up, would apply equally well to any tyrannical regime in history. It is a promise to be obedient and easily controlled, to subordinate oneself to "the republic," rather than a promise to do the right thing. Many other patriotic rituals and songs, as well as the overtly religious reverence given to two pieces of parchment – the Declaration of Independence and the U.S. Constitution – also demonstrate that people do not merely view "government" as a practical necessity; they view it as a god, to be praised and worshiped, honored and obeyed. The main factor distinguishing the belief in "government" from other religions today is that people actually believe in the god called "government." The other gods people claim to believe in, and the churches they attend, are now, by comparison, little more than empty rituals and half-heartedly parroted superstitions. When it comes to their everyday lives, the god that people actually pray to, to save them from misfortune, to smite their enemies, and to shower them with blessings, is "government." It is "government" whose commandments the people most often respect and obey.

Whenever a conflict arises between "government" and the teachings of the lesser gods – such as "pay your fair share" (taxation) versus "Thou shalt not steal," or "duty to country" (military service) versus "Thou shalt not murder" – the commands of "government" supersede all the teachings of the other religions. Politicians, the high priests of the church of "government" – the mouthpieces and representatives of "government," who deliver the sacred "law" from on high – even openly declare that it is permissible for the people to practice whatever religion they wish, as long as they do not run afoul of the supreme religion by disobeying "the law" – meaning the dictates of the god called "government."

Perhaps most telling is that if you suggest to the average person that maybe God does not exist, he will likely respond with less emotion and hostility than if you bring up the idea of life without "government." This indicates which religion people are more deeply emotionally attached to, and which religion they actually believe in more firmly. In fact, they believe so deeply in "government" that they do not even recognize it as being a belief at all. The reason so many people respond to the idea of a stateless society ("anarchy") with insults, apocalyptic predictions and emotional tantrums, rather than with calm reasoning, is because their belief in "government" is not the result of careful, rational consideration of evidence and logic. It is, in every way, a religious faith, believed only because of prolonged indoctrination. And there is almost nothing which state-worshipers find more existentially terrifying than contemplating the possibility that "government" – their savior and protector, teacher and master – does not actually exist, and never did.

Many political rituals have overtly religious overtones to them. The grandiose, cathedral-like buildings, the pomp and circumstance at inaugurations and other "government" ceremonies, the traditional costumes and age-old rituals, the way the members of the ruling class are treated and described (e.g., "honorable"), all give such proceedings an air of holiness and reverence, far more indicative of religious rites than of a practical means of collective organization.

It would be helpful to have some morally superior, all-powerful deity to protect the innocent and to prevent injustice. And that is what statists hope "government" will be: a wise, unbiased, all-knowing and all-powerful "final decider" that will override and supersede the selfish whims of man, and unerringly dispensing justice and fairness. However, there is no such thing, and can be no such thing, and there are many reasons why it is foolish to look to "government" as the solution to human imperfection. People may say they want "government" to enforce objective rules of civilized behavior, but what each statist really wants is to have his *own* idea of justice and morality enforced by "authority." But the statist fails to realize that the moment there is an "authority," it is no longer up to the statist to decide what counts as moral or just—the "authority" will claim the right to do that for him. And so, over and over again, believers in "authority" have tried to create an all-powerful force for good by anointing some people as rulers, only to quickly learn that once the master is on the throne, he does not care what his slaves were hoping he would do with the power they gave him. And this has happened to all kinds of statists, with very different beliefs and agendas. Socialists assert that "government" is needed to "fairly" redistribute wealth; Objectivists assert that "government" is needed to protect individual rights; Constitutionalists assert that a "government" is needed to carry out only those tasks listed in the Constitution; believers in democracy assert that "government" is needed to carry out the will of the majority; many Christians assert that "government" is needed to enforce God's laws; and so on. And in every case the people end up disappointed, because the "authority" always changes the plan in order to serve the interests of the people in power. Once a set of rulers are "in charge," what the masses had intended for them to do with their power does not matter. This fact has been demonstrated by every "government" in history. Once the people create a master, the people, by definition, are no longer in charge.

To expect otherwise, even without all of the historical examples, is absurd. To expect the master to serve the slave—to expect power to be used solely for the benefit of the one being controlled, not the one in control — is ridiculous. What makes it even more insane is that statists claim that appointing rulers is the only way to overcome the imperfections and untrustworthiness of man. Statists look out at a world full of strangers who have questionable motives and dubious morality, and they are afraid of what some of those people might do. That, in and of itself, is a perfectly reasonable concern. But then, as protection against what some of those people might do, the statists advocate giving some of those same people of questionable virtue a huge amount of power, and societal *permission* to rule over everyone else, in the vain hope that, by some miracle, those people will happen to decide to use their newfound power only for good. In other words, the statist looks at his fellow man and thinks, "I do not trust you to be my neighbor, but I do trust you to be my master."

Bizarrely, almost every statist admits that politicians are more dishonest, corrupt, conniving and selfish than most people, but still insists that civilization can exist only if those particularly untrustworthy people are given both the power and the right to forcibly control everyone else. Believers in "government" truly believe that the only thing that can keep them safe from the flaws of human nature is taking *some* of those flawed humans — some of the most flawed, in fact — and appointing them as gods, with the right to dominate all of mankind, in the absurd hope that, if given such tremendous power, such people will use it only for good. And the fact that that has never happened in the history of the world does not stop statists from insisting that it "needs" to happen to ensure peaceful civilization.

(*Author's personal note: I say all of this as a former devout statist, who for most of my life not only accepted the self-contradictory and delusional rationalizations underlying the myth of "government," but vehemently spread the mythology myself. I did not escape my own authoritarian indoctrination quickly or comfortably, but let go of the superstition slowly and reluctantly, with much intellectual "kicking and screaming" along the way. I mention this only so that it may be understood that when I refer to the belief in "authority" as utterly irrational and insane, I am attacking my own prior beliefs as much as anyone else's.*)

Another way to look at it is that statists worry that different people have different beliefs, different viewpoints, different standards of morality. They express concerns such as "What if there is no government and someone thinks it's okay to kill me and steal my stuff?" Yes, if there are conflicting views — as there always have been and always will be — they can lead to conflict. The authoritarian "solution" is that, instead of everyone deciding for himself what is right and what he should do, there should be a central "authority" that will make one set of rules that will be enforced on everyone. Statists obviously hope that the "authority" will issue and enforce the *right* rules, but they never explain how or why this would happen. Since the edicts of "government" are written by mere human beings—usually exceptionally power-hungry, corrupt human beings—why should anyone expect their "rules" to be better than the "rules" each individual would choose for himself?

The belief in "government" does not make everyone agree; it only creates an opportunity to drastically escalate personal disagreements into large-scale wars and mass oppression. Nor does having an "authority" settling a dispute do anything to guarantee that the "right" side wins. Yet statists talk as if "government" will be fair, reasonable, and rational in situations where individuals would not be. Again, this demonstrates that believers in "government" imagine "authority" to have super-human virtues that should be trusted above the virtues of mere mortals. History shows otherwise. A twisted sense of morality in one person, or a few, can result in the murder of one person, or even dozens, but that same twisted sense of morality in just a few people, when they get hold of the machine called "government," can result in the murder of millions. The statist wants his idea of the "good rules" forced on everyone by a central "authority," but has no way to make that happen and no reason to expect that it will happen. In their search for an all-powerful "good guy" to save the day, statists always end up creating all-powerful bad guys. Over and over again, they build giant, unstoppable "government" monsters in the hope that they will defend the innocent, only to find that the monsters become a far greater threat to the innocent than the threats they were created to protect against.

Ironically, what statists actually advocate in their attempts to guarantee justice for all is the legitimization of evil. The truth is that all the belief in "authority" ever does, and all it ever can do, is to *introduce more immoral violence into society*. This is not an unfortunate coincidence, or the side effect of a basically good idea. It is a truism based upon the nature of the belief in "authority," and this is easy to logically prove.

✸ *Adding More Immoral Violence*

Almost everyone agrees that sometimes physical force is justified, and sometimes it is not. Though people may argue about details and "gray areas," it is generally accepted that *aggressive* force — the initiation of violence against another person — is unjustified and immoral. This would include theft, assault and murder, as well as more indirect forms of aggression such as vandalism and fraud. On the other hand, using force in defense of the innocent is widely accepted as justified and moral, even noble. The legitimacy of the use of force is determined by the situation it is used in, not by *who* is using it. To simplify, force which everyone has the right to use can be termed "good force," and force which no one has the right to use can be termed "bad force." (The reader can apply his own standards, and the logic here will still apply.)

Because of the belief in "authority," agents of "government" are imagined to have the right to use force not only in the situations where everyone would have such a right, but in other situations as well, such as using force to collect "taxes." It stands to reason that if everyone has the right to use "good force," but "the law" supposedly authorizes agents of "government" to use force in *other* situations as well, then "the law" is nothing but an attempt to *legitimize* bad force. In short, "authority" is permission to commit evil — to do things that would be recognized as immoral and unjustified if anyone else did them.

Obviously, neither the enthusiastic voter who proudly posts a campaign sign in his yard, nor the well-intentioned citizen who "runs for office," understands this fact. If they did, they would understand that "democracy" is nothing more than majority-approved immoral violence, and cannot possibly fix society or be a tool for freedom or justice. Despite the mythology which claims that a person's vote is his "voice," and that the right to vote is what makes people free, the truth is that all "democracy" does is legitimize aggression and unjustified violence. The logic of this is so simple and obvious that an enormous amount of propaganda is needed in order to train people to *not* see it. If everyone has the right to use inherently righteous force, and "government" agents are allowed to use "force" in *other* situations as well, then, by its very nature, what "government" adds to society is immoral violence.

The problem is that the people are taught that when violence has been made "legal" and is committed by "authority," it changes from immoral violence into righteous "law enforcement." The fundamental premise upon which all "government" rests is the idea that what would be morally wrong for the average person to do can be morally *right* when done by agents of "authority," implying that the standards of moral behavior which apply to human beings *do not apply* to agents of "government" (again, hinting that the thing called "government" is superhuman). Inherently righteous force, which most people generally agree is limited to defensive force, does not require any "law" or special "authority" to make it valid. The only thing that "law" and "government" are needed for is to attempt to legitimize immoral force. And that is exactly what "government" adds, and the only thing it adds, to society: more inherently unjust violence. No one who understands this simple truth would ever claim that "government" is essential to human civilization.

The notion that man-made "law" can negate the usual rules of civilized behavior has some fairly terrifying ramifications. If "government" is not limited by basic human morality, which the very concept of "authority" implies, by what standards or principles would "government" action be limited at all? If 30% "taxation" is valid, why would 100% "taxation" not be valid? If "legal" theft is legitimate and just, why couldn't "legalized" torture and murder be legitimate and just? If some "collective need" requires society to have an institution that has an exemption from morality, why would there be any limits on what it can do? If exterminating an entire race, or outlawing a religion, or forcibly enslaving millions is deemed necessary for the "common good," by what moral standards could anyone complain, once they have accepted the premise of "authority"? All belief in "government" rests on the idea that the "common good" justifies the "legal" initiation of violence against innocents to one degree or another. And once that premise has been accepted, there is no objective moral standard to limit "government" behavior. History shows this all too clearly.

Almost everyone accepts the myth that human beings are not trustworthy enough, not moral enough, not wise enough to exist in peace without a "government" to keep them in line. Even many who agree that there would be no rulers in an ideal society often opine that human beings are not "ready" for such a society. Such sentiments are based on a fundamental misunderstanding of what "authority" is and what it adds to society. The idea of "government" as a "necessary evil" (as Patrick Henry described it) implies that the existence of "government" imposes restraints upon the violent, aggressive nature of human beings, when in reality it does the exact opposite: the belief in "authority" legitimizes and "legalizes" aggression.

Regardless of how foolish or wise human beings are, or how malicious or virtuous they might be, to say that human beings are not "ready" for a stateless society, or cannot be "trusted" to exist without having an "authority" that they bow to, is to say that peaceful civilization can exist only if there is a huge, powerful machine that introduces an enormous amount of immoral violence into society. Of course, statists do not recognize the violence as immoral, because to them, it is not mere mortals committing the violence, but representatives of the deity known as "government," and deities have the right to do things that mortals do not. When described in accurate, literal terms, this nearly universally held belief—that it is necessary to introduce immoral violence into society in order to prevent people from committing immoral violence—is exposed as the patently absurd myth that it is. But everyone who believes in the myth of "government" has to believe exactly that. They do not believe it as a result of rational thought and logic; they accept it as an article of faith, because it is part of the unquestionable doctrine of the church of "government."

Who Gave Them the Right?   ✳

There are several ways to demonstrate that the mythology the public is taught about "government" is self-contradictory and irrational. One of the simplest ways is to ask the question: How does someone acquire the right to rule another? The old superstitions asserted that certain people were specifically ordained by a god, or a group of gods, to rule over others. Various legends tell of supernatural events (the Lady of the Lake, the Sword in the Stone, etc.) that determined who would have the right to rule over others. Thankfully, humanity has, for the most part, outgrown those silly superstitions. Unfortunately, they have been replaced by new superstitions that are even less rational.

At least the old myths attributed to some "higher power" the task of appointing certain people as rulers over others—something a deity could at least theoretically do. The new justifications for "authority," however, claim to accomplish the same amazing feat without supernatural assistance. In short, despite all of the complex rituals and convoluted rationalizations, all modern belief in "government" rests on the notion that mere mortals can, through certain political procedures, bestow upon some people various rights which none of the people possessed to begin with. The inherent lunacy of such a notion should be obvious. There is no ritual or document through which any group of people can delegate to someone else a right which no one in the group possesses. And that self-evident truth, all by itself, demolishes any possibility of legitimate "government."

The average person believes that "government" has the right to do things that the average individual does not have the right to do. The obvious question then is, How, and from whom, did those in "government" acquire such rights? For example — whether you call it "theft" or "taxation" — how did those in "government" acquire the right to forcibly take property from those who have earned it? No voter has such a right. So how could voters possibly have given such a right to politicians? Today, all statism is based entirely upon the assumption that *people can delegate rights they don't have*. Even the U.S. Constitution pretended to give to "Congress" the right to "tax" and "regulate" certain things, though the authors of the Constitution had no such right themselves, and so could not possibly have given such a right to anyone else.

Because each person has the right to "rule" himself (as schizophrenic as that idea may be), he can, at least in theory, authorize someone else to do it. But a right he does not possess, and therefore cannot delegate to anyone else, is the right to rule someone else. And if "government" ruled only those individuals who had each willingly delegated their right to rule themselves, it would not be government.

And the number of people involved does not affect the logic. To claim that a majority can bestow upon someone a right which none of the individuals in that majority possess is just as irrational as claiming that three people, none of whom has a car or money to buy a car, can give a car to someone else. To put it in the simplest terms, you can't give someone something you don't have. And that simple truth, all by itself, rules out *all* "government," because if those in "government" have only those rights possessed by those who elected them, then "government" loses the one ingredient that makes it "government": the right to rule over others ("authority"). If it has the same rights and powers as everyone else, there is no reason to call it "government." If the politicians have no more rights than you have, all of their demands and commands, all of their political rituals, "law" books, courts, and so on, amount to nothing more than the symptoms of a profound delusional psychosis. Nothing they do can have any legitimacy, any more than if you did the same things on your own, unless they somehow acquired rights that you do not have. And that is impossible, since no one on earth, and no group of people on earth, could possibly have given them such superhuman rights.

No political ritual can alter morality. No election can make an evil act into a good act. If it is bad for you to do something, then it is bad for those in "government" to do it.

And if the same morality that applies to you also applies to those in "government" — if those in "public office" have no more rights than you do — then "government" ceases to be government. If judged by the same standards as other mortals are judged, those wearing the label of "government" are just a gang of thugs, terrorists, thieves and murderers, and their actions lack any legitimacy or "authority." They are nothing but a band of crooks who insist that various documents and rituals have given them the *right* to be crooks. Sadly, even most of their victims believe them.

Altering Morality ✳

The concept of "authority" depends upon the concepts of right and wrong (i.e., morality). Having "authority" does not merely mean having the *ability* to forcibly control other people, something possessed by countless thugs, thieves and gangs who are not referred to as "authority"; it means having the *right* to control other people, which implies that those being controlled have a moral *obligation* to obey, not just to avoid punishment but also because such obedience (being "law- abiding") is morally *good* and disobedience ("breaking the law") is morally *bad*. Thus, for there to be such a thing as "authority," there must be such a thing as right and wrong. (How one defines right and wrong, or what one believes to be the source of morality, does not particularly matter for purposes of this discussion. Use your own definitions, and the logic will still apply.) While the concept of "authority" requires the existence of right and wrong, it is also ruled out entirely by the existence of right and wrong. A simple analogy will prove that seemingly odd claim.

The laws of mathematics are an objective, unchanging part of reality. If you add two apples to two apples, you will have four apples. Those who study mathematics seek to understand more about reality, to learn about what already is. One who entered the field of math with the stated goal of altering the laws of mathematics would be seen as insane, and rightfully so. Imagine how absurd it would be for some math professor to proclaim, "I hereby decree that henceforth, two plus two shall equal five." Yet such lunacy is what occurs every time politicians enact "legislation." They are not merely observing the world, and trying to best determine what is right and what is wrong — something every individual should, and must, do for himself. No, they are claiming to be *altering* morality, by issuing some new decree. In other words, like the insane math professor who thinks he can, by mere declaration, *make* two plus two equal five, the politicians speak and act as if they are the *source* of morality, as if they have the power to *make up* (via "legislation") what is right and wrong, as if an act can become bad simply because they declared it to be "illegal."

Whether the issue is math, morality, or anything else, there is a huge difference between trying to *determine* what is true and trying to *dictate* what is true. The former is useful; the latter is insane. And the latter is what those in "government" pretend to do every day. In their "legislation," the politicians do not merely express how they think people should behave, based upon universal standards of morality. Anyone has the right to say, "I think doing this thing is bad, and doing that thing is good," but no one would call such opinions "laws." Instead, the message from the politicians is, "We are *making* that thing bad, and *making* this thing good." In short, every "legislator" suffers from a profoundly delusional god-complex, which leads him to believe that, via political rituals, he actually has the power, along with his fellow "legislators," to *change* right and wrong, by mere decree.

Mortals cannot alter morality any more than they can alter the laws of mathematics. Their understanding of something may change, but they cannot, by decree, change the nature of the universe. Nor would anyone sane attempt to. Yet that is what every new "law" passed by politicians pretends to be: a *change* in what constitutes moral behavior. And as absurd as that notion is, it is a necessary element to the belief in "government": the idea that the masses are morally obligated to obey the "law-makers"—that disobeying ("breaking the law") is morally wrong—not because the politicians' commands happen to match the objective rules of morality, but because their commands *dictate* and *determine* what is moral and what is not.

Understanding the simple fact that mere mortals cannot make good into evil, or evil into good, all by itself makes the myth of "government" disintegrate. Anyone who fully understands that one simple truth cannot continue to believe in "government," because if the politicians lack such a supernatural power, their commands carry no inherent legitimacy, and they cease to be "authority." Unless good is whatever the politicians say it is—unless right and wrong actually come from the whims of the politician-gods—then no one can have any moral obligation to respect or obey the commands of the politicians, and their "laws" become utterly invalid and irrelevant. In short, if there is such a thing as right and wrong at all, however you wish to define those terms, then the "laws" of "government" are always illegitimate and worthless.

Every person is (by definition) morally obligated to do what he feels is right. If a "law" tells him to do otherwise, that "law" is inherently illegitimate, and should be disobeyed. And if a "law" happens to coincide with what is right, the "law" is simply irrelevant. The reason, for example, to refrain from committing murder is because murder is inherently wrong. Whether or not some politicians enacted "legislation" declaring murder to be wrong—whether or not they "outlawed" it—has no effect whatsoever on the morality of the act. "Legislation," no matter what it says, is never the *reason* that something is good or bad. As a result, even "laws" prohibiting evil acts, such as assault, murder and theft, are illegitimate. While people should not commit such acts, it is because the acts themselves are intrinsically evil, not because man-made "laws" say they are wrong. And if there is no obligation to obey the "laws" of the politicians, then, by definition, they have no "authority."

Returning to the math professor analogy, if the professor authoritatively declared that, by his mere decree, he was going to make two plus two equal five, any sane individual would view that decree as incorrect and delusional. If, on the other hand, the professor declared that he was going to *make* two plus two equal four, such a declaration would still be silly and pointless even though two plus two *does* equal four. The professor's declaration is not the *reason* it equals four. Either way, the professor's declaration would and should have no effect on people's ability to add two and two. And so it is with the "laws" of politicians: whether or not they actually coincide with objective right and wrong, they never have "authority," because they are never the *source* of right and wrong, they never *create* an obligation for anyone to behave a certain way, and so should have no bearing on what any individual judges to be moral or immoral.

Consider the example of narcotics "laws." To believe that it is bad to use violence against someone for having a beer (which is "legal"), but good for "law enforcers" to use violence against someone smoking pot (because it is "illegal"), logically implies that politicians actually have the ability to alter morality—to take two essentially identical behaviors and make one into an immoral act that even justifies violent retribution. Moreover, if one accepts the legitimacy of "laws" (politician commands), one must also accept that drinking alcohol was perfectly moral one day, but was immoral the next day—the day "prohibition" was enacted. Then, not many years later, it was immoral one day, and moral the next—the day prohibition was repealed.

Even the gods of most religions do not claim the power to constantly amend and revise their commandments, to regularly *change* what is right and wrong. Only politicians claim such a power. Every act of "legislation" involves such lunacy: the notion that one day an act could be perfectly permissible, and the very next day — the day it was "outlawed" — it would be immoral.

✳ *The Unavoidability of Judging*

Nearly everyone is taught that respect for "the law" is paramount to civilization, and that the good people are those who "play by the rules," meaning they comply with the commands issued by "government." But in reality, morality and obedience are often direct opposites. Unthinking adherence to any "authority" constitutes the greatest betrayal to humanity that there could possibly be, as it seeks to discard the free will and individual judgment that make us human and make us capable of morality, in favor of blind obedience, which reduces human beings to irresponsible robots. The belief in "authority" — the idea that the individual ever has an obligation to ignore his own judgment and decision-making process in favor of obeying someone else — is not just a bad idea; it is self-contradictory and absurd. The profound lunacy involved can be summed up as follows:

"I believe it's good to obey the law. In other words, I judge that I should do as the legislators command. In other words, I judge that, rather than making my own decisions about what I should do, I should subjugate myself to the will of those in government. In other words, I judge that it is better for my actions to be dictated by the judgment of people in power instead of by my own personal judgment. In other words, I judge that it is right for me to follow the judgment of others, and wrong for me to follow my own judgment. In other words, I judge that I should not judge."

In any case in which there is a conflict between a person's own conscience and what "the law" commands, there are only two options: either the person ought to follow his own conscience regardless of what the so-called "law" says, or he is obligated to obey "the law," even though that means doing what he personally thinks is wrong. Regardless of whether the individual's judgment is flawed or not, it is schizophrenic insanity for a person to believe that it is *good* for him to do what he believes is bad. Yet that is the basis of the belief in "authority." If one understands the fact that every individual is obligated, at all times and in all places, to do whatever he thinks is right, then he cannot have any moral obligation to obey any outside "authority." Again, if a "law" coincides with the individual's judgment, the "law" is irrelevant. If, on the other hand, the "law" conflicts with his individual judgment, then the "law" must be viewed as illegitimate. Either way, the "law" has no "authority."

(An obligation to obey an "authority" is not the same as people voluntarily altering their behavior for the sake of peaceful coexistence. For example, a person may think he has every right to play music in his own backyard, but may nonetheless choose not to at his neighbor's request. Or a person may change how he dresses, talks, and behaves when he visits some other culture, or some setting where his usual behavior might offend others. There are many factors which can impact someone's opinion about what he should or should not do. Recognizing "authority" as a myth is not at all the same as not caring what anyone else thinks. Going along with various customs, standards of behavior, and other societal norms, for the sake of getting along and avoiding conflicts, is often a perfectly rational and useful thing to do. What is not rational is for someone to feel morally obliged to do something he does not personally judge to be the right thing to do, given the circumstances.)

To be blunt, the belief in "authority" serves as a mental crutch for people seeking to escape the responsibility involved with being a thinking human being. It is an attempt to pass off the responsibility for decision-making to someone else: those claiming to have "authority." But the attempt to avoid responsibility by "just following orders" is silly, because it requires the person to *choose* to do what he was told. Even what appears as blind obedience is still the result of the individual *choosing* to be obedient. Not choosing anything is not possible. Or, as the band Rush put it, in their song "Free Will," "*If you choose not to decide, you still have made a choice.*"

The excuse "I was only following orders," neatly dodges the fact that the person first had to decide that he would obey "authority." Even if some "authority" proclaims, "You must obey me," as countless conflicting "authorities" have claimed, the individual still must choose which one, if any, to believe. The fact that most people give very little thought to such things does not change the fact that they had the option of not obeying, and are therefore completely responsible for their actions — precisely the responsibility they wanted "authority" to relieve them of. It is impossible not to judge; it is impossible not to make choices. For a person to pretend that someone or something else made his choices for him—that he played no part in the decision, and thus bears no responsibility for the outcome—is utterly insane. Loyal obedience to "authority," while painted by many as a great virtue, is really nothing more than a pathetic attempt to escape the responsibility of being human and reduce oneself to an unthinking, amoral, programmable machine.

Everyone, at all times, makes his own choices and is personally responsible for those choices. Even those who hallucinate an "authority" are still choosing to believe, and choosing to obey, and are still responsible for having done so. "Authority" is merely a delusion whereby people imagine that it is possible to avoid responsibility by merely doing what they were told. Or, to express it in a more personal way:

Your actions are always determined entirely by your own judgment, and your own choices. To try to attribute your behavior to some outside force, such as "authority," is cowardly and dishonest. *You* made the choice, and you are responsible. Even if you just stupidly obeyed some self-proclaimed "authority," *you* decided to do that. The claim that there was something outside of yourself making your choices for you—the claim that you had no choice; that you had to obey "authority"—is a cowardly lie.

There is no shortcut to determining truth, about morality or anything else. All too often, the basis of people's belief system boils down to this: "To know what is true, all I have to do is ask my infallible authority; and I know my authority is always right, because it *tells* me that it is always right." Of course, countless competing, contradictory "authorities" will always exist, and each will declare itself to be the source of truth. It is, therefore, not merely a good idea for people to judge for themselves what is true and what is not; it is completely unavoidable. Even those who consider it a great virtue to have a belief system—political, religious, or otherwise—based upon "faith" fail to realize that only an individual can decide *what* to have faith in. Whether he wants to admit it or not, he is always the ultimate decider; he always uses his own judgment to decide what to believe and what to do.

Part III
The Effects of the Superstition

Effects of the Myth ✸

Throughout the ages, human beings have clung to all sorts of superstitions and false assumptions, many of them relatively harmless. For example, when most people believed the earth to be flat, that factually incorrect notion had little or no impact on how people lived their daily lives, or how they treated one another. Likewise, if children believe in the tooth fairy, or that storks deliver babies, they are not going to become purveyors of evil as a result of accepting such myths. On the other hand, over the years other false assumptions and myths have posed real dangers to humanity. It could be a simple misunderstanding among doctors, which led them to try "cures" that posed a bigger threat to their patients than the maladies they were trying to treat. As a more drastic example, some cultures offered up human sacrifices, in the hope that doing so would win the favor of their imaginary gods.

But nothing else comes close to the level of destruction—mental, emotional and physical—that has occurred throughout the world, and throughout recorded history, as a result of the belief in "authority." By dramatically altering how people *perceive* the world, the myth of "authority" alters their thoughts and actions as well. In fact, the belief in the legitimacy of a ruling class ("government") leads nearly everyone to either condone or commit acts of evil without even realizing it. Having been convinced that "authority" is real, and that by way of it, some human beings have acquired the moral right to initiate violence and commit acts of aggression against others (by way of so-called "laws"), every Democrat, every Republican, every voter, and everyone else who advocates "government" in any form is a proponent of violence and injustice. Of course, they do not see it that way, because their belief in "authority" has warped and perverted their perception of reality.

The trouble is that when something alters a person's perception of reality, the person rarely notices it happening. For example, the world might look very different to someone wearing colored contact lenses, even though he cannot see the lenses themselves. The same is true of mental "lenses." Each person thinks that the world is really the way he sees it. Everyone can point to others and claim that they are out of touch with reality, but almost no one thinks that his own perception is skewed, even when others tell him so. The result is billions of people pointing fingers at each other, telling each other how delusional and misguided they are, with almost none of them willing, or even able, to honestly examine the mental "lenses" that distort their own perceptions.

Everything a person has been exposed to, especially when young, has an impact on how he views the world. What his parents taught him, what he learned in school, how he has seen people behaving, the culture he grew up in, the religion he was raised in, all create a long-lasting set of mental "lenses" that affect how he sees the world. There are countless examples of how mere differences in perspective have led to horrendous consequences. A suicide bomber who intentionally kills civilians imagines that he is doing the right thing. Nearly everyone on both sides of every war imagines himself to be in the right. No one imagines himself to be the bad guy. Military conflicts are entirely the result of differences in perspective resulting from mental "lenses" that have been trained into the soldiers on both sides. It should be self-evident that if thousands of basically good people were all seeing the world as it is, they would not be desperately trying to kill each other. In most cases, the problem is not actual evil or malice, but simply an inability to see things as they are.

Consider, as an analogy, someone who has ingested a strong hallucinogen and who, as a result, becomes convinced that his best friend is really a malicious alien monster in disguise. From the perspective of the one having hallucinations, violently attacking his friend is perfectly reasonable and justified. The problem, in the case of one whose perception of reality has been so distorted, is not that he is immoral, or that he is stupid, or that he is malicious. The problem is that he is not seeing things as they actually are, and as a result, decisions and actions which seem perfectly appropriate to him are, in reality, horribly destructive. And when such a hallucination is shared by many, the results become far worse.

When everyone has the same misperception of reality — when everyone believes something untrue, even something patently absurd — it doesn't feel untrue or absurd to them. When a false or illogical idea is constantly repeated and reinforced by nearly everyone, it rarely occurs to anyone to even begin to question it. In fact, most people become literally incapable of questioning it, because over time it becomes solidified in their minds as a given — an assumption that doesn't need a rational basis and doesn't need to be analyzed or reconsidered, because everyone knows it to be true. In reality, however, each person simply assumes it to be true, because he cannot imagine that everyone else — including all the respectable, well-known, educated people on the radio and TV — could all believe something false. What business does one average individual have doubting something which everyone else seems perfectly comfortable accepting as indisputable truth?

Such a deeply entrenched belief is invisible to those who believe it. When a mind has always thought of something in one way, that mind will imagine evidence and hallucinate experience supporting the idea. A thousand years ago, people would have confidently proclaimed that it was a proven fact that the earth was flat, and they would have said it with just as much certainty and honesty as we now proclaim it to be round. To them, the idea of the world being a giant spherical thing, floating around in space and attached to nothing, was patently ridiculous. And their utterly false assumption about the world being flat would have seemed to them to be a scientific, self-evident fact.

So it is with the belief in "authority" and "government." To most people, "government" feels like an obvious reality, as rational and self-evident as gravity. Few people have ever objectively examined the concept, because they have never had a reason to. "Everyone knows" that "government" is real, and necessary, and legitimate, and unavoidable. Everyone assumes that it is, and talks as if it is, so why would anyone question it? Not only are people rarely given a reason to examine the concept of "government," but they have a very compelling psychological incentive to not examine it. It is exceedingly uncomfortable and disturbing, even existentially terrifying, for someone to call into question one of the bedrock assumptions upon which his entire view of reality, and his entire moral code, has been based for all of his life. One whose perception and judgment have been distorted by the superstition of "authority" (and that describes nearly everyone) will not find it easy or pleasant to contemplate the possibility that his entire belief system is based upon a lie, and that much of what he has done throughout his life, as a result of believing that lie, has been harmful to himself, his friends and family, and humanity in general. In short, the belief in "authority" and "government" warps the perception of almost every person, skews his judgment, and leads him to say and do things which are often irrational, or pointless, or counter-productive, or hypocritical, or even horribly destructive and heinously evil. Of course, the believers in the myth do not see it that way, because they do not see it as a belief at all. They are firmly convinced that "authority" is real, and, based on that false assumption, conclude that their resulting perceptions, thoughts, opinions, and actions are perfectly reasonable, justifiable and proper, just as the Aztecs no doubt believed their human sacrifices to be reasonable, justifiable and proper. A superstition capable of making otherwise decent people view good as evil, and evil as good — which is exactly what the belief in "authority" does — is what poses the real threat to humanity.

The superstition of "authority" affects the perceptions and actions of different people in different ways, whether it be the "lawmakers" who imagine themselves to have the right to rule, the "law enforcers" who imagine themselves to have the right and obligation to enforce the commands of the "lawmakers," the subjects who imagine themselves to have the moral duty to obey, or mere spectators looking on as neutral observers. The effect of the belief in "authority" on these various groups, when taken together, leads to a degree of oppression, injustice, theft and murder which simply could not and would not otherwise exist.

Part III(a)

The Effects on the Masters

The Divine Right of Politicians

In this country, at the top of the gang called "government" are the congressmen, presidents and "judges." (In other countries the rulers are known by other names, such as "kings," "emperors," or "members of parliament.") And, though they are at the top of the authoritarian organization, they are not perceived to be "authority" itself (the way kings used to be). They are still imagined to be acting on behalf of something other than themselves — some abstract entity called "government." As a result of the belief in "authority," they are imagined to have rights to do things in the name of "government" that none of them have the right to do as individuals. The legitimacy of their actions is measured not by what they do, but by how they do it. In most people's eyes, the actions that politicians take in their "official capacity," and the commands they issue by way of the accepted political rituals, are judged by a very different standard than are their actions as private individuals.

If a congressman breaks into his neighbor's home and takes $1,000, he is seen as a criminal. If, on the other hand, together with his fellow politicians, he imposes a "tax," demanding the same $1,000 from the same neighbor, it is seen as legitimate. What would have been armed robbery would then be viewed by almost everyone as legitimate "taxation." Not only would the congressman not be viewed as a crook, but any "tax cheats" who *resisted* his extortionist demands would be considered the "criminals."

But the belief in "authority" not only changes how "lawmakers" are viewed by the masses; it also changes how "lawmakers" view themselves. It should be obvious that if a person becomes convinced that he has the moral right to rule over others, that belief will have a significant effect upon his behavior. If he believes that he has the right to demand a portion of everyone's income, under threat of punishment (provided he does it through accepted "legal" procedures), he will almost certainly do so. If he is convinced that he has the right to coercively control the decisions of his neighbors — that it is moral and legitimate for him to do so — he almost certainly will. And, at least at first, he may even do so with the best of intentions.

A simple mental exercise gives a glimpse into how and why politicians act the way they do. Think about what *you* would do if you were made king of the world. If you were in charge, how would you improve things? Consider the question carefully before reading on.

When asked what they would do if they were in charge, almost no one answers, "I would just leave people alone." Instead, most people start imagining the ways in which they could use the ability to *control* people as a tool for good, for the betterment of mankind. If one starts with the assumption that such control can be legitimate and righteous, the possibilities are nearly endless. One could make a healthier country by forcing people to eat more nutritious foods and exercise regularly. One could help the poor by forcing the rich to give them money. One could make people safer by forcing them to pay for a strong system of defense. One could make things more equitable, and society more compassionate, by forcing people to behave the way they should.

However, while many positive benefits for society can be imagined, if only "government" power were used for good, the potential for tyranny and oppression — in fact, the *inevitability* of tyranny and oppression — is just as easy to imagine. Once someone believes himself to have the right to control others, there is little likelihood that he will choose not to use that power. And, whatever noble intentions he may have had to begin with, what he will actually end up doing is using violence, and the threat of violence, to impose his will upon others. Even seemingly benevolent causes like "giving to the poor" first require "government" to forcibly take wealth from another. Once someone—however virtuous and well-intentioned he may be—has accepted the premise that "legal" aggression is legitimate, and once he has been given the reins of power, and with them the supposed right to rule, the chances of that person choosing *not* to forcibly control his neighbors is almost none. The level of coercion and violence he inflicts upon others may vary, but he will become a tyrant, to one degree or another, because once someone truly believes that he has the right to rule (even if only in a "limited" manner), he will not view others, or treat others, as equals. He will view them, and treat them, as subjects.

And that is if the person started with good intentions. Many of those who seek "high office" do it for purely selfish reasons from the start, because they desire wealth and power for themselves, and delight in dominating other people. Of course, acquiring a position of "authority" is, for such people, a means of achieving an enormous amount of power that they would not otherwise have. The examples, throughout the world and throughout history, of megalomaniacs using the façade of "authority" to commit heinous atrocities are so common and well-known that they hardly require mentioning at all. Putting evil people into positions of "authority" (e.g., Stalin, Lenin, Mao, Hitler, Mussolini, Pol Pot) has resulted in the robbery, assault, harassment, terrorization, torture and outright murder of a nearly incomprehensible number of human beings. It is so obvious that it is almost silly to even say it: giving power to bad people poses a danger to humanity.

But giving power to *good* people—people who, at least initially, intend to use their power for good—can be just as dangerous, because for one to believe that he has the right to rule necessarily requires him to believe that he is exempt from basic morality. When someone imagines himself to be a legitimate "lawmaker," he will try to use the force of "law" to control his neighbors, and will feel no guilt while doing so.

Ironically, though "lawmakers" are at the very top of the authoritarian hierarchy, even they do not accept personal responsibility for what "government" does. Even they speak as if "the law" is something other than the commands they issue. For example, it is very unlikely that any politician would feel justified hiring armed thugs to invade his neighbor's home, and drag his neighbor away and put him in a cage, for the supposed sin of smoking marijuana. Yet many politicians have advocated exactly that, via anti-drug "legislation." They seem to feel no shame or guilt regarding the fact that their "legislation" has resulted in millions of non-violent people being forcibly taken from their friends and families and made to live in cages for years on end—sometimes for the rest of their lives. When they speak of the acts of violence which they are directly responsible for—and "narcotics laws" are only one example—"legislators" use terms such as "the law of the land," as if they themselves are mere spectators and "the land" or "the country" or "the people" were the ones who made such violence occur.

Indeed, the politicians' level of psychological detachment from what they have personally and directly caused via their "laws" borders on insanity. They command armies of "tax collectors" to forcibly confiscate the wealth earned by hundreds of millions of people. They enact one intrusive "law" after another, using threats of violence to control every aspect of the lives of millions of people they have never met and know nothing about. And after they have been directly responsible for initiating violence, on a regular basis, against nearly everyone living within hundreds or thousands of miles of them, they are genuinely shocked and offended if one of their victims threatens to use violence against them. They consider it despicable for a mere peasant to even threaten to do what they, the politicians, do to millions of people every day. At the same time, they do not even seem to notice the millions of people who are imprisoned, whose property is stolen, whose financial lives are ruined, whose freedom and dignity are assaulted, who are harassed, attacked, and sometimes murdered by "government" thugs, as a direct result of the very "laws" those politicians created.

When young men and women are dying by the thousands, in the latest war game waged by politicians, the politicians speak of it as a "sacrifice for freedom," when it is nothing of the sort. The politicians even use scenes of soldiers in caskets—a consequence directly attributable to what those politicians did—as photo-ops, to show the public how concerned and compassionate they are. The very people who sent the young folk off to kill or to die, then speak about what happened as if they themselves were mere observers, saying things like "they died for their country" and "there are casualties in every war," as if the war just happened by itself.

And, of course, the thousands upon thousands of people on "the other side" — the subjects of some other "authority," the citizens of some other "country" — who are killed in the wars waged by the politicians, are barely even mentioned. They are an occasional statistic reported on the evening news. And never do the politicians accept the smallest shred of responsibility for the widespread, large-scale, pro-longed pain and suffering, mental and physical, which their war-mongering has inflicted upon thousands or millions of human beings. Again, the depth of their denial and complete evasion of personal responsibility can be seen in the fact that, if one of the victims of the politicians' war games decides to attack the source, by directly targeting the ones who gave the orders to attack, *all* of the politicians, even those claiming to be against the war, and all of the talking heads on television express shock and outrage that anyone would do something so despicable. This is because, in the eyes of "lawmakers" — due to the amazing power of the "authority" myth to completely warp and distort their perception of reality — when they do things which result in the deaths of thousands of innocents, that is "the unfortunate cost of war," but when one of their victims tries to strike back at the source, it is "terrorism."

It is bad enough for those who are just obeying orders to deny personal responsi-bility for their actions (which is addressed below), but for those actually giving the orders, and making up the orders, to deny any responsibility for what their orders directly caused to happen is sheer lunacy. Yet that is what "lawmakers" always do, on every level. Whether it is the federal government, or some local township or borough council, every time a "legislature" imposes a "tax" on something, or imposes some new "legal" restriction, the politicians are using the threat of violence to control people. But, due to their undying faith in the myth of "authority," they cannot see that that is what they are doing, and they never take personal responsibility for having threatened and extorted their neighbors.

Part III(b)

The Effects on the Enforcers

✳ *Following Orders*

The "lawmakers" give the commands, but it is their faithful enforcers who carry them out. Millions upon millions of otherwise decent, civilized people spend day after day harassing, threatening, extorting, controlling and otherwise oppressing others who have not harmed or threatened anyone. But because the actions of such "law enforcers" are deemed "legal," and because they believe they are acting on behalf of "authority," they imagine themselves to bear no responsibility for their actions. In fact, they do not even view their own actions as *being* their own actions. They speak and act as if their minds and bodies have somehow been taken over by some invisible entity called "the law" or "government." They say things like "Hey, I don't make the laws, I just enforce them; it's not up to me." They speak and act as if it is impossible for them to do anything other than helplessly carry out the will of a power called "authority," and that they are therefore no more personally responsible for their actions than a puppet is responsible for what the puppeteer makes it do.

When acting in their "official" capacity, while seemingly helplessly possessed by the spirit of "authority," "law enforcers" behave in ways which they never otherwise would, and do things that they themselves would recognize as uncivilized, violent and evil if they did such things on their own, without an "authority" telling them to. Examples of this occur all over the world, every hour of every day, in a wide variety of ways. A soldier might shoot a complete stranger, whose only sin was to be out walking in a militarily occupied zone after a declared curfew. A group of heavily armed men might kick down someone's door and drag him away, or shoot a man in front of his wife and children, because the man grew a plant which politicians proclaimed to be forbidden ("illegal"). A bureaucrat might file paperwork instructing a financial institution to take thousands of dollars out of someone's bank account in the name of "tax collection." Another bureaucrat may send in armed thugs upon finding out that someone had the gall to build a deck on his own property, with the approval of his neighbors but without "government" approval (in the form of a "building permit"). A traffic cop may stop and extort someone (via a "ticket") for having a broken tail light. A TSA agent may frisk someone, and rummage through his personal belongings, without the slightest reason to suspect that the person has done, or is going to do, anything wrong. A "judge" may direct armed thugs to put someone in a cage, for weeks, months, or years, for anything from showing contempt for the judge, to driving without the written permission of politicians (in the form of a driver's "license"), to having engaged in any type of mutually voluntary but non-politician-sanctioned ("illegal") commerce.

These examples, and literally millions of others which could be given, are acts of aggression committed by perpetrators who would not have committed them if they had not been directed to do so by a perceived "authority." In short, most instances of theft, assault and murder happen only because "authority" *told* someone to steal, attack, or kill. Most of the time, the people who carry out such orders would not have committed such crimes on their own. Of the 100,000 people who work for the Internal Revenue Service, how many engaged in harassment, extortion and theft *before* becoming IRS agents? Few, if any. How many soldiers went around harassing, threatening, or killing people they did not know *before* joining the military? Few, if any. How many police officers regularly went around stopping, interrogating, and kidnapping non-violent people *before* becoming "law enforcers"? Very few. How many "judges" had people thrown into cages for non-violent behavior *before* being appointed to a "court"? Probably none.

When such acts of aggression become "legal," and are done in the name of "law enforcement," those who commit them imagine such acts to be inherently legitimate and valid, even though they recognize that, had they committed the very same acts on their own, instead of on behalf of "authority," the acts would have constituted crimes, and would have been immoral. While there are obviously more significant and less significant cogs in the wheels of the "government" machine, from low-level paper-pushers to armed mercenaries, they all have two things in common: 1) they inflict unpleasantness on others in a way they would not have done on their own, and 2) they accept no personal responsibility for their actions while in "law enforcer" mode. Nothing makes this more obvious than the fact that, when the properness or morality of their actions is called into question, their response is almost always some variation of "I'm just doing my job." The obvious implication in all such statements is this: "I am not responsible for my actions, because 'authority' *told* me to do this." The only way that makes a shred of sense is if the person is literally incapable of refusing to do something a perceived "authority" tells him to do. Unfortunately, the horrific truth is that most people, as a result of their authoritarian indoctrination, do seem to be psychologically *incapable* of disobeying the commands of an imagined "authority." Most people, given the choice between doing what they know is right and doing what they know is wrong when ordered to do so by a perceived "authority," will do the latter. Nothing demonstrates this more clearly than the results of the psychology experiments done by Dr. Stanley Milgram in the 1960s.

✳ *The Milgram Experiments*

In brief, the Milgram studies were designed to determine to what degree ordinary people would inflict pain upon strangers simply because an "authority" figure told them to. For the complete description of the experiments and the results, see Dr. Milgram's book, *Obedience to Authority*. The following is a short synopsis of his experiments and findings.

Subjects were asked to volunteer for what they were told was an experiment testing human memory. Under the supervision of a scientist (the "authority" figure), one person was strapped into a chair and wired with electrodes, and the other — the actual subject of the study — sat in front of a shock-generating machine. The person in front of the "zapper" machine was told that the goal was to test whether shocking the other person when he gave a wrong answer to a memorization question would affect his ability to remember things. The true goal, however, was to test to what degree the person in front of the zapper machine would inflict pain on an innocent stranger simply because a perceived "authority" told him to. The zapper machine had a series of switches, going up to 450 volts, and the "zapper" was supposed to increase the voltage and administer another shock each time the "zappee" got an answer wrong. The "zappee" in the tests was actually an actor who was not being shocked at all, but at given voltage levels would give out shouts of pain, protests about heart troubles, demands to stop the experiment, screams for mercy, and eventually silence (feigning unconsciousness or death). And the "zapper" machine was clearly marked with danger labels at the upper end of the series of switches.

The results of the experiment shocked even Dr. Milgram. In short, a significant majority of subjects, nearly two out of three, continued through the experiment right to the end, inflicting what they thought were excruciatingly painful — if not lethal — shocks to a complete stranger, despite the screams of agony, the cries for mercy, even the unconsciousness or death of the (pretending) victim. Dr. Milgram himself succinctly sums up the conclusion to be reached:

"With numbing regularity good people were seen to knuckle under the demands of authority and perform actions that were callous and severe. ... A substantial proportion of people do what they are told to do, irrespective of the content of the act and without limitations of conscience, so long as they perceive that the command comes from a legitimate authority."

Of note, in the experiments there was no threat that the "zapper" would be punished for failure to obey, nor was there any special reward promised for obedience. So the findings were not the result of someone harming someone else in order to "save his own neck," or in order to otherwise profit himself. Instead, the results demonstrate that, even absent any promise of reward or punishment, the average person will inflict excruciating pain, even death, upon an innocent stranger, for no other reason than that he was told to do so by a perceived "authority."

This point cannot be over-stressed: there is a particular belief that leads basically good people to do bad things, even heinously evil things. Even the atrocities of Hitler's Third Reich were the result, not of millions of evil people, but of a very small handful of truly evil people who had acquired positions of "authority," and millions of obedient people who merely did what the perceived "authority" told them to do.

In her book about Hitler's top bureaucrat, Adolf Eichmann (sometimes called "the Architect of the Holocaust"), author Hannah Arendt used the phrase "the banality of evil" to refer to the fact that most evil is not the result of personal malice or hatred, but merely the result of blind obedience — individuals giving up their own free will and judgment in favor of unthinking subservience to an imagined "authority."

Interestingly, both Arendt's book and Dr. Milgram's experiments offended a lot of people. The reason is simple: people who have been taught to respect "authority," and have been taught that obedience is a virtue and that cooperating with "authority" is what makes us civilized, do not like to hear the truth, which is that truly evil people, with all their malice and hatred, pose far *less* of a threat to mankind than the basically *good* people who believe in "authority." Anyone who honestly examines the results of Dr. Milgram's experiments cannot escape that fact. But aside from the general lesson to be learned from the Milgram experiments — that most people will intentionally hurt other people if a perceived "authority" tells them to — several other findings from Milgram's work are worth noting:

1) Many of the subjects of the experiments showed signs of stress, guilt, and anguish while inflicting pain on others, and yet continued doing so. This fact demonstrates that these were not simply nasty sadists waiting for an excuse to hurt others; they did not enjoy doing it. Furthermore, it shows that the people *knew* that they were doing something wrong, and did it anyway because "authority" told them to. Some subjects protested, begged to be allowed to stop, trembled uncontrollably, even cried, and yet most continued to the end of the experiment. The conclusion could hardly be more obvious: *The belief in "authority" makes good people commit evil.*

2) The subject's income level, education level, age, sex, and other demographic factors seemed to have little or no influence on the results. Statistically speaking, a rich, cultured, educated young woman will obey an authoritarian command to hurt someone else just as readily as an illiterate, poor, male manual laborer will. The one common factor shared by all of those who continued to the end of the experiment is that they believed in "authority" (obviously). Again, the message to be learned, however troubling it may be, is logically inescapable: *Regardless of almost any other factors, the belief in authority turns good people into agents of evil.*

3) The average person, when the experiment is described to him, not including the results, guesses that the compassion and conscience of most people would prevent

them from continuing through the entire experiment. Professional psychiatrists predicted that only about one in a thousand would obey to the end of the experiment, when in reality it was about 65%. And when the average person, who has not actually been tested, is asked if he personally would have gone to the end of the study if he had been tested, he usually insists that he would not have. Yet the majority do. Again, the message is troubling but indisputable: *Almost everyone hugely underestimates the degree to which the belief in "authority," even in himself, can be used to persuade good people to commit evil.*

4) Dr. Milgram also found that some test subjects, defying all reason, were determined to blame the results of their own blind obedience on the victim: the one being shocked. In other words, through whatever twisted mentality it took, some of those doing the shocking imagined that the one being shocked was somehow to blame for his own suffering. With that in mind, it should come as no surprise that when police officers are caught assaulting innocent civilians, or when soldiers are caught terrorizing or murdering civilians, or when prison guards are caught torturing prisoners, their defense is often to blame the *victim*, no matter how much the authoritarian aggressors have to mangle the truth and logic in order to do so.

Interestingly, even though at the Nuremberg trials, "just following orders" was not accepted as a valid excuse for what the Nazis did, it is still the standard response from soldiers, police, tax collectors, bureaucrats, and other agents of "authority" whenever the morality of their behavior is questioned. In Milgram's experiments and in countless real-life abuses of power, those who intentionally hurt others simply fall back on the standard excuse, claiming that they were not personally responsible because they were merely following orders. In the Milgram experiments, several subjects even directly asked the "authority" figure which of them was responsible for what was happening. When the "authority" figure said that he was the one responsible, most subjects went on without further debate, apparently comfortable with the notion that whatever happened from then on was not their fault and they would not be held liable. Again, the message is difficult to escape: *The belief in "authority" allows basically good people to disassociate themselves from the evil acts they themselves commit, relieving them of any feeling of personal responsibility.*

5) When it was left up to the "zapper" what voltage to use, only very rarely would he go above 150 volts, the point at which the one pretending to be shocked said he

did not want to go on. It is very important to note that up to that point—and almost all subjects made it to that point—the "zappee" let out grunts of pain but did not ask for the experiment to stop. As a result, the one doing the zapping could quite reasonably say that the one being zapped had agreed to the arrangement, and up to that point was still a willing participant. Interestingly, of the few subjects who did not go all the way to the end, many of them stopped as soon as the "zappee" said he wanted out. This could be dubbed the "libertarian line," since, once the "zappee" asks to be unstrapped, for the zapper to continue anyway constitutes initiating violence against another—the exact thing libertarians oppose.

Unfortunately, those who stop at the "libertarian line" are only a small minority of the population. As for the rest, the findings are disturbingly clear: of the people who would, at the behest of "authority," shock someone who calmly said, "I don't want to do this anymore," most would continue inflicting pain even if the victim was screaming in agony. Is this because most people are evil? No. It is because they have been conditioned to do as they are told and have been indoctrinated into the most dangerous superstition of all: the belief in "authority."

It should be noted that even Dr. Milgram could not escape his own indoctrination into the cult of "authority" worship. In passing, and with very little comment, even he opined that *"we cannot have a society without some structure of authority."* He made a weak attempt to defend teaching obedience to "authority" by saying: *"Obedience is often rational. It makes good sense to follow the doctor's orders, to obey traffic signs, and to clear the building when the police inform us of a bomb threat."* Yet none of those examples actually requires or justifies a belief in "authority." Despite the way people often talk, doctors do not give "orders." They are "authorities" in the sense that they are knowledgeable in the field of medicine, but not in the sense of having any right to rule. As for the other examples, the main reason to observe the rules of the road, or to leave a building with a bomb in it, is not because obedience to "authority" is a virtue, but because the alternative is injury or death. If some non-authority in a theater pulled a bomb from under his seat, held it up for all to see, and said, "A bomb! Let's get out of here!" would everyone else stay where they were because the person was not perceived as an "authority"? Of course not. And if "government" repealed the "law" saying which side of the road everyone should drive on, would people start randomly swerving around? Of course not. They would keep driving on the right side, because they do not want to crash into each other. So, although even Dr. Milgram clung to the notion that the belief in "authority" is sometimes necessary and good, he gave no rational argument to support such an assertion. It is a testament to the strength of the myth of "authority" that even someone who had witnessed what Dr. Milgram had witnessed was still unable to completely give up the superstition.

After Dr. Milgram publicized his findings, many were shocked and dismayed by the extent to which normal people were willing to inflict pain or death upon innocent strangers when instructed to do so by a perceived "authority." Similar tests performed since Dr. Milgram's experiments have yielded similar results, which continue to shock some people. However, the results really should not be surprising to anyone who has taken a look at how most human beings are raised.

Teaching Blind Obedience ✸

The purported purpose of schools is to teach reading, writing, mathematics, and other academic fields of thought. But the message that institutions of "education" actually teach, far more effectively than any useful knowledge or skills, is the idea that subservience and blind obedience to "authority" are virtues. Simply consider the environment in which the majority of people spend most of their formative years. Year after year, students live in a world in which:

• They receive approval, praise and reward for being where "authority" tells them to be, when "authority" tells them to be there. They receive disapproval, reproach and punishment for being anywhere else. (This includes the fact that they are coerced into being in school to begin with.)

• They receive approval, praise and reward for doing what "authority" tells them to do. They receive disapproval, reproach and punishment for doing anything else, or for failing to do what "authority" tells them to do.

• They receive approval, praise and reward for speaking when and how "authority" tells them to speak, and receive disapproval, reproach and punishment for speaking at any other time, in any other way, or about any subject other than what "authority" tells them to speak about, or for failing to speak when "authority" tells them to speak.

• They receive approval, praise and reward for repeating back whatever ideas the "authority" declares to be true and important, and receive disapproval, reproach and punishment for disagreeing, verbally or on a written test, with the opinions of those claiming to be "authority," or for thinking or writing about subjects other than what "authority" tells them to think or write about.

• They receive approval, praise and reward for immediately telling "authority" about any problems or personal conflicts they encounter, and receive disapproval, reproach and punishment for trying to solve any problems or settle any disagreements on their own.

• They receive approval, praise and reward for complying with whatever rules, however arbitrary, "authority" decides to impose upon them. They receive disapproval, reproach and punishment for disobeying any such rules. These rules can be about almost anything, including what clothes to wear, what hairstyles to have, what facial expression to have, how to sit in a chair, what to have on a desk, what direction to face, and what words to use.

• They receive approval, praise and reward for telling the "authority" when another student has disobeyed "the rules," and receive disapproval, reproach and punishment for failing to do so.

The students clearly and immediately see that, in their world, there are two distinct classes of people, masters ("teachers") and subjects ("students"), and that the rules of proper behavior are drastically different for the two groups. The masters constantly do things that they tell the subjects *not* to do: boss people around, control others via threats, take property from others, etc. This constant and obvious double standard teaches the subjects that there is a very different standard of morality for the masters than there is for the subjects. The subjects must do whatever the masters tell them to, and only what the masters tell them to, while the masters can do pretty much anything they want.

Not long ago, the masters would even routinely commit physical assault (i.e., "corporal punishment") against subjects who did not quickly and unquestioningly do as they were told, while telling the subjects that it was completely unacceptable for *them* to ever use physical violence, even in self-defense, especially in self-defense against the masters. Thankfully, the use of regular, overt physical violence by "teachers" has become uncommon. However, though the force has become less obvious, the basic methods of authoritarian control and punishment remain.

In the classroom setting, the "authority" can change the rules at will, can punish the entire group for what one student does, and can question or search any student—or all students—at any time. The "authority" is never seen as having any obligation to justify or explain to the students the rules it makes, or anything else it does. And it is of no concern to "authority" whether a student has a good reason to think that his time would be better spent being somewhere else, doing something else, or thinking about something else. The "grades" the student receives, the way he is treated, the signals he is sent—written, verbal, and otherwise—all depend upon one factor: his ability and willingness to unquestioningly subvert his own desires, judgment and decisions to those of "authority." If he does that, he is deemed "good." If he does not, he is deemed "bad."

This method of indoctrination was not accidental. Schooling in the United States, and in fact in much of the world, was deliberately modeled after the Prussian system of "education," which was *designed* with the express *purpose* of training people to be obedient tools of the ruling class, easy to manage and quick to unthinkingly obey, especially for military purposes. As it was explained by Johann Fichte, one of the *designers* of the Prussian system, the goal of this method was to "fashion" the student in such a way that he "simply cannot will otherwise" than what those in "authority" *want* him to will. At the time, the system was openly admitted to be a means of psychologically enslaving the general populace to the will of the ruling class. And it continues to accomplish exactly that, all over the world, including in the U.S.

The reason most people do whatever "authority" tells them to, regardless of whether the command is moral or rational, is because that is exactly what they were trained to do. Everything about authoritarian "schooling" (and authoritarian parenting), even the modern version that pretends to be caring and open-minded, continually hammers into the heads of the youngsters the notion that their success, their goodness, their very worth as human beings, is measured by how well they obey "authority."

Is it any wonder, then, that rather than applying logic to evidence to reach their own conclusions, most adults look for an "authority" to tell them what to think? Is it any wonder that when a man with a badge starts barking orders, most adults timidly obey without question, even if they have done nothing wrong? Is it any wonder that most adults sheepishly submit to whatever interrogations and searches "law enforcers" want to inflict upon them? Is it any wonder that many adults will run to the nearest "authority" to solve any problem or settle any dispute? Is it any wonder that most adults will comply with any order, however irrational, unfair, or immoral it may be, if they imagine the one giving the order to be "authority"? Should any of this be surprising in light of the fact that nearly everyone went through many years of being deliberately trained to behave that way?

Dr. Milgram's experiments made it quite clear that the kind of people produced even by our modern, supposedly enlightened society, even in the good old U.S.A. — that supposed bastion of liberty and justice — are, for the most part, callous, irresponsible, unthinking tools for whichever megalomaniac claims the right to rule. When the people are intentionally trained to humbly submit to the beast called "authority" — when they are taught that it is more important to obey than it is to judge — why should we be at all surprised at the extortion, oppression, terrorism and mass murder that are committed just because a self-proclaimed "authority" commanded it? All of human history makes the deadly formula as plain as it could possibly be: A few evil rulers + many obedient subjects = widespread injustice and oppression.

✳ *Making Monsters*

There should also be at least some mention here about the psychological study done at Stanford University in 1971, in which a sort of mock prison was set up, with dozens of students appointed as mock prisoners and others as mock prison guards. The experiment had to be terminated early, after only six days, because those who had been given "authority" (the guards) had become shockingly callous, abusive and sadistic toward their prisoners.

It must be noted that the abuse committed by the "guards" even went beyond what they were told to do by those running the experiment, which was *designed* to humiliate and degrade the prisoners. This shows that the personal malicious or sadistic tendencies in an individual is a significant contributing factor to such abuse, but that most people openly act out such tendencies only when given a position of "authority" that they believe gives them permission to do so. The same phenomenon can be seen in all sorts of abuses of power, whether by a bureaucrat on a power trip, a soldier or police officer who likes to bully or assault civilians, or any other official who enjoys lording his power over others. These demonstrate that not only does the belief in "authority" allow basically good people to become tools of oppression and injustice, but it also brings out and dramatically amplifies whatever potential for malice, hatred, sadism and love of dominion those people may possess. The superstition of "authority" begins by making average people mere *agents* of evil (which Arendt described as the "banality of evil"), but then goes on to make such people *personally* evil, by convincing them that they have the right, or even the duty, to abuse and oppress other people. This can be seen in the behavior of soldiers, police, prosecutors, judges, even petty bureaucrats. Anyone whose job consists of harassing, extorting, threatening, coercing and controlling decent people will, sooner or later, become at least callous, if not downright sadistic. One cannot continually act like a monster without eventually *becoming* one.

Another important thing to note, as shown in countless examples of abuses of power, is that, while a belief in "authority" can lead people to inflict harm on others, that same belief often cannot *limit* the extent to which the agents of "authority" hurt other people. For example, many individuals who would never oppress an innocent person on their own become "police officers," thereby acquiring the "legal" power to commit a certain degree of oppression. Yet, on many occasions, they end up going well beyond the "legal" oppression they are "authorized" to commit, and become sadistic, power-happy monsters. The same is true, perhaps even more so, of soldiers.

Perhaps the reason so many combat veterans end up being deeply emotionally traumatized is not so much a result of thinking about what they have witnessed as it is a result of thinking about what they themselves have done. The high rate of suicide among combat veterans supports this thesis. It makes little sense for someone to wish for his own death simply because he has *seen* something horrible. It makes a lot more sense for someone to wish for his own death because he himself has *done* something horrible, and has in fact *become* something horrible.

The reason that the belief in "authority" can drive people to commit evil, but in the end cannot limit the evil they commit, is simple. Aside from whatever "technical" limitations there are supposed to be on an agent of "authority," the primary concept that the enforcer is taught, and the primary concept that he must accept in order to do his job, is that, as a representative of "authority," he is above the common folk and has the moral right to forcibly control them. In short, he is taught that his badge and his position make him the rightful master of all the "average" people. Once he is convinced of that lie, it should be expected that he will despise the average citizen and treat him with contempt, in the same way—and for the same reason—that a slave owner will treat his slaves not as human beings, but as property, whose feelings and opinions matter no more than the feelings and opinions of the master's cattle or his furniture.

It is very telling that many modern "law enforcers" quickly become angry, even violent, when an average citizen simply speaks to the "officer" as an equal, instead of assuming the tone and demeanor of a subjugated underling. Again, this reaction is precisely the same—and has the same cause—as the reaction a slave master would have to an "uppity" slave speaking to him as an equal. There are plenty of examples, depicted in numerous police abuse videos on the internet, of supposed representatives of "authority" going into a rage and resorting to open violence, simply because someone they approached spoke to them as one adult would speak to another instead of speaking as a subject would speak to a master. The state mercenaries refer to this lack of groveling as someone having an "attitude." In their eyes, someone treating them as mere mortals, as if they are on the same level as everyone else, amounts to showing disrespect for their alleged "authority."

Similarly, anyone who does not consent to be detained, questioned, or searched by "officers of the law" is automatically perceived, by the state mercenaries, as some sort of troublemaker who has something to hide. Again, the real reason such lack of "cooperation" annoys authoritarian enforcers is because it amounts to people treating them as mere humans instead of treating them as superior beings, which is what they imagine themselves to be. If, for example, someone was confronted by a stranger *without* a badge, who started interrogating the person in an obviously accusatory way, and asked to be allowed to search the person's pockets, his car, and his home, not only would the person being accosted almost certainly refuse, but he also would probably be outraged at the request. "Of course you can't rummage through my stuff! Who do you think you are?" But when strangers with badges make such requests, they are the ones offended when the targets of their intrusive, unjustified harassments, accusations and searches object, and refuse to "cooperate." Even when the "officers" know full well that the Fourth and Fifth Amendments to the U.S. Constitution specifically dictate that a person has no "legal" duty to answer questions or consent to searches, such "lack of cooperation"—i.e., the failure to unquestioningly bow to the enforcer's every whim and request—is still seen by the "police" as a sign that the person must be some sort of criminal and enemy of the state. From the perspective of "law enforcers," only a despicable lowlife would ever treat representatives of "authority" in the same manner as he treats everyone else.

Again, this is not how most of these people view the world before becoming "officers of the law." In their authoritarian enforcement training, they are specifically taught to treat people as inferiors, to always try to gain control of everyone and everything the moment they arrive on a scene, telling everyone where to go, what to do, when they can speak, and so on. They are not merely told that they have the right to boss everyone around, which would be dangerous enough; they are trained to believe that they *must*, in every situation, use whatever it takes—commands, intimidation, or outright violence—to get everyone present to bow to their "authority," and are taught that it is a crime for anyone to fail to unquestioningly bow to their will, which they characterize as "disobeying a lawful order."

It is also very significant that it is customary for the police, as soon as they arrive at any scene, to make sure that no one else is armed with any sort of weapon, and to disarm anyone who is, before knowing anything else about who the people are or what is going on, and even regardless of whether the people are "legally" armed. The obvious purpose of this practice is to immediately create a huge imbalance of power, where only the "law enforcers" have the ability to forcibly impose their will on others. Imagine the arrogance required for an average citizen to arrive on some scene, unfamiliar with the situation and the people involved, and have his very first thought be, "Nobody is allowed to have a weapon, except me."

In short, "law enforcers" are *trained* to be oppressive megalomaniacs and to treat everyone else as cattle. And, human nature being what it is, anyone who routinely treats others that way—the way "law enforcers" are required to treat everyone else—will learn to despise others and treat them with contempt, disrespect and hostility. However good or bad at heart an individual is to begin with, the way to bring out the *worst* in him is to give him "authority" over others.

(Author's personal note: Several former police officers have personally told me that they quit the force after they noticed that the job, and their supposed "authority," was slowly turning them into monsters — one of them using that exact word.)

In fairness, many "law enforcers" make an effort to be "nice guys," and attempt to treat others with respect. But ultimately they cannot treat others as equals and still be "law enforcers." They can be friendly, and even apologetic about it (e.g., "Sorry, but I'm going to have to ask you to..."), but their job still requires them to coercively control and extort others, and not just those who have actually harmed someone. A cop cannot treat others as equals without losing his job. Imagine an officer who would do traffic stops, or search places, or detain and interrogate people, or use physical force against someone *only* in situations in which *you* would feel justified in doing such things yourself, without any badge or "law" telling you you could.

The same holds true of "government" investigators, prosecutors and judges. Any "government" employee who refused to investigate, prosecute, or sentence someone for a victimless "crime" would quickly lose his job. It is not up to the agents of "authority" to decide which "laws" to enforce. If there are morally illegitimate "laws" (as there always are), all branches of authoritarian "law enforcement" are required to enforce them, thereby assisting in the extortion and oppression of innocent people. Even if much of what he does is aimed at actual criminals — those who have committed acts of aggression against others — every "law enforcer," as part of his job, is required to commit acts of aggression himself. There are some who do almost nothing *other* than initiating violence, such as "tax" collectors, narcotics agents, and immigration agents. This makes it literally impossible, in almost all cases, to work for "government" without committing immoral acts of aggression. Being a "law enforcer" and being a moral person are almost always mutually exclusive.

However politely they may do the job, and despite the fact that they also go after actual criminals (the kind who have victims), "law enforcers" are always professional aggressors, subjugating the people to the will of the politicians by way of violence and the threat of violence. And anyone who does that, if he did not already have a certain degree of contempt and hatred for his fellow man, will almost certainly develop it. To put it another way, even the nicest, most friendly slave owner, if he continues to believe in the legitimacy of slavery and continues to practice it, will be committing evil and will inflict harm upon the people he imagines to be his rightful property. And he will naturally develop a degree of contempt toward the victims of his aggression, and will behave contemptuously toward them.

The ability of the belief in "authority" to create harm, and the simultaneous *inability* of it to *limit* the harm, once the master imagines himself to have the right to rule over his "inferiors," can be seen not only on an individual basis but on a large scale as well. Most of the debates and writings that led up to the ratification of the U.S. Constitution focused on *limiting* the powers that the federal government would have, and on discussing all of the things that it was *not* allowed to do. The Bill of Rights, for example, is a list of things the U.S. government is constitutionally *prohibited* from doing. In fact, the Ninth and Tenth Amendments make it an open-ended list, so that the federal "government," in theory, was not supposed to do anything except what the Constitution specifically "authorized" it to do. Nonetheless, with the exception of the Third Amendment, the "Bill of Rights" also happens to be a list of rights that federal agents violate every single day, in every state in the union. In reality, whether on an individual or national level, telling someone "You have the right to rule others, but only within these limits" will, sooner or later, result in that person dominating others without recognizing *any* limits to his power.

In the long run, there is no such thing, and can be no such thing, as "limited government," because once someone is accepted by others as a rightful master, and believes himself to have the moral right to rule, there will be nothing and no one "above" him with the power to restrain him. Inside a "government," a higher "authority" might choose to limit a lower "authority," but logic and experience show that an authoritarian hierarchy, taken as a whole, will never limit itself for long. Why would it? Why would a master ever put his own interests below the interests of his slaves?

The Constitution is a perfect example of this: a piece of parchment which purported to grant very limited "authority" to certain people but which utterly failed to stop those people from going beyond those limits, creating something that eventually grew into the most powerful authoritarian empire in history. And the problem cannot be solved by appointing another set of masters (e.g., a "court system") inside the same authoritarian structure, with the supposed purpose of enforcing limits upon the first set of masters. "Separation of powers" and "checks and balances" and "due process" are meaningless if the masters and those assigned to limit them are both part of the same authoritarian organization.

✷ _Demonizing the Victim_

It is important to stress the fact that in the Milgram experiments, the subjects thought they were shocking innocent strangers. There was no accusation that the one being shocked was a bad person, or had done anything immoral. It should be obvious that if the average person will, at the behest of "authority," inflict pain upon an innocent person, he will also inflict such pain — with less hesitation and less guilt — upon someone he imagines to be _deserving_ of such pain.

The U.S. military (and presumably many other militaries) has done a lot of research to determine what can be done to overcome a soldier's natural aversion to killing, so that he will kill on command. And one of the most effective ways of achieving this is to demonize and dehumanize the one he is being told to shoot. In modern wars the "governments" of both sides feed their soldiers constant propaganda designed to paint "the enemy" as a bunch of heartless, vicious, sadistic, inhuman monsters. Ironically, this becomes a self-fulfilling prophecy, because such propaganda makes _both_ sides into gangs of heartless monsters, zealously trying to exterminate enemies that they do not view as being fully human.

Similar tactics are used in "law enforcement." The hired mercenaries of "government" are far more likely to inflict injustice and oppression upon someone if that person has first been dehumanized and demonized. Even the terminology used — by the masters, the enforcers, and everyone else — constitutes a very effective form of mind control, which alters how both enforcers and their targets perceive reality, thereby affecting how both groups behave. Such terms reinforce the premise that obedience to "authority" is a virtue, and that disobedience is a sin.

What literally happens is that one group of people issues a command, and their enforcers impose it upon the masses, by punishing disobedience. This is what the Mafia does, what street gangs do, what schoolyard bullies do, and what all "governments" do. The difference is that when "government" does it, it uses not only threats but also indoctrination, of both the enforcers and the general public. Where the message of most thugs is usually direct and honest ("Do what I say or I hurt you"), the "government" message involves a great deal of psychology and mind control, which is essential to making the state mercenaries feel righteous about inflicting oppression on others. The controllers in "government" portray themselves as "law-makers" who have the *right* to "govern" society, portray their commands as "laws," and portray any who disobey as "criminals." And, unlike Mafia "heavies," those who administer retribution against any who disobey the politicians are portrayed, not merely as hired thugs, but as noble "law enforcers," who are righteously protecting society from all the uncivilized, contemptuous "law-breakers."

Such propaganda goes a long way, not only toward making the authoritarian enforcers carry out violence against innocent people, but also toward making them feel proud of it. They are convinced, via their authoritarian indoctrination, that they are bringing "criminals" to "justice," thereby maintaining "law and order" for the benefit of society. But what they are actually doing, more often than not, is using violence to coerce everyone into obeying whatever commands the politicians issue, however immoral, arbitrary, socially or economically destructive, or downright idiotic those commands may be.

There is a big difference in the connotations of the two terms "law enforcer" and "politician's thug." There is no difference, however, in what they literally mean. But by persuading the enforcers that the violence they use constitutes righteous and noble "law enforcement," their perceptions can be altered in such a way that they will gladly and proudly impose the ruling class's will upon their fellow man. There are as many examples of this as there are "laws," but they all fall into one of two categories: *prohibitions* (whereby politicians proclaim that their subjects may not do certain things) and *demands* (whereby politicians proclaim that their subjects *must* do certain things). One example of each will suffice to demonstrate the point.

Prohibition: The controllers issue a decree that their subjects may not possess marijuana. That prohibition is proclaimed to be "the law," and any who disobey it are deemed to be "criminals." The controllers then spend huge amounts of money (taken from their subjects by way of a different "law") to pay for mercenaries, guns, armored vehicles, prisons, and so on, for the sole purpose of taking captive any who are caught disobeying their "law."

Consider the perspective of the "police officer" assigned the duty of enforcing that "law" who discovers that someone has been selling marijuana to willing customers.

If the "officer" could objectively consider the situation, without the myth of "authority" distorting his perception, he would immediately see that his "job" is not only immoral but utterly idiotic and hypocritical—his "job" being to physically capture someone for the purpose of putting that person in a cage for a long time, for doing something that was neither fraudulent nor violent. In fact, until the cop showed up, all of the people involved—grower, dealer, seller, buyer and user—interacted peacefully and voluntarily. Furthermore, if the officer has ever consumed alcohol, he would be guilty of something morally identical to what the "criminal" has done. Nonetheless, he will see himself as the brave, righteous, noble "law enforcer" as he participates in a paramilitary, armed invasion of the person's home and forcibly captures and drags the "criminal" away from his friends and family. Then the officer will go home and have a beer, and of course would not react kindly to anyone who tried to forcibly stop him from doing so. The only difference—which is no real difference at all—is that politicians made up a command about one mind-altering substance (marijuana) and not the other (alcohol). As a result, the "officer" will truly believe that using one mind-altering substance is a good, wholesome, all-American behavior, while using another is shady, immoral and "criminal," and even justifies violent assault and kidnapping of the "perpetrators."

Demand: The controllers enact a "law" saying that any of their subjects who own property must give to the controllers, every year, a payment in the amount of two percent of the value of the subject's property. That demand is called a "property tax" and is proclaimed to be "the law," and any who disobey it are "criminals" and "tax cheats." The controllers then set up an organization of "tax collectors" to find any who disobey, to either forcibly extract money from them or to forcibly evict them from their properties and seize such properties and give them to the controllers.

Of course if anyone did that without all of the authoritarian propaganda, it would be called extortion: "You have to pay me a bunch of money, every year, or I won't let you live in your own house." And very few people, including those who now work as "tax collectors," would want to be part of such a racketeering scheme. Yet when the exact same thing is done "legally," not only will average people accept a job being part of such an extortion racket but they will show disdain for any who resist it. Those who then try *not* to be robbed are viewed as greedy "tax cheats" who don't want to pay their "fair share." And those whose job it is to forcibly take money or property from such "tax cheats" usually do so with a feeling of righteousness, because they truly believe that the "authority" of "law" can take what is usually an immoral act—theft, extortion and racketeering—and transform it into something righteous and legitimate. So they commit mass robbery, feel good about it, and feel contempt for their victims. That is the power of the most dangerous superstition.

Statists often argue that taxation is not theft because "governments" use tax revenue for things that are for the "common good," so it's just a matter of people paying for goods and services they receive. Such an argument ignores the fundamental nature of the situation. A simple example makes the double standard obvious. Suppose a stranger came up to you and said he had mowed your lawn, or left an item for you at your house, and now demanded that you give him $1,000, though you had never agreed to any such arrangement. Obviously that would constitute extortion, and you would have no duty to pay, even if he really had mowed your lawn or left you something. No one has the right, without your consent, to provide you some item or service—when you didn't ask for it and didn't want to buy it—and then forcibly take from you whatever he declares the item or service to be worth. And yet that is exactly what every "government," at every level, always does.

When targets of authoritarian aggression are successfully demonized and dehumanized, there are essentially no limits to the degree of violence and injustice which those who believe in "authority" will commit. For any who might still have hope that the consciences of American soldiers and "law enforcers" might limit the level of injustice they are willing to inflict upon complete strangers, there are plenty of real-world examples that prove otherwise. Perhaps the most well known is the massacre at My Lai during the Vietnam war, where U.S. troops not only murdered hundreds of unarmed civilians, mostly women and children, but also sexually assaulted and tortured some, and some soldiers openly delighted in the suffering and deaths of their victims, by the soldiers' own testimonies. This is what *American* soldiers did, as a result of their loyalty to the myth of "authority," combined with the demonization and dehumanization of their victims. The soldiers themselves put it perfectly bluntly, one saying they were "just following orders," and another saying that most of the U.S. soldiers there "*didn't consider the Vietnamese human.*" (It should be noted that there were some American soldiers who tried, with little success, to stop or limit the massacre.) While this is one of the most famous examples of wartime atrocities committed by American troops, it is certainly not the only one. In fact, examples of sadistic behavior by some American soldiers keep coming to light. Whereas in the Milgram experiments, some test subjects would demonstrate—verbally or by their behavior—that they felt bad about inflicting harm upon an innocent stranger, "law enforcers" and soldiers who are first taught to despise an "enemy," obey authoritarian commands even more eagerly, often in a way that shows that they *delight* in inflicting pain and death on their victims.

This was plainly displayed in the images that came out of the Abu Ghraib prison in Iraq showing that American troops, male and female, not only carried out mental and physical torture, but exhibited delight and amusement at the suffering of their victims, happily posing for the camera while humiliating, assaulting, torturing and raping their prisoners. (Both the Bush and Obama administrations prevented much of the photographic evidence of this torture from being made public, for fear of the effect that those images would have on the opinion of the military and the "country," among Americans and foreigners alike.) Though such torture was carried out at the behest of the highest levels of "government," it is important to note that the ones who carried out these commands of "authority" clearly exhibited a sadistic enjoyment of the pain and suffering they were inflicting on other human beings. They had been told, by someone they perceived as "authority," that it was noble and righteous to hate and hurt "the enemy." So they did, and they enjoyed it.

The same attitude and mentality can be seen in various "law enforcement" actions, such as the assault on Ruby Ridge in 1992, and the raid, standoff, and eventual massacre near Waco, Texas, in 1993. In neither case was "authority" going after someone who had actually harmed or threatened anyone else. Instead, both events involved paramilitary assaults based upon the alleged possession of "illegal" firearms. In the Waco incident, eighty people, including men, women and children, eventually died, after being mentally and physically tortured for weeks with sleep deprivation and CS gas, among other things. The victims were demonized, to the public and to those in "law enforcement," and the "government" aggressors exhibited both contempt for their victims and enthusiasm at the thought of killing them. The same general attitude can be seen in dozens of "police abuse" videos depicting police enthusiastically bullying and even physically assaulting people who are not a threat to anyone, and who are not even fighting back or resisting. This is the direct result of convincing "law enforcers" that everyone else is beneath them and that, as agents of "authority," they have the right to have everyone else treat them like superiors, groveling before them and unquestioningly obeying their commands. The same pattern can also be seen among "tax collectors" and other bureaucrats.

To what extent the belief in "authority" actually *creates* sadistic tendencies, and to what extent it simply unleashes tendencies which were already there, hardly matters. The point is that, by pretending to relieve the individual of responsibility for his own actions, and by ordering him to inflict harm on others and telling him that it not just permissible but *virtuous* to harm a particular target, the myth of "authority" converts millions of average, otherwise decent people into monsters and sadistic agents of evil. Whatever factors normally compel people to behave civilly and nonviolently — whether it be the individual's internal virtues, his devotion to moral principles or religious beliefs, or simply his concern about what others might think of him or might do to him — are easily defeated and overridden by the belief in "authority." In short, the most effective way to shut down the humanity and decency of any individual is to teach him to respect and obey "authority."

What the Badge Means   ✸

Those who claim to act under the "authority" of "government" usually go out of their way to make it clear that they are doing so. When a soldier dons his military attire, marches in formation, or gets into a military vehicle; when a cop puts on his uniform and gets into the car marked "POLICE"; when a plainclothes "government" agent — whether from the FBI, IRS, U.S. Marshals, or any other agency — shows his "badge" or announces his "official" title, he is making a very specific statement, which can be summed up as follows:

"I am not acting as a thinking, responsible, independent human being, and should not be treated as such. I am not personally responsible for my actions, because I am not acting from my own free will or my own judgment of right and wrong. I am, instead, acting as the tool of something superhuman, something with the right to rule you and control you. As such, I can do things that you can't. I have rights that you don't. You must do as I say, submit to my commands, and treat me as your superior, because I am not a mere human being. I have risen above that. Through my unquestioning obedience and loyalty to my masters, I have

become a piece of the superhuman entity called 'government' and act on its 'authority.' As a result, the rules of human morality do not apply to me, and my actions should not be judged by the usual standards of human behavior."

This bizarre, mystical, cult-like belief is held by *every* "law enforcer" in the world. It is horribly dangerous for anyone to imagine himself to have an exemption from the basic rules of right and wrong, yet that is exactly what every agent of "government" imagines. Despite the fact that soldiers and "law enforcers" usually display their "official" uniforms with great pride, what they are actually doing is publicly displaying the fact that they are delusional, have a completely warped and demented view of reality, and have betrayed the very thing that made them human: their free will and the personal responsibility that goes along with it. Every person who claims to act on behalf of "authority" is demonstrating that he has accepted an utterly ridiculous lie: that his position, his badge, his office dramatically *changes* what behaviors are moral and what behaviors are immoral. The idea is patently insane, but is rarely recognized as such because even the victims of the enforcers share in this delusion.

❋ *Noble Motives, Evil Actions*

It is important to again stress the fact that, of those who become "law enforcers" and soldiers, most do so out of a desire to fight for justice. Nonetheless, because of their belief in "authority," their noble intentions often end up being used to harm the innocent and protect the guilty. Because a police officer is supposed to "enforce the law," and a soldier is supposed to follow orders, their own values and intentions get trumped by the agendas of those giving the orders. Notwithstanding the military recruiting propaganda encouraging young men and women to join up to fight for truth and justice, the true job of a soldier is to kill whomever the masters tell him to kill. It is as simple as that. How many Americans would, on their own, choose to go to foreign lands and kill complete strangers? Very few. How many Americans, on their own, if they were in a foreign land, would feel justified in going door to door, interrogating strangers at gunpoint, invading and searching their homes, because they thought some truly bad people *might* be in the area? Very few. These are actions which almost every individual's sense of morality would tell him are wrong. But when someone voluntarily joins an authoritarian military, he intentionally shuts off his own judgment and conscience in favor of simply doing as he is told.

Though soldiers sometimes use legitimate force, such as combatting aggressors and invaders, they also routinely act as aggressors and invaders themselves. It would be impossible for a "government" military to function any other way. Imagine an army going door to door, politely asking each homeowner for permission to cross his land. Simply calling the situation "war" causes the believers in "government" to imagine that the usual standards of human behavior do not apply. Under the excuse of necessity, soldiers trespass, steal, intimidate, threaten, assault, interrogate, torture, and murder. And they do this even against people they consider to be their allies. The military invasion and occupation of Iraq by the mercenaries of the U.S. "government," which was purportedly done to defend the people of Iraq, was an example of large-scale aggression and coercion—and thus was immoral—even if it displaced a regime guilty of an even worse level of intimidation and murder (the regime of Saddam Hussein). Yet the supposed evil of the enemy is often cited as the justification for authoritarian coercion. In truth, today and throughout history, large-scale violence against innocents has always been done in the name of "fighting for freedom" or "fighting against injustice." Even when the Nazis invaded Poland, they first staged a series of false-flag events and propaganda stunts, collectively known as "Operation Himmler," so they could pretend that the invasion was a justifiable act of self-defense. The truth is that, even when the evil of an enemy regime is easy to see, making the overall fight seem righteous to one side, the violence committed by authoritarian militaries is never directed only at the actual aggressors on the other side. The structure and methodology of hierarchical armies make it so that innocents are *always* victimized in one way or another, and not just by accident, but by design. The pack mentality that is such a big part of patriotism makes this unavoidable.

In World War II, the American troops saw "the Krauts" (the Germans) and "the Japs" (the Japanese) as the enemy, rather than seeing the enemy as those individuals who actually committed acts of aggression against innocent people—a concept which would require each soldier to constantly use his own individual perception and moral judgment to assess each situation as he confronted it, which is incompatible with an authoritarian chain of command. Of course, of the people who fit the definition of "the Krauts" or "the Japs," many played no part in the conflict (aside from funding it through paying "taxes," as discussed below). But on both sides in every war, "government" militaries, and the propaganda they use, always target and demonize a general *category* of people rather than just the individuals who have actually initiated violence. The result is that huge demographic groups end up being ordered to subjugate or exterminate each other, making it so that neither side is ever the "good guy" in any war between "nations," as both militaries always use violence against innocent people, as well as against other soldiers.

Perhaps one of the most heinous examples of this was the dropping of nuclear bombs on Nagasaki and Hiroshima, which constituted by far the two worst individual acts of terrorism and mass murder in history. Together, they resulted in the deaths of around two hundred thousand civilians—about seventy times worse than the number of deaths from the 9/11 attacks on the World Trade Center. The admitted goal was to inflict fear, pain and death on the population of an entire country, in order to coerce the ruling class of that country to bend to the will of another ruling class. Ironically, this fits perfectly the United States "government's" own definition of "terrorism," except that that definition conveniently *exempts* acts that are "legal" and/or committed by "governments." If those in "government" advocate and carry out violent activities that are intended to *"intimidate or coerce a civilian population"* or to *"influence the policy of a government by intimidation or coercion,"* then it is considered legitimate and just. If anyone else does the exact same thing, it is "terrorism." (See Section 2331 of Title 18 of the United States Code.)

As an aside, the existence of nuclear weapons is entirely the result of the belief in "authority." Unlike many weapons, it is impossible to use them for purely defensive purposes. The only reason the nuclear bomb was invented and manufactured in the first place was because of the authoritarian, nationalistic, pack-mentality idea that it is possible, and righteous, to be at war with an entire country, and that therefore indiscriminately exterminating thousands of people at once can be justifiable.

Being a member of a "government" military requires one to contribute to anti-human acts, even if only indirectly, regardless of whatever noble motives the individual may have had for joining the armed forces. The reason is simple: acting based on one's own perception and judgment, and abiding by one's own conscience and one's own sense of right and wrong, is utterly incompatible with being a member of any "government" military. Sadly, the result is that *both* sides of every war are wrong, in that they both initiate violence against innocents. At the same time, both sides of every war are also right, in that they each condemn the *other* side for initiating violence against innocents. In short, as long as there are soldiers willing to subjugate themselves to a claimed "authority," and even to commit murder when it tells them to, lasting peace will be impossible. Those who fight for any "government," even if they believe they are "fighting for their country," can never achieve freedom and justice, because a ruling class, by its very nature, never wants freedom and justice, even for its own subjects, or it would cease to exist. However noble their motives, and however courageous their actions, ultimately the only thing "government" soldiers can ever achieve is subjugation and domination.

Many Americans are under the impression that U.S. soldiers are allowed to (or even required to) disobey any illegal or immoral order, a belief which allows Americans to imagine that the U.S. "government" mercenaries are fundamentally different from the mercenaries of other regimes. The grain of truth behind this belief is that U.S. soldiers are (at least in theory) required to disobey "unlawful" orders, but the rule says nothing about morality. And because the rulers define what is "lawful," ultimately the rule does not mean much. In combat, nearly everything every military does constitutes violent aggression, and nearly every order a soldier receives is an immoral (even if "lawful") order, whether it is to trespass on private property, blow up a bridge, block a road, disarm civilians, detain and interrogate people at random, or kill complete strangers. A soldier who disobeyed such commands would almost certainly be court-martialed. The idea that one should sometimes disobey orders — whether because they are immoral or "unlawful" — while fine in principle, goes directly against the entire concept of "authority," and against the methods used to train soldiers to be blindly obedient tools of whatever regime they serve.

Even when the rules of engagement are only to fire if fired upon, that is still often unjustified. When someone commits aggression, the target of that aggression has the right to use whatever force is necessary to stop the aggressor. This means that in a lot of situations, shooting at soldiers — including American soldiers — is inherently justified. Killing someone for defending himself against aggressors is murder, even when the aggressors are U.S. soldiers. And almost every soldier routinely commits immoral acts of aggression, believing that commands from "authority" make it okay for him to do so. If any soldier actually took seriously the idea that he should disobey an immoral order, the first thing he would do would be to quit the military.

Those who act as mercenaries for "government," even if they do so with the best intentions, will always be part of a machine that commits aggression as often as, or more often than, it defends the innocent. That being the case, nearly every combat soldier does things which would justify the use of defensive violence against him. However, as invading armies always do, the American military commanders label anyone who resists their acts of aggression as an "enemy combatant," an "insurgent," or a "terrorist." When aggression is committed in the name of "authority," many then view any act of self-*defense* against such aggression as a sin. As much as American authoritarians might be outraged at the suggestion, the truth is that many thousands of people the world over have had good cause to shoot at American soldiers.

When a person who has not harmed or threatened anyone is in his own home, minding his own business, and heavily armed thugs break down his door, point machine guns at him and his family, threatening and ordering them around, the homeowner has the absolute right to protect himself and his family by any means necessary, including killing the armed intruders. The average American, if he were the *victim* of such an assault by foreign mercenaries, would feel perfectly justified in using whatever violence was necessary to repel the attackers, but if his fellow Americans were the ones *committing* such assaults in a foreign land, that same American, having been steeped in "authority"-worship and pack mentality, will "support the troops," and will cheer when American soldiers murder a homeowner who attempts to forcibly resist such aggression and thuggery.

Authoritarian military actions are *never* purely defensive. When "governments" declare war, it is never to defend the innocent or to preserve freedom, though that is always the *stated* purpose. When "governments" engage in war, it is always to protect or add to the territory or other resources controlled by that "government." The ruling class, by its very nature, does not even want its *own* subjects to be free, much less the subjects of some foreign ruler. As a result, though one who dies in combat is often said to have given his life for his country, in reality those who die in war are simply resources spent by tyrants, in various turf wars with other, competing gangs of tyrants. The people are fed propaganda about heroism, sacrifice and patriotism, to hide the fact that "governments" never enter wars to serve justice or freedom. They do it to serve their own power. An objective examination of history makes this obvious.

Even one of the most apparently justifiable military endeavors in history — the Allies in World War II fighting against the Axis powers — while it resulted in the defeat of the *third* worst mass murderer in history (Adolph Hitler), it also resulted in an even *worse* mass murderer (Josef Stalin) essentially being given half of Europe by the rulers of the Allied nations. The motive of most of the American soldiers who fought in the war was undoubtedly to protect the good from the evil; but the motives of those who commanded them, and therefore the actual results of the brave soldiers' efforts, was nothing more than authoritarian conquest and power.

In World War II, one could have at least suggested (with some imagination) the possibility of an invasion of the United States, and thereby claim that it was an act of self-defense because "national security" was at stake. But most U.S. military operations have involved no direct threat at all to the U.S. Thirty-some thousand Americans died in the Korean war. No one imagined that North Korea was going to invade the U.S. Fifty-some thousand Americans died in the Vietnam war. No one imagined that North Vietnam was going to invade the U.S. No one imagined that the armies of Iraq or Afghanistan were going to invade the U.S. The excuse for such conflicts has always been a vague cause such as "fighting communism," or the even more ethereal excuse of having a "war on terror" (which is made more ironic by the fact that terrorist tactics were and continue to be routinely used by U.S. forces).

The sad irony is that the American ruling class, because of the legitimacy its victims imagine it to have, is the *only* gang actually capable of conquering and subjugating the American people. The gigantic military machine, and all of the war games it has engaged in, rather than providing a shred of real protection for the American public, is what *created* most existing foreign threats, and what is still used as the excuse to justify the oppression of Americans by their *own* "government," via the Orwellian-named "Patriot Act," among other things. The popular bumper sticker that says "If you love your freedom, thank a veteran" is a continuing symptom of the pack-mentality, state-worshiping propaganda that ruling classes feed to their subjects so that the masters will continue to have pawns to play in their sadistic, destructive power games. Even when a slave master fights to prevent some other slave master from stealing his slaves, he is still no friend of the slaves themselves.

It is quite understandable that someone who has risked his life, gone through hell, harmed or killed other human beings, possibly including innocents, and suffered physical or emotional trauma as a result, would be reluctant to accept that all his courage, his suffering, and the damage he inflicted on others ultimately served only the schemes of megalomaniacs. However, even some of the most famous military personalities in history have eventually come to acknowledge that "governments" engage in war, not for any noble purpose, but for profits and power. Major General Smedley Butler, who at the time of his death in 1940 was the most decorated U.S. Marine in history, wrote a book titled "War Is a Racket" that criticized the military-industrial complex, saying that war "*is conducted for the benefit of the very few, at the expense of the very many*," even going so far as to describe his *own* military "service" as the actions of "*a high class muscle man*," a "racketeer" and a "gangster." Likewise, General Douglas MacArthur opined that military expansion is driven by an "*artificially induced psychosis of war hysteria*" and "*an incessant propaganda of fear*." General MacArthur also said the following: "*The powers in charge keep us in a perpetual state of fear — keep us in a continuous stampede of patriotic fervor with the cry of grave national emergency. Always there has been some terrible evil to gobble us up if we did not blindly rally behind it by furnishing the exorbitant sums demanded. Yet, in retrospect, these disasters seem never to have happened, seem never to have been quite real.*"

Of course, to criticize war as a racket which benefits only the ruling class is not to say that the ruling class on the other side is not also evil, or should not be resisted. The atrocities committed by the enforcers of the regimes of Stalin, Mao, Hitler, Lenin, Pol Pot, and many others were extremely serious, and the use of *defensive* violence against the acts of aggression committed by the agents of such regimes was certainly justified. But authoritarian warfare pits pawn against pawn in large-scale bloody combat which covers huge geographical areas, always victimizing civilian populations in the process, while the ruling classes on both sides watch from a safe distance.

Further evidence that war is never about ideals or principles is the fact that the U.S. "government" has often waged war against tyrants it put into place, such as Manuel Noriega and Saddam Hussein. An even more blatant example of how war is not about principles is the fact that at the beginning of World War II, Josef Stalin and his Soviet Union were sworn enemies of the United States. By the end of the war, the psychotic mass murderer was referred to as "Uncle Joe" by the U.S. "government" propagandists, and was treated as a noble ally. Stalin's crimes against humanity, resulting in tens of million of deaths, went largely unmentioned in the U.S. at the time. In light of that fact, it is absurd to claim that the U.S. "government" decided to enter World War II based on any moral principle, or to defeat evil.

It is important to note what does and what does *not* occur in traditional international warfare. Competing ruling classes, including the American rulers, are content to watch their respective pawns slaughtering each other by the thousands, but it has long been the official policy of many "governments," including the U.S. "government," not to attempt to kill foreign "rulers"—i.e., the ones most responsible for making the war happen. In truth, the most moral, the most rational, and the most cost-effective means of defense against any invading "authority" is the assassination of those who command it. Targeting "governments," instead of their loyal enforcers, would serve humanity wonderfully, not only ending most violent conflicts a lot more quickly but creating a huge deterrent to any megalomaniac tempted to start conflicts in the first place. Yet there is an open, mutual, standing agreement between most high-level tyrants that, while it is okay to play games with the lives of their subjects, they will rarely target each other.

And so, over and over again, huge numbers of soldiers march out onto battlefields to kill each other while the real enemies of humanity—the rulers on *both* sides— remain out of harm's way. Thus the lives of the well-intentioned soldiers, the brave "government" enforcers who loyally follow orders to the bitter end, are utterly wasted in endeavors which, by design, ultimately achieve real freedom and justice for no one. And if a soldier manages to recognize and target the ones most responsible for injustice and oppression—those who wear the label of "government" on both sides of every war—he is condemned as a traitor and a terrorist.

Proudly Committing Evil ✺

Whether it is a soldier or some low-level bureaucrat, the job of all "law enforcers" is to forcibly inflict the will of the ruling class upon the general public. Nonetheless, most imagine that as they do so they are "serving the people." Of course, the idea of "serving" someone by initiating violence against him is ridiculous. (Consider the oxymoron of the absurdly named "Internal Revenue Service," which does nothing but rob hundreds of millions of people of trillions of dollars every year.) Rather than ever considering the possibility that what they do on a regular basis—participating in a system of aggression and coercion—is immoral and uncivilized, most state mercenaries, from the paper-pusher to the hired killer, simply say that they are "just doing their jobs," and imagine that that absolves them of all personal responsibility for their actions and the results of those actions.

This, above all else, has been the downfall of human society. Most of the evil and injustice committed by human beings is not the result of greed, or malice, or hatred. It is the result of people doing what they were told, people following orders, people "doing their jobs." In short, most of man's inhumanity to man is a direct result of the belief in "authority." The damage done by the merely obedient is just as real, and just as destructive, as if they had each done it from personal malice. Whether an old lady is robbed by an armed street thug or by a well-dressed, well-educated "tax collector" makes no difference, morally or in practical terms. Whether a family in Iraq is killed by soldiers of Saddam Hussein or by soldiers of the United States "government" makes no difference, morally or in practical terms. Whether someone's personal choices are coercively controlled by a neighborhood thug or by the "police" makes no difference, morally or in practical terms.

The only difference is that the authoritarian thug, as a result of his delusional belief in the mythical entity called "government," refuses to accept personal responsibility for his own actions. His belief in the most dangerous superstition renders him unable to recognize evil as evil. In fact, he will feel *proud* of his loyal obedience to his masters as he spends day after day inflicting hardship and suffering upon innocent people, because he has been taught, for all of his life, that when evil becomes "law," it ceases to be evil and becomes good.

In truth, if anything is a sin, it is blind obedience to "authority." Acting as an enforcer for "government" amounts to spiritual suicide — actually *worse* than physical suicide, because every authoritarian "enforcer" not only shuts off the free will and ability to judge which make him human (thus "killing" his own humanity) but also leaves his body intact, to be used by tyrants as a tool for oppression. To be a "law enforcer" is to willingly change one's self from a person into a robot — a robot which is then given to some of the most evil people in the world, to be used to dominate and subjugate the human race. Wearing the uniform of a soldier or the badge of a "law enforcer" is not a reason for pride; it should be cause for great shame at having forsaken one's own humanity in favor of becoming a pawn of oppressors.

Part III(c)

The Effects on the Targets

Proud to Be Robbed ✸

One of the more bizarre results of the belief in "authority" is that it causes the victims of "government" aggression to feel *obligated* to be victimized, and causes them to feel bad if they *avoid* being victimized. A prime example is the citizen who proclaims that he is proud to pay his "taxes." Even if one believes that some of what he surrenders is used to fund useful things (roads, helping the poor, etc.), to be proud of having been threatened and coerced into funding such things is still strange. Pride in being a "law-abiding taxpayer" is not the result of having helped people, which the person could have done far more effectively on a voluntary basis; the pride comes from having faithfully obeyed the commands of a perceived "authority." By analogy, a man may feel good about having freely given to someone in need, but he would not take pride in getting robbed by a poor man. Probably the only situation in which anyone brags about having been forced to do something occurs in the context of one who believes he is obligated to obey a perceived "authority."

Having been trained to view obedience as a virtue, people want to feel good about surrendering what they earn to "government." And so, with the help of political propaganda, they hallucinate that their "contributions" are actually helping society as a whole. They speak as if paying "taxes" means "giving back to society" or "investing in the country." Such rhetoric, as common as it is, is logically nonsensical, since it implies that every one of the individuals who make up "society" and "the country" somehow each owes a debt to the group as a whole, but is owed nothing. What people are actually doing when they pay "taxes" is giving money, not to "society" or "the country," but to the politicians who make up the ruling class, to spend however they please. The implication, as odd as it is, is that "the people" can benefit as a whole, by every one of "the people" being robbed individually. The idea that the "common good" is better served by politicians spending everyone's money than it would be served by each person spending his own money is strange, to say the least. Recently, the lie of "taxes" serving the common good has become more transparent as "governments" have spent astronomical amounts of money on things which obviously serve the elite at the expense of society and humanity. This would include war-mongering, direct multi-billion-dollar redistribution schemes benefiting the richest people in the world ("bailouts"), and "government" takeovers of various segments of the economy (e.g., the health-care industry), among other things.

In fact, there is almost nothing average people could financially support that would be *less* helpful to society and humanity in general than paying "taxes." Whatever things a person views as worthwhile — schools, roads, defense, helping the poor, etc. — he could just as easily support without going through politicians and "government." Yet many people specifically express pride for having surrendered the fruits of their labors to their masters, having "paid their taxes." Consider how someone would be viewed who proudly proclaimed, "I lied on my tax return, avoided giving $3,000 to the government, and gave the $3,000 to a really good charity instead." Many people would still condemn such a person for his "criminal" disloyalty to the masters, even if the person's actions better served humanity than "paying his taxes" would have. This is because the pride expressed by many people does not come from helping humanity, but from obeying "authority."

There is little or no chance that anyone would voluntarily contribute his own wealth to every one of the programs and schemes now funded via "government." And if he hands over money only because some "law" or other "authority" compelled him to, and then expresses pride in having done so, he is in essence boasting about having been forcibly dominated, precisely the way a thoroughly indoctrinated slave might take pride in serving his master well. There is a big difference between feeling good about having voluntarily supported some worthy cause, and taking pride in being subjugated. Instead of being offended at the insult and injustice of being coercively controlled and exploited—in fact, instead of even recognizing that as injustice—many victims of "government" oppression feel profound loyalty to their controllers.

Proud to Be Controlled ✴

If a slave can be convinced that he *should* be a slave, that his enslavement is both proper and legitimate, that he is the rightful property of his master and that he has an obligation to produce as much as possible for his master, then he does not need to be physically oppressed. In other words, enslaving the mind makes enslaving the body unnecessary. And that is exactly what the belief in "authority" does: it teaches people that it is morally virtuous that they surrender their time, effort and property, as well as their freedom and control over their own lives, to a ruling class.

Many people express pride at being "law-abiding taxpayers," which means only that they do what the politicians tell them to do, and give the politicians money. When confronted with the idea that it is wrong for them to be forcibly deprived of the fruits of their labor, even if it is done "legally," such people often vehemently defend those who continue to rob them, insisting that such robbery is essential to human civilization. (Of course, they do not use the term "robbery" to describe the situation, though they are well aware of what would be done to them if they refused to pay.) Likewise, when one person objects to the level of taxation or other forcible control being inflicted upon him by those in "government," others who are also being oppressed will often condemn the one who is objecting, telling him that if he does not like how he is being treated, he should leave the country. Maligning a fellow *victim* of coercion for complaining about it, is a sure sign that a person actually takes *pride* in his own enslavement.

Frederick Douglass, a former slave, witnessed and described that exact phenomenon among his fellow slaves, many of whom were proud of how hard they worked for their masters and how faithfully they did as they were told. From their perspective, a runaway slave was a shameful thief, having "stolen" himself from the master.

Douglass described how thoroughly indoctrinated many slaves were, to the point where they truly believed that their own enslavement was just and righteous:

"I have found that, to make a contented slave, it is necessary to make a thoughtless one. It is necessary to darken his moral and mental vision, and, as far as possible, to annihilate the power of reason. He must be able to detect no inconsistencies in slavery; he must be made to feel that slavery is right; and he can be brought to that only when he ceases to be a man."

Though slavery is no longer practiced openly, the mentality of loyal subservience remains. Most people today detect no inconsistencies in allowing a ruling class to forcibly extort and control everyone else, and in fact feel that such extortion and oppression is right, to the point where many feel actual shame if they are caught keeping what they earn and running their own lives. It is one thing to feel shame at having been caught stealing, or defrauding, or committing aggression. But it is quite another for someone to feel shame about having done something which, if not for politician decrees ("laws"), he would have seen as perfectly permissible. Such shame does not come from the immorality of the act itself; it comes only from the imagined immorality of disobeying "authority," i.e., "breaking the law."

When, for example, the average citizen is caught "cheating" on his "taxes," or not having a registration sticker on his car, or smoking marijuana, or doing any one of a thousand other things which do not constitute aggression against anyone else, but which have nonetheless been declared "illegal" by the ruling class, there is usually some feeling of guilt in the person's own mind. Without a feeling of being obligated to obey, being caught and punished by agents of "government" would be regarded in the same way that being bitten by a dog would be regarded: as an unpleasant consequence to be avoided, but having no moral element to it at all. Instead, most people feel, at least to some extent, that being caught committing a victimless "crime" indicates some sort of moral failing in themselves, because they did not do as they were told. The desire to have the approval of "authority" is extremely powerful in almost everyone, to a degree that they themselves do not even realize. The ubiquitous message of authoritarianism has a psychological impact far deeper than most people imagine, as the Milgram experiments demonstrated. Nearly everyone experiences dramatic emotional stress and discomfort any time he comes into conflict with "authority," and will go to great lengths, no matter what acts of evil he must commit, in order to earn the approval of his masters.

Even the terminology people use illustrates how effectively they have been trained to feel morally obligated to obey "authority." This can be seen in such simple phrases as "You're not allowed to do that" or even "You can't do that" when referring to some behavior that has been declared "illegal" by the ruling class. Such phrases do not simply express a potential adverse consequence, but also imply that, because some act has been forbidden by the masters, committing that act is bad, not allowable, or even impossible (i.e., "You can't do that!").

Looking at the statistical facts demonstrates the power of the belief in "authority." In the United States, about 100,000 IRS employees extort about 200,000,000 victims. Those being robbed outnumber the robbers by about *two thousand* to one. This could never be accomplished by brute force alone; it continues only because most of those being robbed feel a *duty* to be robbed, and imagine such robberies to be legitimate and valid. The same is true of many other "laws," which are generally obeyed even though the enforcers are always hugely outnumbered by those they seek to control. The high levels of compliance do not come so much from a fear of punishment as from the feeling among those being controlled that they have a moral obligation to cooperate with their own subjugation.

The Good Funding the Evil   ❋

Even if an individual is never personally victimized by "law enforcement," never has a run-in with the police, and sees little if any direct impact by "government" upon his day-to-day life, the myth of "authority" still has a dramatic impact, not only on his own life but also on how his existence affects the world around him. For example, the millions of compliant subjects who feel an obligation to surrender a portion of what they earn to the state, to pay their "fair share" of "taxes," continually fund all manner of endeavors and activities which those people would not otherwise fund — which almost no one would otherwise fund, and which therefore would not otherwise exist. By way of "taxes," those claiming to be "government" confiscate an almost incomprehensible amount of time and effort from millions of victims and convert it into fuel for the agenda of the ruling class. For example, millions of people who oppose war are compelled to fund it via "taxation." The product of their time and effort is used to make possible something they morally oppose.

The same is true of state-controlled wealth-redistribution programs (e.g., "welfare"), Ponzi schemes (e.g., "Social Security"), the so-called "war on drugs," and so on. Most of the programs of "government" would not exist if not for the belief among the general population in a moral obligation to pay one's "taxes." Even "government" programs purported to have noble goals — such as protecting the public and helping the poor — become bloated, inefficient and corrupt monstrosities, which almost no one would willingly support if there was no "law" requiring them to do so.

In addition to the waste, corruption, and destructive things which "government" does with the wealth it confiscates, there is also the less obvious issue of what the people would have done with their money otherwise. As "government" takes the wealth of the producers to serve its own purposes, it also deprives the producers of the ability to further their own goals. Someone who surrenders $1,000 in "taxes" to the ruling class may not only be funding a war he morally opposes, but he is also being deprived of the ability to put $1,000 into savings, or donate $1,000 to some charity he considers worthwhile, or pay someone $1,000 to do some landscaping work. So the damage done by the myth of "authority" is twofold: it forces people to fund things that they do not believe are good for themselves or society, while simultaneously preventing them from funding things that they do view as worthwhile. In other words, subservience to "authority" causes people to act in a manner which is, to one extent or another, directly opposed to their own priorities and values.

Even the people who imagine that their "tax" dollars are doing good by building roads, helping the poor, paying for police, and so on, would almost certainly not fund the "government" version of those services, at least not to the same degree, if they did not feel compelled to do so. Any private charity that had the inefficiency, corruption, and record of abuse that AFDC, HUD, Medicare, and other "government" programs have, would quickly lose all of its donors. Any private company as expensive, corrupt, and inefficient as "government" infrastructure programs would lose all of its customers. Any private protection service which was so often caught abusing, assaulting, and even killing unarmed, innocent people would have no customers. Any private company that claimed to be providing defense, but told its customers it needed a billion dollars every week to wage a prolonged war on the other side of the world, would have few, if any, contributors, including among those who now verbally support such military operations.

The feeling of obligation to pay "taxes" seems to be little hampered by the fact that "government" is notoriously wasteful and inefficient. While millions of "taxpayers" struggle to make ends meet while paying their "fair share" of "taxes," politicians waste millions on laughably silly projects—everything from studying cow farts, to building bridges to nowhere, to paying farmers to *not* grow certain crops, and so on, ad infinitum—and billions more are simply "lost," with no accounting of where they went. But much of what people make possible through payment of "taxes" is not just wasted but is quite destructive to society. The "war on drugs" is an obvious example. How many people would voluntarily donate to a private organization which had the stated goal of dragging millions of non-violent individuals away from their friends and families, to be put into cages? Even the many Americans who now recognize the "war on drugs" as a complete failure continue, via "taxes," to provide the funding which allows it to continue to destroy literally millions of lives.

Even the most vocal critics of the various abuses being perpetrated by the ever-growing police state are often among those making that abuse possible, by providing the funding for it. Whether the issue is blatant oppression, or corruption, or mere bungling bureaucratic inefficiency, everyone can point to at least a few things about "government" that do not meet with his approval. And yet, having been trained to obey "authority," he will continue to feel obligated to provide the funding which enables the same bungling, corrupt, oppressive "government" activities that he criticizes and opposes. Rarely does anyone notice the obvious inherent contradiction in someone feeling *obligated* to fund things that he thinks are bad.

Of course, people who work for non-authoritarian organizations can also be inefficient or corrupt, but when what they are doing comes to light, their customers can simply stop funding them. That is the natural correction mechanism in human interaction, but it is completely defeated by the belief in "authority." How many people are there who are not currently being forced to fund some "government" program or activity that they morally oppose? Very few, if any. So why do those people keep funding things which they feel are destructive to society? Because "authority" tells them to, and because they believe that it is good to obey "authority." As a result, they continue to surrender the fruits of their labors to fuel the machine of oppression—a machine which otherwise would not and could not exist. "Governments" produce no wealth; what they spend they first must take from someone else. Every "government," including the most oppressive regimes in history, has been funded by the payment of "taxes" by loyal, productive subjects. Thanks to the belief in "authority," the wealth created by billions of people will continue to be used, not to serve the values and priorities of the people who worked to produce it, but to serve the agendas of those who, above all else, desire dominion over their fellow man. The Third Reich was made possible by millions of German "taxpayers" who felt an obligation to pay up. The Soviet empire was made possible by millions of people who felt an obligation to give to the state whatever it demanded. Every invading army, every conquering empire, has been constructed out of wealth that was taken from productive people. The destroyers have always been funded by the creators; the thieves have always been funded by the producers; through the belief in "authority," the agendas of the evil have always been funded by the efforts of the good. And this will continue, unless and until the most dangerous superstition is dismantled. When the producers no longer feel a moral obligation to fund the parasites and usurpers, the destroyers and controllers, tyranny will wither away, having been starved out of existence. Until then, good people will continue to supply the resources which the bad people need in order to carry out their destructive schemes.

✳ *Digging Their Own Graves*

Sadly, the belief in "authority" even makes people feel obligated to assist in their *own* enslavement, oppression and sometimes death. In fact, only a small percentage of the coercion of "government" is implemented by the enforcers of "authority"; most of it is implemented by its *victims*. The ruling class merely tells people that they are required to do certain things, and most people comply without any actual enforcement taking place. As one impressive example, tens of millions of Americans, every year, fill out lengthy, confusing forms known as "tax returns," essentially extorting themselves. If the victims of the IRS agreed to pay, but only if the "government" figured out their alleged tax liabilities, the system would collapse. Every tax return is basically a signed confession, with the victim of the extortion racket not only revealing everything about his finances — essentially interrogating himself — but also even figuring out the amount that will be stolen, so the thieves do not have to.

But all the unproductive and unpleasant inconveniences and bureaucratic hassles that people subject themselves to, simply because they were told that "the law" requires it, are nothing compared to the more serious symptoms of the belief in "authority." Based upon the mythology about "duty to country" and the "laws" imposing military conscription ("the draft"), millions of people throughout history have become *murderers* for the state. Only a small fraction (so-called "draft-dodgers") ever resisted, and they have usually been despised by their fellow countrymen, for being cowards or for lacking "patriotism."

In the case of many "laws," it can be difficult to distinguish between people who obey because of a simple fear of punishment, and those who obey out of a feeling of moral obligation to bow to the commands of politicians ("the law"). With military conscription, however, it is easy to tell the difference, because "compliance" is usually far *more* dangerous than any punishment "government" threatens against those who refuse to comply. If the choices are to "comply" and possibly die a gruesome death on some battlefield on the other side of the world, or to disobey and possibly go to prison, it is unlikely that the threat alone is why so many people "register" and show up for "duty" when called. In short, the level of compliance with "the draft," at least in the past, shows quite clearly that most people would rather commit murder or die than disobey "authority." There could hardly be a better indication of just how powerful the superstition of "authority" is: that thousands upon thousands of otherwise civilized, peaceful human beings will leave home, sometimes traveling halfway around the world, to kill or die simply because their respective ruling classes told them to.

Every soldier is both an enforcer and a victim of the superstition of "authority," whether he volunteered or was drafted. Fighting to defend innocents against aggressors is a noble cause, and is often the intention of those who join the military. But in a hierarchical military regime, the soldier becomes a tool of the machine rather than a responsible individual. Rather than being guided by his own conscience, he is controlled entirely by the orders he receives through the chain of command. And every time his obedience leads him to do something immoral (which is quite often), he not only harms his victims, he also harms himself. After the Vietnam war, as one example, many American soldiers came home with their bodies intact but with deep psychological problems. How much of the mental damage was a result of witnessing carnage and how much was the result of personally *creating* carnage is difficult to say. A prolonged fear of imminent death can, of course, cause serious psychological problems, as can inflicting death upon others.

Violent confrontations can be quite stressful, even when the individual feels entirely justified, such as when defending his family from an attacker. But to engage in mortal combat where no one, including the combatants, seems to have any clear idea what the purpose or justification for the conflict is, as occurred in Vietnam, seems to add an additional degree of psychological trauma. As many combat soldiers have attested to, once in the hell of war, any vague but noble cause or justification for the fight is usually forgotten, and all that is left is the desire to stay alive and to help one's friends stay alive—both of which are served much better by going home, or by not joining the military in the first place. And yet the number of people who simply walk away is quite small, for one simple reason: because it would constitute an act of disobedience to a perceived "authority." And the average soldier, though he may have the courage and strength to throw himself into mortal combat, does *not* have the courage and strength to disobey a perceived "authority." As in many cases of authoritarian coercion, the victims of military conscription almost always far outnumber those trying to implement it. Even when people are "legally" commanded to sacrifice their minds and bodies for the sake of turf wars between tyrants, simple passive disobedience by any significant portion of "draftees" would make the war machine grind to a halt. What punishment is there to fear that is worse than the result of compliance? The usual results of fighting in war are prolonged terror, physical and mental pain and suffering, dismemberment or death. Nonetheless, even after witnessing the horrors of war first hand, very few people can bring themselves to disobey "authority," take off the uniform and walk away.

A testament to the power of the belief in "authority" is the well-documented (if seldom discussed) fact that the atrocities committed against the German Jews by the Nazis were often carried out with the cooperation and assistance of *Jewish* police, such as occurred in the Warsaw Ghetto. In their culture, just as in almost every other culture, the people had been so thoroughly convinced that obedience is a virtue that, even though someone new was "in charge," they still felt obligated to do as they were told, even if it meant violently oppressing their own kinsmen. But what may be even more disturbing (but indisputable) is the fact that many millions of people in history have assisted in their *own* extermination, because "authority" told them to. For example, during the Holocaust, many hundreds of thousands of Jews, on their own power, boarded the cattle cars of the very trains that would take them away to their deaths, without trying to hide, run away, or resist. Why? Because those pretending to be "authority" told them to. While it was no doubt true that they were not all aware of exactly what lay in store for them at the other end, they still handed themselves into the custody of a machine that obviously meant them harm.

There is a certain feeling of comfort and safety that one gets by conforming and obeying. Believing that things are in someone else's hands, and having trust that someone else will make things right, is a way to avoid responsibility. Authoritarian indoctrination stresses the idea that, no matter what happens, if you simply do as you are told, and do what everyone else does, everything will be okay, and those in charge will reward and protect you. The body counts from one "government" atrocity after another show how misguided such a belief truly is. Had the victims of "legal" oppression and murder simply *withheld their assistance*, even if they did not lift a finger to forcibly resist, the world would be a very different place today. If the Nazis had had to physically carry each Jew, dead or alive, to the gas chambers or crematoriums, the level of murder would have been dramatically lower. If every slave sold into bondage had refused to work, there would soon have been no slave trade. If the IRS had to calculate the tax due and then directly take it from each "taxpayer," there would be no more federal "taxation." In short, if the *victims* of authoritarian extortion, harassment, surveillance, assault, kidnapping, and murder simply stopped *assisting* in their own oppression, tyranny would crumble. And if the people went a step further and forcibly resisted, tyranny would collapse even more quickly. But resistance, whether passive or violent, requires the people to disobey a perceived "authority," and that is something that most people are psychologically incapable of doing. Ultimately, it is the belief in "authority" among the *victims* of oppression, even more than the beliefs of the ruling class and their enforcers, which allows tyranny, and man's inhumanity to man, to continue on such a large scale.

The Effects on Actual Criminals ✽

Ironically, in situations where obedience would actually improve human behavior, "authority" has no effect. Those individuals, for example, whose own consciences do not stop them from robbing or assaulting their neighbors, because they do not care about the usual standards of right and wrong, also do not care what "authority" tells them to do. It is only those who are trying to be good who ever feel compelled to obey "authority." The belief in "authority" is a belief about morality—it is the idea that obedience is morally good. To those who do not care about what is deemed "good"—the very people whose consciences are not enough to make them behave in a civilized manner—the myth of "authority" has no effect. To put it another way, only those who do not need to be controlled—i.e., those already trying to live moral lives—feel any obligation to obey the controllers. Meanwhile, those who pose a real threat to peaceful society feel no moral obligation to obey any "authority" anyway. Generally speaking, all commands from "authority," including inherently justifiable commands such as "do not steal" and "do not murder," are always either unnecessary (when directed at good people) or ineffectual (when directed at bad people). It is difficult to imagine any situation in which an individual would otherwise have no qualms about committing theft, assault, or murder, but would feel guilty about violating "laws" which prohibit such actions.

A distinction should be made here between moral obligation and fear of retaliation. A thief who feels no moral obligation to refrain from stealing will also feel no moral obligation to obey "laws" against stealing. However, if he perceives a threat to his own safety, whether from the "police" or anyone else, he might be deterred from robbing someone. But that deterrent effect comes entirely from the threat of violence, not from the claimed "authority" underlying the threat. This means that supposed "authority" is never what stops actual crimes from happening, and that an effective deterrent system does not require "authority" at all. This is discussed in further detail below.

Part III(d)

The Effects on the Spectators

The Sin of Non-Resistance   ✹

It is obvious that the belief in "authority" affects the perceptions and actions of "law enforcers," and also affects the perceptions and actions of those against whom "laws" are enforced. But even the perceptions and actions of the *onlookers*, those who are not directly involved, also play a huge role in determining the state of human society. More specifically, the *inaction* of spectators, who quietly allow "legal" coercion to be inflicted upon others, has an enormous impact. History is full of examples proving that Edmund Burke was right when he said that all that is necessary for evil to triumph is for good people to do nothing.

The mass murder committed by the regimes of Stalin, Mao, Hitler, and many others was made possible not just by the willingness of the "enforcers" to carry out their orders but also by their victims' imagined obligation to obey "authority," and by the belief held by almost all onlookers that they should not interfere with "the law" being carried out. The perpetrators of mass injustice, including mass murder, are always hugely outnumbered by their victims, and if you add in the number of spectators —

all those people who could have intervened — it becomes obvious how significant the actions (or inaction) of mere "spectators" can be.

Of course, some people will fail to intervene in a situation simply as a result of basic fear. A witness to a mugging who does not dare to intervene is not condoning mugging by his inaction. He simply values the benefit to his own safety that comes from inaction more than he values whatever benefit he thinks he could be to the victim by stepping in. But there are many cases in which the belief in "authority" makes people hesitate to get involved in a conflict, not just out of fear but out of a deep psychological aversion to going against "authority." There are two ways this can cause spectators to stand idly by while "legal" injustice is inflicted upon someone else: 1) the spectator can believe that the injustice is actually a good thing, because it is "the law," or 2) the spectator can disapprove, but his willingness to actually act out against "law enforcers," or even to speak out against "authority," is stifled by his trained-in subservience. Either way, the outcome is the same: the spectator does nothing to stop the injustice. But the two phenomena will be addressed separately.

✳ *Imagining "Legal" Evil to Be Good*

There are literally millions of examples that could be used to demonstrate how the perception of the general public is dramatically affected by the belief in "authority." Just consider how the average person views and judges an act when it is committed by one claiming to be "authority," as opposed to how he views and judges the exact same act when it is committed by anyone else. Here are a few examples:

1) Scenario A: An American soldier in a foreign country is going house to house, kicking in doors, carrying a machine gun and pointing it at complete strangers, ordering them around and interrogating them, while searching for "insurgents." Scenario B: An average citizen, in his own country, is going house to house, kicking in doors, carrying a machine gun and pointing it at complete strangers, ordering them around and interrogating them, while searching for people he doesn't like. The first is viewed by most people to be a brave and noble soldier "serving his country," while the latter is viewed as a horribly dangerous, probably mentally disturbed individual who should be disarmed and subdued at all costs.

2) Scenario A: An "officer of the law" is manning a "sobriety checkpoint" or a border checkpoint, stopping everyone to ask if they are in the country "legally" or if they have been drinking, or to otherwise see if any indication or evidence of "criminal" activity can be found. Scenario B: A man without a badge is stopping every car that drives down his street, asking every driver if he is an American, asking whether he has been drinking, and looking into his car for anything that appears suspicious. The cop who engages in such intrusive, obnoxious harassment, detainment, interrogation and searching is viewed by many as a brave "law enforcer" doing his job, while anyone else behaving that way would be viewed as psychotic and dangerous.

3) Scenario A: A "Child Protective Services" worker receives a case file and, based upon an anonymous tip, shows up at a house to question the homeowners, with the stated purpose of deciding whether they are fit parents or whether the state should forcibly take their children away from them. Scenario B: An average person, based upon a rumor he heard from a stranger, shows up at the home of other strangers, asking them questions and threatening to take their children away if the questioner is not satisfied with the answers.

Again, the "government" worker is imagined to just be "doing his job," while the average individual who does the same thing is seen as a dangerous, probably mentally unstable person. This is not to say that there could never be a situation in which a child should be taken away from his parents for the child's own protection, but such matters would be taken extremely seriously by any individual who had to take personal responsibility for his actions. A bureaucrat who is merely acting as a cog in the machine of "government," on the other hand, will do such things with far less hesitation and less justification, because he will imagine that something called "the law" is solely responsible for whatever he does.

4) Scenario A: A pilot in the United States Air Force, having been given orders to do so, flies to the proper coordinates and delivers his payload to the intended target. The result is that some mercenaries of a different "authority" are killed, along with a number of civilians who happened to be in the area. Scenario B: An American citizen, acting on his own, loads up a plane with homemade explosives, flies over a building in the city where a vicious street gang is known to reside, and drops the ordnance. The result is that several gang members are killed, as are a dozen innocent bystanders who happened to be passing by on the street.

The average American views the civilian casualties from the first scenario as unfortunate, but chalks them up to the hazards of war. The military pilot is viewed as a hero for having served his country, and is given a medal. In the latter scenario, however, the average American views the pilot as a lunatic, a terrorist and a murderer, and demands that he be put in prison for the rest of his life.

Whether an act has been formally declared "legal" by politicians, and whether it is being done at the behest of "authority," has a huge impact on the perceived morality and legitimacy of the act. In a very real sense, those who do the bidding of "authority" are not even regarded as people, in that their behaviors and actions are judged by such a drastically different standard from those of average human beings. As another example, a lot of people would be alarmed at a report of "a man with a gun" in their neighborhood, unless they heard that the man also had a badge.

People judge behavior based largely upon whether such behavior has been authorized or forbidden by "authority" rather than whether the behavior is inherently legitimate. When citizens are called into an authoritarian court to serve as jurors in a "criminal" trial, for example, it is routine for the "judge" to tell the jury that they are *not* to concern themselves with whether the accused did anything *wrong;* they are to decide only whether or not his actions were in accordance with whatever the "judge" declares "the law" to be. Of note, those in positions of power have, over the years, deliberately and methodically worn away at an old tradition known as "jury nullification," whereby a jury could, in essence, overturn what they viewed as a bad "law" by returning a verdict of "not guilty" even if they believed the accused had actually broken "the law." Every jury still has that power, but authoritarian judges do everything they can to keep jurors from realizing it.

Even when not on a jury, most people still judge others through authoritarian-colored glasses, judging the goodness of another based heavily upon whether he obeys the commands of politicians — i.e., whether he is a "law-abiding taxpayer." Compare how the average citizen would view the two individuals described below.

Individual A has no driver's license, works "under the table" to avoid paying "taxes," never registered for the "Selective Services," owns an unregistered, unlicensed firearm, occasionally smokes pot, sometimes gambles ("illegally"), and lives in a cabin which he owns but for which he has no "occupancy permit," and which has a deck on the back that he built without first getting a building permit.

Individual B has a driver's license, pays taxes on what he earns, registered for the draft, owns a registered firearm, occasionally drinks beer, sometimes plays the state lottery, and lives in a "government"-inspected and approved house with a "government"-inspected and approved deck out back.

The two live otherwise similar lives, with both being productive, and with neither robbing or assaulting anyone else. Their behaviors, choices and lifestyles are very similar in almost every way, except that there are "laws" against the actions of Individual A, but not against those of Individual B. That alone, without any other substantive difference in what they do or how they treat other people, would cause a lot of people to view Individual A with a degree of contempt, while viewing Individual B with respect and approval. In fact, if Individual A was accosted, detained, and even physically assaulted (e.g., tasered, beaten and handcuffed) by "law enforcers," even if he had never threatened or harmed anyone, many believers in "government" would opine that he "had it coming," that he *deserved* to be attacked and caged for having disobeyed the commands of politicians.

This tendency of onlookers to blame the *victims* of authoritarian violence is incredibly strong. One who accepts the superstition of "authority" — the idea that some individuals have the right to forcibly dominate others, and that those others have a duty to comply — will assume that if "authority" is using violence against a person, it must be justified, and therefore the victim of such violence must have done something wrong. This pattern shows up in different situations. When, for example, U.S. troops kill civilians in some foreign country, many Americans are desperate to believe, and therefore automatically assume, without a shred of evidence, that the dead victims must have been "insurgents," or collaborators, or at least sympathizers with "the enemy." As another example, when the Branch Davidians near Waco, Texas, were subjected to a military assault, follow by prolonged physical and mental torture, followed by mass extermination, many Americans were quick to assume that anyone that "government" would do that to must have deserved it. The American tyrants fostered this attitude by fabricating various rumors and accusations, in order to demonize the victims of that violent, fascistic assault on non-violent people. Actually, the incident was the result of a publicity stunt by the ATF, based upon rumors that some people in the group possessed "illegal" gun parts. Many people assume that if someone was assaulted, prosecuted, or imprisoned by agents of "authority," then that person must have done something wrong, and must have deserved what was done to him. This assumption may come from a refusal of people to consider the possibility that the "government" they rely on for protection is actually an aggressor, or it may come from not wanting to consider the possibility that anyone, including himself, could be the next helpless victim of authoritarian violence, even if he has done nothing wrong. Regardless of the cause, the end result is that, when evil is committed in the name of "law," many spectators immediately hate the victims, and rejoice at the pain and suffering that is inflicted upon them.

✳   *Obligation to Do Wrong*

While everyone is aware that there are "laws" against robbery and murder (except when they are committed in the name of "authority"), the average person is completely unaware of the tens of thousands of pages of other "government"-issued statutes, rules and regulations—federal, state and local. But even when they have very little idea exactly what "the law" does and does not allow, most people still hold a general belief that "obeying the law" is a good thing, and that "breaking the law" is a bad thing. In fact, even when a person is strongly opposed to a particular "law," believing it to be unjust, he may still hold a general, conflicting belief that "laws" ought to be obeyed and that it is justified to punish those who disobey. This psychological paradox is quite common, in fact, with many people vehemently lobbying to change what they view to be bad "laws," while supporting the idea that as long as it is the law, people should obey it.

Such mental contradictions are common in the context of the belief in "authority," but are rare outside of it. For example, no one would argue that it is morally wrong to try to steal an old lady's purse but also morally wrong for the old lady to hang on to her purse. But the concept of a "bad law," in the mind of one who believes in "authority," boils down to a similar paradox: a *bad* command which also is *bad* to disobey. The spectator who believes in "authority" may view a particular command, enacted by the masters and implemented by the enforcers, as being unimportant, unnecessary, counter-productive, or even stupid or unjust, while at the same time believing that people still have a moral obligation to obey that command, simply because it is "the law." Examples of the effects of such a viewpoint abound, ranging from the mundane to the horrific. Here are a few.

1) At 2:00 a.m., on a wide-open, straight, empty road running through unpopulated farmland, a driver slows down, but does not stop, at the stop sign at a cross street. A motorcycle cop, hiding a hundred yards away behind some bushes, turns on his lights. Almost everyone, given those facts, would agree that the driver did not harm or endanger anyone, or anyone's property, and yet most people would agree that the cop would have the right to demand money from the driver, via a traffic "ticket." In other words, even though they would concede that the only thing "bad" about what the driver did was that it was technically "illegal," they believe that that alone justifies the forcible robbery of the driver. Taking it one step further, if the driver attempted to leave the scene, rather than accept the "ticket," most spectators would agree that the cop would be right to chase down, capture and imprison the driver.

2) A "government" inspector, from a state "Board of Health," conducts an inspection of a restaurant. The restaurant is perfectly clean and organized, and the inspector finds no indication that anything there poses any risk to anyone's health. However, he nonetheless finds several technical violations of the local "code" for restaurants. As a result of those violations — not because they create a danger to anyone, but because they are "against the rules" — the restaurant owner is fined hundreds of dollars. Again, even though the restaurant owner did not harm or endanger anyone or anyone's property, most people would view it as legitimate for the owner to be robbed by those acting on behalf of "government." And if the owner attempted to resist such robbery — whether by trying to conceal the technical "violations," or by bribing the "inspector," or by refusing to pay the fine — he would be seen as immoral by most people, and the enforcers would be seen as having the right to use whatever means necessary to achieve compliance with "the law."

3) A man drives his friend home from a party. Knowing he would have to drive, he did not have any alcohol to drink, though his friend did. He drops his friend off and heads home. He notices the police doing a sobriety checkpoint traffic stop ahead, and remembers that his friend left his half-full beer bottle in the car. Knowing that it is "illegal" to have an open container of alcohol in his car, he covers it up. He has not harmed or endangered anyone, and in fact has acted quite responsibly, acting as designated driver to make sure his friend would arrive home safely. However, he still "broke the law" (albeit accidentally) by driving a car with an open bottle of beer in it, and then tried to hide evidence of that fact. If he was caught doing so and arrested, few people would view the cop as the bad guy in the situation.

4) A man sells a shotgun with a barrel a quarter of an inch shorter than "the law" allows. The weapon is no more lethal than a shotgun a quarter of an inch longer, and no one who was involved threatened or used violence against anyone. But the man, having been caught with the "illegal" item, is subjected to a para-military invasion of his property, followed by an armed standoff, in which several people are killed.

Unfortunately, this example is not hypothetical. It happened to Randy Weaver at Ruby Ridge in 1992. And he was not merely "caught" selling an "illegal" shotgun; he was enticed into doing so by undercover "law enforcers." The result of the armed invasion of the Weavers' property, and the subsequent shootout and siege, was that Mr. Weaver's wife and son were killed, and he and a friend were wounded. Though it would be absurd for anyone to claim that there is a moral difference between possessing a shotgun with an 18-inch barrel and possessing a shotgun with a 17¾-inch barrel, and even though that allegation was the entire "legal" justification for the armed assault and confrontation, many spectators would still fault Randy Weaver, viewing him as the bad guy for having allowed himself to be coaxed into breaking an arbitrary, completely irrational (not to mention unconstitutional) "law." That is the power of the belief in "authority": it can lead many people to view a gang of sadistic, murderous thugs as the good guys, and to view their *victims* as the bad guys.

To most people, "breaking the law," without specifying *which* "law," has an automatic negative connotation. They view disobedience to "authority" not merely as dangerous but as immoral. But to the "government" believer, something even worse than committing a minor, victimless "crime" is openly disobeying an agent of "authority."

The average spectator, when observing the interaction between an "authority" figure and anyone else, will often view with disdain anyone who does not immediately and unquestioningly answer any questions and comply with any requests from a man with a badge. Even if the person complies, but exhibits an "attitude" toward the "authority" figure—any attitude other than meek subservience—many spectators will be quick to condemn the one who fails to grovel. And one who runs away from the police, even if he had done nothing wrong in the first place, is viewed with scorn by most. And when someone who runs, or hides, or refuses to cooperate is beaten up, tortured, or even murdered by "law enforcers," many spectators opine that the victim should have done what the police told him to do. And when someone actively *resists* an "authority" figure, few have the gumption to take that person's side under any circumstances, even with mere words. Just as a well-trained dog will not bite its master, even when sadistically maltreated, so those who have been trained to bow to "authority" are usually psychologically incapable of bringing themselves to lift a finger to defend themselves, much less someone else, from any aggression committed in the name of "law" and "government" and "authority." Indeed, due to their authoritarian indoctrination, most people would more eagerly condemn their fellow victims than join together with their fellow victims to actually resist tyranny.

There is, of course, a difference between saying that it is not smart for someone to do something, and saying that it is immoral to do something. It is one thing to say that it is stupid for someone to "mouth off" to a cop, and another to say that doing so is actually immoral and that one who does so therefore *deserves* whatever abuse or punishment he receives. The believers in "authority" often express the latter opinion about anyone who "defies the police," regardless of the reason.

The idea of average people imposing justice upon wayward "law enforcers" existentially terrifies statists, even when a "law enforcer" has done something as serious as committing murder. In the eyes of the well indoctrinated, the only "civilized" course of action in such a situation is to beg some *other* "authority" to make things right, but never to "take the law into one's own hands." People may complain about and condemn "legal" injustice, but few are even able to consider the possibility of engaging in premeditated, "illegal" resistance, even when agents of "government" are inflicting vicious brutality upon unarmed, non-violent targets. And if, through prolonged brainwashing, a people can be rendered psychologically unable to resist the oppressions done in the name of "authority," then it makes no difference whether those people have the physical means to resist. Modern tyrants and their enforcers are always outnumbered (and often outgunned) by their victims by a factor of hundreds or thousands. Yet tyrants still maintain power, not because people lack the *physical* ability to resist, but because, as a result of their deeply inculcated belief in "authority," they lack the *mental* ability to resist. As Stephen Biko put it, "The most potent weapon in the hands of the oppressor is the mind of the oppressed."

Double Standard on Violence ❈

The double standard in the minds of those who have been indoctrinated into authoritarianism, when it comes to the use of physical force, is enormous. When, for example, a "law enforcer" is caught on film brutally assaulting an unarmed, innocent person, the talk is usually about whether the officer should be reprimanded, or maybe even lose his job. If, on the other hand, some citizen assaults a "police officer," nearly everyone will enthusiastically demand—often without even wondering or asking why the person did it—that the person be caged for many years. And if a person resorts to the use of deadly force against a supposed agent of "authority," hardly anyone even bothers to ask why he did it. In their minds, no matter what the agent of "authority" did, it is never okay to kill a representative of the god called "government." To the believers in "authority," nothing is worse than a "cop-killer," regardless of why he did it.

In reality, using deadly force against one who pretends to be acting on behalf of "authority" is morally identical to using deadly force against anyone else. An act of aggression does not become any more legitimate or righteous simply because it is "legalized" and committed by those claiming to act on behalf of "authority." And using whatever force is necessary to stop or prevent an act of aggression, whether the aggression is "legal" or not, and whether the aggressor is a "law enforcer" or not, is justified. (Of course, the risks involved with resisting "legal" aggression are often much higher, but that does not make it any less moral or justified.) Many of the reasons now used by "law enforcers" to forcibly take people captive—such as engaging in peaceful public demonstrations without a "permit," or photographing "law enforcers" or "government" buildings, or not submitting to random stops and questioning by "law enforcers"—have no shred of justification when viewed without the "authority" myth. As such, resisting such fascist thuggery, even if it requires deadly force to do so, is morally justified, albeit extremely dangerous. But most people are literally incapable of even considering such an idea. Even when they recognize unjust oppression, they imagine that the "civilized" response is to let the injustice happen, and then later beg some other "authority" to make amends.

When faced with "legal" aggression and oppression, there are only two possibilities: either the people are obliged to *allow* "law enforcers" to inflict all manner of injustice and oppression upon them (and then complain later), or the people have the right to use whatever level of force is necessary to stop such injustice and oppression from occurring. To say, for example, that someone has a "right" to be free from unreasonable searches and seizures by "government" agents (as the Fourth Amendment states) would mean nothing if a victim of such tyranny was obliged to allow it to happen at the time and then complain about it later. To have a "right" to be free from such oppression logically implies the right to use whatever force is required to stop such oppression from happening in the first place, even if that requires the killing of police officers. But the very thought terrifies those who have been trained to always bow to "authority." Most of those who speak of "unalienable" rights still balk at the thought of forcibly defending those rights against authoritarian assaults.

To say that someone has a "right" to do something, while also saying that he would not be justified in forcibly defending such a right against "government" incursions, is a contradiction. In truth, what most people call "rights" they actually perceive as "government"-granted privileges, which they hope their masters will allow, but which they have no intention of forcibly protecting if such "rights" are "outlawed" by "government." For example, to have an unalienable right to speak one's mind (the right to freedom of speech) means that the person also has the right to use whatever level of violence it takes, up to and including deadly force, to defend against "government" agents who try to silence him. Though the point makes loyal believers in "authority" very uncomfortable, the very concept of a person having an unalienable right to do something also implies the right, if all else fails, to kill any "law enforcers" who attempt to stop him from doing it. But in truth, there is almost nothing that "government" can do, whether it be censorship, assault, kidnapping, torture, or even murder, which would make the average statist advocate violent, "illegal" resistance.

(The reader is invited to test the depths of his own loyalty to the myth of "authority" by considering the question of what would have to happen before he himself would feel justified in killing a "law enforcer.")

"Law enforcers" constantly escalate disagreements to the level of violence, every time they try to arrest someone, or force their way into someone's home, or forcibly take someone's property. And authoritarian enforcers will then keep increasing the level of violence they use, until they get their way. The result is that the people, unless they are willing to engage in open revolution against the entire system, will sooner or later bow to the will of the ruling class, or be killed. And though the mercenaries of the state are always using force, or the threat of force, to subdue and subjugate average people, the moment their intended victims respond to violence with violence, most spectators will instantly identify the *victim* of aggression—the one who used force only to *defend* against an attack—as the "bad guy." This glaring double standard—the idea that it is okay for "authority" to commit violent acts of aggression on a regular basis, but horribly evil for the common folk to ever respond with defensive violence—shows how drastically the belief in "authority" can warp people's perception of reality.

Ironically, in considering other places and other times, almost everyone accepts and even praises the use of "illegal" violence, including deadly violence, against agents of "government." Few people would still insist that the Jews who lived in 1940 Germany should have continued to try to "work within the system" by voting and petitioning the Third Reich for justice. Instead, those who "illegally" hid, ran away, or even forcibly resisted (as occurred in the Warsaw Ghetto) are now seen by almost everyone as having been justified in doing so, even though they were technically "criminals," "law-breakers," and even "cop-killers." But authoritarians, in their own time and in their own country, not only continue to condemn any who "illegally" try to avoid or resist oppression, but cheerfully gloat over the suffering of such people when they are punished by "government." To delight in a "tax cheat" being punished, for example, as many Americans do, is akin to a slave taking pleasure in the whipping of a fellow slave who tried to escape.

There may be an aspect of simple envy in this: a feeling that, if one subject has been victimized, it is not "fair" that another escaped such suffering. This contributes to the fact that "taxpayers"—i.e., those who have been forcibly extorted by the ruling class—often express resentment of anyone who has avoided being similarly extorted. Oddly, the victims of "legal" robbery often imagine themselves to be virtuous for having been robbed, and look down on those who, for whatever reason, have not been robbed.

✳ *The Danger of Inaction*

One who views "breaking the law" as inherently bad, regardless of what the "law" is, may be quick to report to the "authorities" any "illegal" activities he is aware of, even if the activities are victimless and constitute neither force nor fraud. Likewise, those who sit on juries in "government" courtrooms, if they imagine disobedience to "authority" ("breaking the law") to be inherently immoral, are likely to give their blessing to someone being punished, sometimes quite harshly, for doing something which harmed no one and did not constitute either fraud or violence. In the case of the "snitch" and the juror, however, such actions take one out of the role of a mere spectator and move him into the role of a *collaborator* of oppression.

The damage done by the belief in "authority" among the spectators of oppression comes more often from their inaction, rather than from their action. Time after time, oppressions—large and small—have been committed right under the noses of basically good people who did nothing about it. To a certain degree, this is the result of simple self-preservation: a person may avoid getting involved simply because he fears for his own safety. But the Milgram experiments showed quite clearly that even without any underlying threat to themselves, most people feel irresistibly compelled to obey "authority" even when they know that what they are being told to do is wrong and harmful to others. And if they find it difficult to disobey a perceived "authority," they will find it even more difficult, if not impossible, to bring themselves to intervene when an "authority" is exerting its will on someone else.

The result of the *spectators* having been trained to be passive, obedient, and non-confrontational can be seen in the many instances, throughout the world and throughout history, of dozens, hundreds, or even thousands of spectators, standing around like zombies, watching as agents of "authority" assault or murder innocent people. Even in the United States, the supposed "land of the free and the home of the brave," videos continue to surface depicting police brutality occurring right in front of crowds of onlookers, who simply stand and watch, not lifting a finger to protect their fellow man against the evils committed in the name of "authority."

Part III(e)

The Effects on the Advocates

✳ *"Legalized" Aggression*

While most people probably imagine themselves to be "spectators" when it comes to authoritarian oppression and injustice, in truth nearly everyone is actually an advocate of "government" violence, in one form or another. Anyone who votes, regardless of the candidate, or even verbally supports some "policy" or "program" of the "government," is condoning the initiation of violence against his neighbors, even if he does not recognize it as such. This is because "law" is not about friendly suggestions, or polite requests. Every so-called "law" enacted by politicians is a command, backed by the *threat of violence* against those who do not obey. (As George Washington put it, *"Government is not reason; it is not eloquence; it is force."*)

Most people, in their day-to-day lives, are very reluctant to use threats or physical force against their fellow man. Only a tiny fraction of the many personal disagreements that occur lead to violent conflicts. However, because of their belief in "government," nearly everyone advocates widespread violence without even realizing it. And they feel no guilt about doing so, because they perceive threats and coercion to be inherently legitimate when they are called "law enforcement."

Everyone knows what happens if someone gets caught "breaking the law." It may only be a "fine" (a demand for payment under threat of force), or it may be an "arrest" (forcibly taking someone captive), or it may even result in "law enforcers" killing someone who continues to resist. But *every "law" is a threat, backed by the ability and willingness to use deadly force against those who disobey,* and anyone who honestly considers the idea will recognize that fact.

But the belief in "authority" leads to a strange contradiction in how people see the world. Almost everyone advocates that "law" be used to coerce others to do certain things, or to fund certain things. However, while advocating such actions, knowing full well the consequences to any who are caught disobeying, those same advocates fail to recognize that what they are advocating is violence. There are millions, for example, who consider themselves to be peaceful, civilized people—some even proudly wear the label of "pacifist"—while advocating armed robbery against every-one they know, as well as millions of strangers. They see no contradiction, because the robbery is given the euphemism "taxation" and is carried out by people who are imagined to have the *right* to commit robbery, in the name of "government."

The level of denial which the belief in "authority" creates is profound. When advoca-ting "political" violence, people accept no responsibility for the results. Those who apply for "government benefits," for example, are asking to receive loot forcibly stolen from their neighbors via "taxation." Likewise, applying for a "government" job amounts to asking that one's neighbors be *forced* to pay one's salary. Whether the person receives a direct payment or some service, program, or other benefit, he will usually accept the stolen property without the slightest hint of shame or guilt. He may otherwise be perfectly neighborly to the people whom he asked the state to rob. In no other situation does such a strange mental disconnect occur, not only for the one advocating the act of aggression, but also for the *victim* of it. If, for example, one person had paid an armed thief to break into his neighbor's house and steal some of his valuables, and the neighbor knew he had done so, such neighbors would probably not be on friendly terms (to say the least). Yet when the same thing is done using "authority," via elections followed by "legislative" theft, neither the thief nor the victim usually perceives anything wrong with it.

(Author's personal note: I've lost count of how many people have expressed sympathy for me and my wife because we were imprisoned for not bowing to the IRS. But it never seems to

occur to our non-anarchist acquaintances that we were caged by the very people they voted for, for disobeying commands which they advocated. As far as I know, not one statist we know has even noticed the schizophrenia and hypocrisy of actively supporting mass extortion ("taxation") and then giving heart-felt condolences to the victims of that same extortion.)

One can see the supernatural essence of "authority" in the fact that, among the people who will eagerly vote for their neighbors to be "legally" extorted and robbed, few would ask or pay mere mortals to do the same thing. Few people would feel justified in hiring a street gang to rob his neighbors in order to pay for his own child's schooling, but many millions advocate the same thing when they condone "property taxes" to fund "public" schools. Why do the two feel so morally different to them? Because those who believe in "government" believe it consists of something more than the people in it. It is imagined to have rights that no mere mortal has.

From the perspective of the statist, asking "government" to do something has far more in common with praying for the gods to do something than it does with asking people to do something. A statist who demands certain "legislation" would be horrified and offended if some group of average people offered to provide similar services. Imagine if a street gang made the following offer to a local resident:

"We'll do a shakedown of your neighbors and use what we get to pay for things you want — your kid going to school, fixing the roads, stuff like that. We have to keep a cut ourselves, of course. And tell us how you wish your neighbors would behave, and we'll make sure they behave that way. If they don't do what we say, we take their stuff or stick them in a cage."

If average people made such an offer, they would be condemned for their attempted thuggery. But when the same things are proposed in a campaign speech by someone running for a position in "government," and when such things are done in the name of vague political abstractions such as "the common good" or "the will of the people," they are seen not only as allowable but as noble and virtuous. When the politician says, "We need to provide adequate funding for our children's education, and we need to invest in our infrastructure," he is literally talking about forcibly taking money away from the people (via "taxes") and spending it the way *he* thinks it should be spent. Such aggression is accepted as justified when done in the name of "authority," but recognized as immoral if done by mere mortals. This shows that, in the mind of the statist, "government" is something more than a collection of human beings. Paradoxically, the statist will insist that everything that "government" is allowed to do, and everything it is, comes from "the people." All belief in "govern-ment" requires the absurd, cult-like belief that, by way of pseudo-religious political documents and rituals (constitutions, elections, appointments, legislation, and so on) a bunch of mere mortals can conjure into existence an entity that possesses superhuman rights—rights not possessed by any of the people who created it. And once the people hallucinate the existence of such a thing, they will eagerly beg that thing to forcibly control and extort their neighbors. People recognize that mere mortals have no right to do such things, but truly believe that the deity called "government" has every right to do such things.

Excuses for Aggression ✳

Though "democracy" is often praised as the height of civilization, cooperation, and "getting along," it is the exact opposite. Voting is an act of aggression, and loving "democracy" amounts to loving widespread violence and constant conflict. Political elections are not about togetherness, unity or tolerance; they are about arguing over how everyone should be *forced* to behave and what everyone should be *forced* to financially support, via the control machine called "government." The abundance of campaign signs littering lawns prior to every election are not the sign of an enlightened, free society; they are the sign of a mentally and physically enslaved society, bickering over which slave master they want holding the whip. Every single person who votes (Democrat, Republican, or third party) is attempting to put people into power who will carry out large-scale extortion ("taxation") to fund various "government" programs. Any candidate who suggested doing away with all such robbery entirely—repealing all "taxes"—would be ridiculed as an extremist kook. All voters attempt to empower a gang that they know will commit mass robbery, yet none of those voters accept any responsibility for doing so. They know what their candidates will do if put into power, they know what the consequences will be to any who then disobey the commands of those politicians, but the belief in "author-ity" makes the voters psychologically incapable of recognizing that what they are doing is advocating widespread violence.

In fact, notwithstanding the traditional mythology and rhetoric, no one who believes in "government" actually *wants* it to be administered with the so-called "consent of the governed." If it were actually done via genuine consent, it would mean that each person's political preferences would be imposed only upon himself, unless others happened to advocate the exact same agenda. Obviously, the goal of the voter is not to compel himself to financially support things he likes, nor is it to control his own choices and behaviors; the goal of every voter is always to use the mechanism of "government" to coerce *other* people into making certain choices, funding certain things, and behaving in certain ways.

Indeed, the individual statist sometimes has a fairly lax view of his *own* obligation to obey the myriad of political commands ("laws"), feeling that he is competent to rely on his own common sense and judgment regardless of "the law," while at the same time feeling that everyone *else* needs to be controlled and micromanaged by "authority." He believes that he himself is trustworthy and moral, and can make his own decisions, and that the purpose of "law" is to keep everyone *else* in line.

The degree to which different voters want "authority" controlling others varies significantly. The Constitutionalist wants the federal "government" to force others to fund only those things specifically designated as federal matters by the U.S. Constitution. Meanwhile, the "progressive" wants "government" to force others to fund all sorts of things, from art, to defense, to caring for the poor, to education, to retirement programs, and so on. But while the two types of voters differ in the degree and types of aggression they support, they do not differ in principle: they have both accepted the premise that "authority" has the right to forcibly extort money for "government" functions that are deemed necessary; they differ only on what counts as "necessary."

The thinking of almost every statist is paradoxical. On the one hand, statists know that every "law" they condone is a command backed by a threat of violence. They are fully aware of the things that are done to any "law-breaker" who gets caught, but the average statist, when asked, will vehemently *deny* that he condones the initiation of violence against his neighbors. On a practical level, the statist knows that any "political" agenda he supports will, if enacted, be administered by whatever level of intimidation or brute force is necessary to obtain compliance from the people. Yet the average statist, while being fully aware of this, will also exhibit a huge logical disconnect, refusing to admit that he is openly and directly advocating the forcible extortion and coercive control of millions of innocent people. The reason for this is that the statist believes that the entity called "authority" has the *right* to rule, and as a result, when it commits violence, it does not *count* as violence.

As long as the violence is done by those claiming to be "authority," who are imagined to have an exemption from the usual rules of morality (don't steal, don't assault, don't murder, etc.) even those who are the most ardent proponents of various "taxes" and other "laws" can continue to imagine themselves to be peaceful, compassionate, non-violent people. Some even imagine themselves to be pacifists. (Because everything "government" does is done via force, or threat of force, there is no such thing, and can be no such thing, as a statist pacifist. While obviously not all anarchists are pacifists, all true pacifists are anarchists.) There are many ways—a few of which are addressed below—in which otherwise decent, virtuous people condone aggression and assault, intimidation and robbery, because they believe that it is perfectly allowable for the superhuman, mythical deity known as "government" to commit such acts, and therefore believe that it is perfectly moral and virtuous for them to *ask* "government" to commit such acts.

Charity Through Violence ✳

The typical statist is profoundly schizophrenic, being both completely aware, and completely unaware, that he personally advocates the widespread use of violence against others. A dramatic example of this would be those who view themselves as loving and compassionate for supporting "government" programs to help the poor. What they are literally advocating, via their support of "welfare" programs, is a massive extortion racket, in which many millions of human beings are robbed of billions of dollars via the threat of being caged. Proponents of such "charity through violence" imagine themselves to be virtuous and caring because of what the needy may receive, while completely disassociating themselves from the threats, intimidation, harassment, forced seizures and imprisonments which they know occur and which they know are essential to any "welfare" program. Because of this bizarre selective denial, those who believe in "government" can be totally aware of the brute force by which such "laws" are implemented, while being seemingly unaware that they themselves are *condoning* such brute force, when they demand such "laws."

The belief in "authority" is what allows for this strange psychological contradiction, as it convinces the advocates of wealth redistribution schemes that the victims of "legal" extortion have an *obligation* to cooperate, and that the use of violence against those who do not pay "their taxes" is therefore justified. As a result, the basic measure of morality and virtue is turned completely on its head, with "welfare" advocates viewing themselves as compassionate for advocating violent theft, while viewing as despicable criminals any who try to avoid or resist that violence.

Similarly, advocates of "Social Security," a Ponzi-style wealth-redistribution scheme, imagine themselves to be caring and compassionate. Blinded by their belief in "government," they fail to recognize that they are not only forcing people into what is (falsely) represented as a "government"-run retirement scheme, but are also adding insult to injury by insinuating that people cannot and should not be trusted to plan for their own futures. It takes a serious disconnect with reality for someone to vehemently support coercing people into participating in an "investment" program which invests in nothing and has no assets, and which has a return far worse than most real investments (and actually does not guarantee any return at all) and then to feel noble and charitable for having forced people into such a scheme. (Not only is there no Social Security "account" — individually or collectively — that is "paid into," but the U.S. Supreme Court (in *Flemming v. Nestor*, 363 U.S. 603) has made it clear that no one has any contractual rights to any Social Security "benefits" at all, regardless of how much they may have "paid into" the system, and that Congress can cut off any or all "benefits" anytime it wants.)

✳ *Advocates of Brutality*

Quite often throughout history, heinous oppression has been supported by the people, in part because the people were unable to recognize evil as evil when it was committed in the name of "law" and "authority." If the people truly believe that "government" has the right to rule, as almost everyone now believes, all sorts of authoritarian "solutions" will be supported, or at least passively accepted, by most people. For example, many Germans in the 1940s, who themselves would never commit or condone private intimidation or assault, much less murder, nonetheless eagerly supported the idea of a "legislative," "government"-approved and "government"-administered "solution" to the so-called "Jewish problem" (as Hitler called it). It was officially sanctioned, and done via "law," so the people imagined themselves to be blameless for whatever happened, even if they vehemently advocated it.

Americans today, suffering from selective denial, are quick to righteously condemn what *other* violent, oppressive regimes have done but slow to recognize that, as a result of their own belief in "authority," they too condone widespread draconian brutality, in the name of "law." Even when oppression goes beyond mere threats and intimidation, and leads to constant, widespread, open violence and brutality, most people, as a result of their belief in "authority," are still unable to recognize it as evil.

An obvious example is war. The nationalism that is so strong in authoritarians blinds them to the absolute evil which they condone and support in the name of "national defense." In many cases, this blindness is intentional. Politicians and conservative voters alike complain when the blunt realities of war are shown to the American people. They want to wave their flag and cheer for their team, enthusiastically participating in the pack mentality, but they do not want to have to actually *see* the real-world results of what it is they support. They can be persuaded to proudly "support the troops," and believe in a supposedly righteous war in the abstract, as long as they are sheltered from having to see the carnage — blood, guts and body parts — which their "patriotism" is causing.

Though love of one's "country" is still portrayed as a great virtue, the truth is that the killers on *both* sides of every war, including those who fought for the most brutal, ruthless regimes in history, have been motivated by the feeling of righteousness that nationalistic pack mentality gives them. War could not happen at all without soldiers putting their devotion and loyalty to their own gang, tribe or "country" above doing what is right. "Patriotism" and the belief in "authority" are the two key ingredients to war. The easiest way to dupe basically good people into committing evil is by portraying acts of aggression and conquest as "fighting for one's country."

While rulers have long been practicing mind control over their subjects, in many cases the mind control of those who believe in "authority" is self-inflicted. They want to believe in "their country," and in some righteous, abstract principle, some ideal, some noble cause (e.g., "spreading democracy"), without having to think of what is happening in simple, literal terms. It is easier to support mass murder when it is called "war," and more so when it is called "national defense." When it is cloaked in authoritarian, pack-mentality terminology, it allows its proponents — and those actually making it happen — to imagine themselves to be supporting something brave and righteous. While individual soldiers may truly believe they are fighting for a noble cause, it is impossible to be a "good guy" and be at war with an entire country, as discussed previously. The way "governments" wage war is *never* justified, and *never* moral, as it always involves widespread violence against innocents. But that is a fact that nationalists, left and right, refuse to see.

Another example of modern draconian brutality, "legally" committed in the "free world," comes from the campaign of violence known as "the war on drugs." In the name of trying to stamp out a habit—not violence, or theft, or fraud, but a mere *habit*—millions of non-violent, peaceful, productive human beings have been assaulted, terrorized, and caged. Enforcement of "narcotics laws" occurs in a particularly brutal, vicious way, with paramilitary invasions of private homes being commonplace, and many-year imprisonments for victimless "crimes" being abundant. And the advocates of the "war on drugs" are well aware, not only of the overtly violent enforcement actions but also of the fact that the only measurable effects have been higher prices for certain mind-altering substances, more crime committed to pay for such substances, violent conflict between rival sellers of the substances, and more funds, weapons, power, and "legislative" permission for those who wear the label of "authority" to harass and assault innocents. Even if it actually worked, and eliminated or significantly reduced the use of certain drugs, such brutality would be absolutely unjustified and immoral. But even though it has utterly failed to get an inch closer to the stated goal, many "conservatives" enthusiastically cheer for more harassment, terrorism and violence. (To add hypocrisy to fascism, most of those "conservatives" drink alcohol: an act morally identical to the behaviors they want "authority" to violently stamp out.)

And while millions of lives continue to be destroyed by that brutal, draconian crusade, many statists eagerly blame the victims, by declaring that they "broke the law" and therefore deserve whatever is done to them. So, to the supposedly moral and responsible "conservative," even if a person has harmed no one, and committed neither force nor fraud, if he has simply disobeyed the arbitrary decrees of his masters, he *deserves* to be assaulted, caged or killed. And, of course, such "conservatives" view it as unforgivable if one of the targets of such fascist thuggery decides to fight back. From the twisted, delusional viewpoint of the devout nationalist authoritarian, it is noble and virtuous for state mercenaries to violently assault, and attempt to kidnap and cage, a productive, peace-loving pot-smoker, but heinously evil for that pot-smoker to use violence to defend himself against such aggression. Such is the insanity caused by the superstition of "authority."

Forced Benefits ✳

Statists often defend "taxation" by arguing that the forced confiscation of wealth by "government" becomes retroactively justified when some of the confiscated money is spent in a way that benefits the one from whom the money was taken, or at least benefits society in general. For example, a statist may argue that if someone drives on a road that was funded in part by money taken from that person, or indirectly benefits from others being able to use the road, then that person should not complain about having been "taxed" to fund it. Ignoring the true nature of the situation, statists mischaracterize this as simply paying for services. But no one would make a similar argument when "authority" is not involved. Suppose, for example, that a restaurant delivered a meal to someone who had not ordered it, and then sent over armed thugs to collect a hundred dollars from that person. If the person, after being extorted in that way, chose to eat the meal, no rational person would argue that that would make the restaurant's actions morally acceptable. Yet that is exactly analogous to the usual view of statists: that if someone benefits from "government" services, he should not complain about "taxes." The unstated premise is that "legal" robbery is perfectly legitimate, as long as "authority" afterward provides some benefit to the one who was robbed. And it seems to make little difference to statists whether such a "benefit" is only indirect, or is horrendously expensive, or is combined with all sorts of other things which do not benefit the person at all, or which the person morally opposes (e.g., funding war, or abortion, or some religious or anti-religious agenda). This is because statists believe that ultimately it is the prerogative of those in "authority," not of those who earned the money, to decide how wealth should be spent, and that, as long as the ruling class claims to be robbing and controlling the people for their own good, the peasants have no right to resist whatever coercion and violence the masters deem necessary.

Attacking to Defend ✳

An offshoot of the notion that "government" providing "benefits" retroactively justifies theft and extortion is the patently ridiculous argument that it is necessary for the people to be forcibly controlled and robbed so that "government" can *protect* them from the bad people who might otherwise forcibly control and rob them. This absurd, contorted rationalization is quite common, whether the discussion relates to an authoritarian military or domestic "law enforcement." And statists rely on fear-mongering to bolster such lunacy, making dire predictions about all the unpleasant things they theorize would occur if the people were *not* forcibly robbed via a massive authoritarian extortion racket.

Again, such silly arguments are never made in situations where "authority" is not involved. No one would accept a claim that it is okay for a restaurant to force someone to pay for food he did not order, on the grounds that otherwise the person might starve. No one would accept a claim that it is okay for a builder to force someone to pay for a building he did not order, on the grounds that otherwise the person might be homeless. But even more ridiculous would be to claim that it is okay for one street gang to run a "protection" racket so that they have the resources to keep all the other dangerous street gangs out of their city. Yet that is exactly the attempted justification for all "government": that it must be allowed to commit aggression against everyone, so that it can *protect* them from others who might commit aggression against them. Supporters of a strong police force or a powerful military—both of which are funded via forcibly confiscated wealth—have accepted the premise that it is not only okay but necessary for people to be oppressed, controlled and extorted by "government" as long as it is done for their own good. And the fact that authoritarian "protectors" not only fail to prevent crime or war, but dramatically *increase* both via war-mongering and creating "illegal" markets, seems to go unnoticed by those who advocate defense via "government." Again, it is only because "authority" is imagined to have the right to commit aggression that anyone would ever make the inane argument that it is proper to initiate violence against people in order to "protect" them.

✳ *Violence by Default*

Much of the time, people will even advocate a forcibly imposed authoritarian plan simply because they are not sure what would happen if they did not, or are not sure how something would be accomplished if people were left in freedom. For example, if someone has a hard time picturing how a completely private road system would function, he will usually advocate a "government" plan, funded by coercion. If he is not sure how well free people could defend themselves without a standing army, he will likely advocate an authoritarian military solution, funded by coercive "taxation." Those who believe in "government" advocate violence by default. All it takes is a little uncertainty and ignorance to cause the average person to advocate a coercive "government" plan for just about anything.

This is not how people behave in their day-to-day lives. The average person does not go around initiating violence against everyone he meets because he is not sure that everyone he meets will otherwise behave properly and make the right decisions. But that is precisely what most statists do via "government": they advocate the widespread, forcible control of millions of human beings, simply because they are not entirely sure that people, if left in freedom, would spend their money the way they should, treat others the way they should, find peaceful, effective solutions to problems, etc. By way of the superstition of "authority," statists can comfortably advocate the violent subjugation of their neighbors, simply because they are not quite sure how their neighbors would otherwise behave.

And those who crave power exploit that fact to their advantage. All the politician needs to do, in order to get support for an authoritarian power-grab, is to tell the public that things might not work very well if he left people in freedom. He does not even need to wait until someone actually does something dishonest, or malicious, or negligent, or otherwise destructive. All he has to do is suggest the possibility that if the people are left in freedom, bad things *might* happen. Because advocates of "government" violence do not recognize "law" as violence, the threshold at which they will support an authoritarian, coerced "solution" is very low. Those who crave power can simply suggest that some "plan" might help someone somewhere, and many people will condone "legal" violence based upon that premise alone.

A lot of "government" violence is based upon guesses about what *might* happen as a result of what people *might* do. For example, much of the state coercion done in the name of "environmentalism" is based upon the idea that the state must forcibly control the choices of everyone because otherwise people might make choices that contribute to global warming, the end of the rain forests, the extinction of animals, and so on. Few people, acting on their own, would commit aggression based upon a guess about possible indirect consequences of the non-malicious, non-violent actions of others. Yet that is commonplace in "government" policy.

As another example of advocating "government" violence by default, consider the practice of forcibly preventing foreigners from setting foot anywhere in an entire "country" without the written permission of the ruling class of that "country." Such immigration "laws" create something akin to the war mentality, where an entire demographic category of people is criminalized and demonized, and subjected to acts of aggression, based upon concerns about what *some* of those people *might* do.

People opine that many "illegals" are criminals, or come into the country just to receive "benefits." Regardless of how often such allegations are accurate, the result is that all "illegals" — anyone who is in the country without the permission of the politicians — are forcibly controlled. This is the result of pack-mentality guilt by association. It should go without saying that using violence against one person because he is of the same race, or from the same country, or in some other way similar to someone else who has actually caused harm, is utterly unjustified. Of note, the attempts by "government" to quell "illegal immigration" also result in aggression being perpetrated against many "legal" residents (as well as "illegals") at "border patrol" checkpoints, many of which are not even at the borders. To stop and question everyone driving down a road because someone *might* be there "illegally" is precisely the kind of unjustified aggression commonly committed by "government" agents and rarely committed by anyone else.

This violence-by-default can also be seen in the intrusive searches and interrogations of anyone who attempts to fly on a plane in the "land of the free." For the owner of a plane to put conditions on anyone who wants to ride in his plane (and this would also apply to a train, a car, or anything else) is very different from a third party forcibly preventing anyone from riding on any plane anywhere in an entire country unless the would-be passengers first subject themselves to questioning, searches of their luggage, and even strip searches of themselves, by the agents of the third party. People would never tolerate any private individual behaving this way (with the attitude of "I'd better force my will on everyone else, just in case"), but for agents of "authority," the tactic is commonplace. And people imagine it to be legitimate. In fact, they often *demand* that "authority" do such things.

In their day-to-day lives, non-violence is the "default" type of behavior for most people. While there are occasional physical conflicts, most people go to great lengths to avoid them, not only by trying not to start a fight but also by trying to defuse tense situations. Even when a fight does occur, both sides usually end up walking away. Each day, billions of people find ways to peacefully coexist, even when they have significantly different viewpoints, beliefs and attitudes. But that is in their *personal* lives. When it comes to "politics," violence is the default. Every voter, to one extent or another, seeks to have his own views and ideas forcibly inflicted upon everyone else, through the mechanism of "government." The default is not to let others "do their own thing," or to try to get along peacefully; the default is to advocate aggression against absolutely everyone, by way of the authoritarian coercion called "law."

There is a mind-bogglingly huge disconnect between what the average person views as "civilized behavior" on an individual basis, and what he views as legitimate and civilized when it comes to the actions of "authority." It is difficult to imagine anyone behaving in his personal life the way voters behave when it comes to "politics." Such a person would constantly be robbing others — friends and strangers alike — of huge sums of money to fund things he deems important, as well as using threats, physical force, and even kidnapping to coerce others into making whatever decisions he thinks would be best, for his victims or for society in general. In short, anyone who acted in his private life the way *all* statists act in the "political" arena would be immediately recognized as a thug, a thief and a lunatic. But doing exactly the same things via "government," advocating mass extortion and thuggery, is accepted by most as something that normal, civilized people *should* do. In fact, they sometimes refer to voting as a duty, as if it is actually immoral to *not* advocate the coercive controlling of one's neighbors. Amazingly, and ironically, the *only* people who do *not* advocate constant widespread violence and coercion via "government" — known as voluntaryists, or anarchists — are usually viewed by the majority as being weird, uncivilized and dangerous.

How the Myth Defeats Virtue ✳

Almost all parents routinely send their children two completely contradictory messages: 1) it is inherently wrong to steal, hit, bully, etc., and 2) it is good to obey "authority." Almost everything that "authority" does constitutes bullying: using violence or the threat of violence to control the behavior of others and take their property. Every "authority" figure, from a school teacher to the dictator of a country, not only coercively controls his underlings on a regular basis but also speaks and acts as if he has the absolute, unquestionable right to do so. So the teacher is always forcibly imposing his will on the students while at the same time telling them that it is wrong for *them* to forcibly impose their will on others. It is the ultimate example of the hypocritical message "Do as I say, not as I do."

If children were raised with the idea that it is inherently wrong to steal, hit, bully, etc., why would there be any societal need for them to also be taught "respect for authority"? It only trains them to be easier to manage and control, which is of benefit to those who seek dominion over them (whether parents, teachers, or politicians), but does not train them to be any more civilized, compassionate, or humane. It does exactly the opposite, as the Milgram experiments demonstrated. In short, children are taught how to be civilized human beings, and then taught an insane superstition which overrides and renders obsolete everything they were taught about being civilized. This bizarre paradox can be seen all over the place in modern society.

The average person would feel shame and guilt if he stole a hundred dollars from his neighbor, but has no qualms about advocating, by way of voting, that "government" take many thousands of dollars from that same neighbor. The average person will hold a door open for a stranger but will, at the same time, advocate that that same stranger have much of his life forcibly controlled via "the law." The superficial politeness and consideration most people exhibit is rendered meaningless and worthless by the massive levels of state coercion and aggression they advocate. Even the Nazis had proper table manners, said "please" and "thank you" (in German), showed proper etiquette and were generally courteous, when they were not committing mass murder.

There is a dramatic contrast between how nearly all statists treat others in their personal lives and how they advocate that "government" treat others via "the law." Millions of people who would be very reluctant to physically hit another human being nonetheless proudly condone the violent subjugation or outright murder of thousands of people. They call it "supporting the troops." Some statists even say that they oppose the war but support the troops. This is comparable to saying that one opposes rape but supports rapists. Because "government" troops *always* use coercion and violence against innocents, in addition to whatever defensive force they use, "supporting the troops" necessarily means supporting oppression. But because of pack mentality and an emotional attachment to one's fellow countrymen, many people try to disassociate "the troops" from what it is that all "troops" do.

As another example of how the belief in "authority" distorts perception, many "welfare" recipients openly admit that, given the choice between accepting voluntarily donated gifts from people they know and receiving something that "government" forcibly took from a complete stranger, they prefer the latter, because it is, in their mind, the *less* shameful of the two options. The fact that anyone would ever prefer accepting stolen property over accepting compassion and generosity shows just how profoundly the belief in "authority" warps people's sense of morality.

In short, every statist — everyone who believes in "government" — deceives himself into believing that he is a good person who supports good things and opposes injustice, hallucinating in himself a respect for his fellow man, while at the same time advocating that his fellow man be forcibly controlled, extorted, imprisoned, or even killed. The "authority" superstition is burrowed into the minds of the masses so deeply that they can advocate evil on a massive, nearly incomprehensible level, while still imagining themselves to be charitable and compassionate. They demand that "government" do things they would never dream of doing on their own. They imagine themselves to be non-violent, civilized, enlightened beings while routinely advocating that all of their neighbors be robbed and forcibly controlled, and put into cages or killed if they resist. In truth, mankind's superficial charity, compassion and civility is nothing but a cruel joke when compared to what almost everyone will do, or what they will ask others to do, in the name of "authority."

Many parents and teachers regularly repeat what is perhaps the most basic rule of humanity, sometimes called "The Golden Rule": Treat others the way you want to be treated. However, *none* of the teachers, and almost none of the parents, who preach that rule actually live by it, because they condone that "authority" forcibly control underlings, inside the classroom and out. "The Golden Rule" is essentially a formula for anarchy: if someone does not like to be dominated and forcibly controlled, he should not advocate that others be dominated and forcibly controlled. If one wants to be left in peace, he should leave others in peace. If one desires the freedom to run his own life, he should allow others the freedom to do likewise. To put it bluntly, advocating aggression against others, including via any form of "government," is utterly incompatible with being a charitable, considerate, compassionate, kind, decent, loving human being. And the only reason so many otherwise good people continue to advocate widespread constant aggression via "government" is because they have been duped into accepting the lie that there is a creature called "authority" that is not bound by the moral standards that apply to human beings.

✳ *"Liberal" Cowardice*

To be blunt, people want "authority" to exist because they themselves are immature cowards. They want an all-powerful entity to impose their will upon others. This takes different forms in different varieties of political advocacy, but the basic motivation is always the same. The "liberal," for example, resents reality. He does not want a world in which suffering and injustice are possible. But instead of doing what he can as a human being, he wants a "government" to do it for him. He wants some magical entity to make sure that everyone, himself included, is fed, housed, and taken care of, no matter how lazy or irresponsible they are. Instead of trusting human beings to take care of each other, he wants a superhuman "authority" to guarantee housing, food, health care, and all sorts of other things, for everyone. He wants it so badly that he refuses to accept the obvious truth that no such guarantee is ever possible, and that if mere mortals do not take care of themselves and each other, nothing else will take care of them.

The liberal views the world as a continuation of the classroom, where there is always an "authority" in charge and in control who will make sure that the good kids are rewarded and protected from the bad kids. Each child is told what to do and taken care of, and all that is asked of him is that he does as he is told. He is expected to bear no responsibility at all for his own well-being, except through his obedience to the "authority." He does not provide his own food, or his own shelter, or his own protection, or anything else. He simply has faith that "authorities" (e.g., teachers and parents) will provide for him. He is raised in a setting which bears no resemblance to reality and is taught to look to "authority" for all of his needs.

And the liberal continues to do exactly that long after he leaves school. He speaks of each person having a "right" to housing, food, health care, and other things, as if some giant tooth fairy is obliged to make such things magically appear for everyone. The nature of reality, though it stares him in the face every day, is too disturbing for him to acknowledge, because it is so different from the world he grew up in, where "authority" was responsible for everything. The "government" programs supported by "liberals" are a manifestation of their own delusional terror of reality and refusal to see the world as it is. They fear uncertainty so much that they try to hallucinate into existence a superhuman entity ("government") that can somehow overcome all the uncertainties of reality and create an always safe, always predictable world. And when the mythological savior not only fails to fix the world but makes everything far worse (as happened with the collectivist regimes of the Soviet Union, Cuba, China, and many others), the "liberal" still refuses to let go of his blind faith in the omniscient, omnipotent god called "government."

A simple analogy makes all "liberal" political theory collapse. If a hundred people were shipwrecked on an island, what would it even mean to say that everyone there has a "right" to food, or that everyone has a "right" to health care, or the "right" to a job, or the "right" to a "living wage"? If, for example, someone has a "right" to housing, and housing comes only from the knowledge, skills and efforts of other people, it means that one person has the right to *force* another person to build him a house. This is exactly what happens in a larger context, when "liberals" advocate that some people be forcibly robbed via "taxation" in order to provide "benefits" for others. The notion that people, by virtue of their mere existence, are entitled to all sorts of things — things which come into being only as the result of human knowledge and effort — is delusional. The logical result of this supposedly loving and compassionate viewpoint is violence and slavery, because if one's "need" entitles him to something, that means that it must be forcibly taken from anyone else who has it or can produce it, if he will not supply it willingly.

The fact that such a short-sighted, animalistic attitude ("collectivism") is portrayed as a "progressive," compassionate philosophy does not change the fact that it is, in reality, indistinguishable from the "philosophy" of rats and cockroaches: regardless of who produced something, if someone else wants it (or claims to "need" it), he should forcibly take it. (The Communist Manifesto expresses this as "from each according to his ability, to each according to his need.") Of course, there is a fundamental difference between suggesting that people who have wealth to spare ought to *voluntarily* help the less fortunate, and advocating that *violence* should be used to make things "fair." "Government" programs are never about *asking* people to help each other; they are always about using threats and aggression to *force* people to do certain things and behave in certain ways. But the myth of "authority" allows "liberals" to advocate widespread, constant violence and intimidation, while still imagining themselves to be caring and compassionate. In essence, what political "leftists" want is an all-knowing, all-powerful "mommy" to *force* people to share and play nice, and they ignore the fact that there is no such thing, and that imagining such a thing only adds violence, suffering and misery to society.

❋ *"Conservative" Cowardice*

As much as political "liberals" want a giant mommy-state to protect and take care of everyone, political "conservatives" want a giant daddy-state doing the same thing. The results are slightly different, but the underlying delusion is the same: the desire for an all-powerful "authority" to protect humanity from reality. The "right-wing" delusion focuses less on motherly pampering and hand-holding, and focuses more on fatherly protection and discipline. "Conservatives" want "authority" to be used to create a big, powerful protection machine, and to firmly impose morality upon the population, which they imagine to be necessary for the survival of mankind. Their denial of reality is just as strong as that of the leftists. Again, the island analogy demonstrates the point well. If a hundred people were shipwrecked on an island, who would imagine that forcing most of them to serve and obey a "protector" would be necessary or useful? And who would imagine that letting one or two of them forcibly impose their morals on the rest would make such a group more virtuous?

A conservative "daddy" form of "government" is the equivalent of a disciplinarian father, who acts as protector of the family from outside forces (the equivalent to a "government" military), and protector of each member of the family from others in the family (the equivalent of domestic "law enforcement"), and the one who keeps "undesirables" away from the family (the equivalent of immigration "laws"), as well as the enforcer of morality, who punishes family members who disobey the rules. This last item equates to "laws" against pornography, prostitution, gambling, drug use, and other habits and behaviors which, although they do not constitute force or fraud against anyone, are thought by many to be destructive — physically, morally, or spiritually — to those who engage in them.

126

But trying to forcibly impose morality is more damaging than the behaviors themselves. Aside from the fact that no one has the right to forcibly control the non-violent choices of another, it is also horribly dangerous to set the precedent that it is okay to use violence to stamp out unseemly or distasteful behavior. Once such a premise is accepted in principle, human society will be a constant war of everyone against everyone. There will never be a time when everyone shares the same values and viewpoints. Peace and freedom cannot exist if every difference of opinion, and every difference in lifestyles or behaviors, leads to violent conflict via "government" coercion. Civilization, a state of peaceful coexistence, is not the result of everyone believing the same thing, but of people agreeing to refrain from initiating violence, even against people who do *not* believe the same things. "Conservative" statism, just as much as the "liberal" version, guarantees perpetual strife and conflict because it seeks to override free will and individual judgment with the so-called morality of a ruling class, whose first principle is forced conformity and sameness. Of course, violence cannot create virtue, even if it sometimes creates obedience, so all attempts by "authority" to coerce people into being moral and virtuous are doomed to fail, and ultimately do nothing but increase the levels of violence and conflict in society.

True Tolerance ✳

The belief in "authority" is so strong that many people automatically associate disapproving of something with wanting to have "government" make it "illegal." In their private lives, most people would never dream of resorting to violence against every person they encounter who has a habit or lifestyle they find unpleasant.

Nearly everyone, on a regular basis, tolerates choices and behaviors from others that he does not approve of. Of course, to "tolerate" something merely means to allow it to exist (i.e., to refrain from trying to forcibly stamp it out); it does not mean to condone it or approve of it. True tolerance is what allows people with different viewpoints and belief systems to coexist peacefully.

Ironically, "tolerance" is often used by statists as an excuse to engage in intolerance. For example, if an employer chooses not to do business with someone based upon that person's race, religion, sexual orientation, or some other general characteristic, some call that "intolerance" (which it is not), and then advocate that "authority" use the force of "law" to coerce the employer to hire whomever "authority" thinks he should. And that *is* intolerance, because it amounts to refusing to allow a person to make his own choices about who to associate with and who to trade with.

This is only one of many examples of how the belief in "authority" exacerbates differences, and introduces violence where it would not otherwise occur. There are several non-violent ways in which people can discourage behavior they disapprove of. Consider the example of a business owner who refuses to hire blacks (which, as repugnant as it may be, is *not* an act of aggression). Those who find such a policy offensive could boycott the person's business, or speak out against his practices or beliefs. Instead, the common response to such a situation is for statists to petition those in "authority" to *force* supposedly fair and enlightened choices upon everyone.

The same holds true for many other societal problems. The fight over whether same-sex marriage should be "legally" recognized or "outlawed" is nothing but a competition in intolerance from both sides. It is not justified to forcibly prevent two men from saying they are married, nor is it justified to force anyone else to recognize such a relationship as "marriage." The notion that everyone has to have the same idea of what constitutes marriage (or anything else) is a symptom of conformity-fascism. Likewise, "obscenity" laws seek to forcibly limit what people may read or view. "Narcotics laws," as well as much of what the FDA does, constitute attempts to forcibly limit which substances people may ingest. "Minimum wage laws" try to forcibly control what two people are allowed to agree upon. "Anti-discrimination" laws attempt to force people into making deals and associations they do not want to make. "Laws" such as the "Americans with Disabilities Act," are attempts to use force, in the name of "fairness," to control what services people can offer, such as shutting down a business if the owner cannot afford to install a wheelchair ramp. All such "laws," all such acts of "authority" and "government," are acts of aggression, the exact *opposite* of tolerance. It is absurd to try to force people to be nice, or fair, or compassionate, not only because aggression is inherently wrong but also because there will never be only *one* idea of what is nice, fair and compassionate. To have millions of people constantly fighting over the sword of "authority," each hoping to forcibly impose his view of "goodness" upon everyone else, has been the direct cause of most of the violence and oppression in history. Though it may seem counter-intuitive, this fact is historically indisputable: most of the evil committed throughout history has come from attempts to use "authority" to accomplish *good* things.

The constitution of the Soviet Union, for example, described an "authority" which was to treat everyone equally, regardless of race or religion, occupation or sex, and to preserve the individual rights of all citizens in their economic, political and social lives. The "rights" enumerated in the Soviet constitution included freedom of speech and freedom of religion, the right to work, the right to rest and leisure, the right to housing, the right to education, the right to health care, and the right of citizens to be cared for in their old age, among other things. The real-world *result* of that noble-sounding experiment, however, was constant, violent repression, harassment and intimidation, economic enslavement, forced suppression of thoughts and opinions, widespread poverty, and the murder of tens of millions of human beings, many via intentionally orchestrated starvation. The constitution of the People's Republic of China is very similar to that of the Soviet Union, and the results were similar as well: widespread violent repression and tyranny, as well as mass murder. (The attempt by Chinese "authorities" to use the violence of the state to reduce population growth has had particularly horrendous and deplorable results.)

Tyrants have always professed to have the noblest intentions for what they do. But even good intentions, when added to the belief in "authority," always result in immoral violence, sometimes to an almost incomprehensible degree. Even without all of the historical examples, it should be obvious that trying to achieve compassion and fairness, love and virtue, cooperation and brotherhood, by way of authoritarian *aggression and violence*, is insane, and that "government," by its very nature, as a tool of forcible control, can never and will never lead to justice, peace and harmony.

It is also worth noting that the political left *and* right are both enamored with the concept of "equality," with the political right pushing for "equality under the law," and the left pushing for equality of outcomes. But neither actually wants true equality, because they both *exempt* the ruling class from such "equality." True equality rules out all "government," because a ruler and a subject obviously can never be equals. What statists actually want is equality among the slaves, but enormous inequality between the slaves and the masters. This again shows that they view "government" as being superhuman, because it never occurs to them, as they push "equality for all," that the equality should also include the politicians and the police.

✹   *Big or Small, Left or Right, It's Still Evil*

Each and every person who advocates "government" in any form—whether liberal, conservative, moderate, independent, communist, fascist, constitutionalist, or any other flavor—believes that representatives of "authority" should, on a large scale, commit acts which, if done by anyone else, would be widely recognized as unjust and immoral. All statists believe that the people who make up "government" have an *exemption* from basic human morality, and not only *may* do things which others have no right to do, but should and *must* do such things, for the (supposed) good of society. The type and degree of aggression varies, but *all* statists advocate aggression.

In statist mythology, the political "left wing" and the political "right wing" are opposites. In reality, they are two sides of the same coin. The difference lies only in what the different voters hope those in power will do with that power. But in practice, "left" and "right" politicians all engage in wealth redistribution, war-mongering, centralized control of commerce, and numerous coercive restrictions upon the behavior of their subjects. As "right-wing" and "left-wing" states approach complete power, they become utterly indistinguishable from each other. Hitler's supposedly "far right" regime and Stalin's supposedly "far left" regime were virtually identical. Whatever the original stated purpose of either, the end result was complete power and control for the politicians, and complete helplessness and enslavement of everyone else. Being allowed to choose between the political "left" and the political "right" provides the people with exactly as much power and freedom as allowing them to choose between death by hanging and death by firing squad. And adding an independent third party only adds the option of death by electrocution. As long as the people bicker only about *which* gang should enslave everyone (also known as "democracy"), the people will remain enslaved.

Ironically, statists of all political stripes lament the influence that "lobbyists" and "special interests" have over politicians, ignoring the fact that *every* voter is a special interest, and every campaign contributor is a lobbyist. Once people accept the premise that "government" has the right to forcibly micromanage society, perpetual competition between groups, each throwing money and favors at politicians to try to get their way, is inevitable. It is silly to advocate authoritarian control ("govern-ment") only to then complain about the unavoidable *effect* of authoritarian control: people trying to buy influence. Politicians can be bought only because they have the power to sell, and they have the power to sell only because people believe in "government." State power will always be used to serve one person's agenda at the expensive of another (how else could coercion be used?), making the idea of "government corruption" redundant. Every statist *wants* "government" to forcibly impose his will on others, but dubs it "corruption" if someone *else's* agenda wins out. The hypocrisy is astounding.

Likewise, conservative pundits, on talk radio and elsewhere, sanctimoniously chastise liberals for advocating the forced redistribution of wealth, while the pundits do exactly the same thing for slightly different purposes. To criticize welfare while supporting corporate subsidies, or to criticize attempts to legislate "fairness" while supporting the "war on drugs," or to criticize liberal plans to nationalize industry while supporting a giant, forcibly funded "government" military (which amounts to nationalizing the protection industry) shows a complete absence of philosophical principles. At the same time, it is equally hypocritical for liberals to righteously condemn "right-wing" war-mongering while supporting a giant, intrusive, vicious extortion racket ("taxation"), or to complain about the "intolerance" of the "right" while advocating all manner of authoritarian behavioral controls. In truth, there is no real difference between the philosophical principles of one statist and another, because they both accept the premise that a ruling class, with the right to control and rob the population, is necessary and legitimate. The only argument after that is not one of principle, but simply a debate over how the loot should be distributed and what choices should be forced upon the peasants. There is no such thing as a tolerant liberal or a tolerant conservative because not *one* of them tolerates people spending their own money and controlling their own lives.

It is true that the degree of evil and the types of immoral aggression advocated vary based upon the different styles of statism. Constitutionalists, for example, advocate relatively low levels of robbery and extortion ("taxation") and advocate that only certain, limited activities and behaviors should be controlled via threats and coercion ("regulation"). But every power which any constitution pretends to grant to any legislature is a power *not* possessed by mere mortal individuals. Who would bother writing into a constitution a line pretending to delegate to *certain* people a right already possessed by everyone else? All such "grants of power," and any document purporting to create a "government" or empower any "legislature" to do anything, are attempts to issue a license to commit evil. However, as should be patently self-evident, no person or group of people—regardless of what documents they create or rituals they perform—can grant to someone else moral permission to commit evil. And putting supposed "limits" on such permission does not make it any more sane or legitimate. In short, to advocate "government" is always to advocate evil.

Liberals and conservatives both insist that someone needs to be "in charge," because that is the reality they were raised in: the only thing required of them was that they remain obedient to authority. From that training, they have little or no idea what to do if left to their own devices, if no one is telling them what to do. So they refuse to grow up, and try to hallucinate into existence a superhuman "authority." Paradoxically, even though there is no earthly species above human beings, they seek to fabricate this superhuman entity out of nothing but human beings, and then try to bestow upon it superhuman qualities, rights and virtues.

The entire concept is delusional, but it is shared by the vast majority of people the world over, who refuse to accept the fact that there is no shortcut to determining right and wrong, there is no magic trick which will make truth and justice automatically prevail, there is no "system" that can guarantee safety or fairness, and that everyday mortal human beings, with all of their deficiencies and shortcomings, are the best and only hope for civilization. There is no tooth fairy, or Santa Claus, or magical entity called "government," which can make an immoral species behave morally, or make a group of imperfect people function perfectly. And the belief in such an entity, rather than being merely pointless and ineffective, drastically *increases* the overall conflict, injustice, intolerance, violence, oppression and murder in human society. Nonetheless, most of those indoctrinated into the worship of "government" would rather cling to their familiar, horribly destructive, heinously evil, profoundly anti-human superstitions than grow up and accept the fact that there is no one above them, that there is no giant mommy or daddy to save the day, that they are at the top, and that each of them is personally responsible for deciding what he should do and then doing it. Sadly, they would rather suffer the hell of perpetual war and total enslavement than face the uncertainty and responsibility that comes with freedom.

The belief in "authority" negates and overrides nearly all of the positive effects of religious and moral beliefs. What most people call their "religion" is empty window-dressing, and what most people tout as their moral virtue is irrelevant, as long as they believe in the myth of "authority." Christians, for example, are taught things such as "If someone strikes you, turn the other cheek," "Love your neighbor" (and even "Love your enemy") and "Do unto others as you would have them do unto you." Yet every so-called Christian who believes in "government" constantly forsakes these principles, advocating constant aggression against everyone—friend and enemy, neighbor and stranger—via the cult of "government." To put on a show of being pious, religious, compassionate, loving and virtuous, while "voting" for a gang that promises to use violence to control the actions of everyone you know, is the height of hypocrisy. To refrain from personally robbing one's neighbor, while pushing for someone *else* to do it, is both cowardly and hypocritical. Yet almost every Christian (and every member of every other religion) does such things on a regular basis, by way of "political" advocacy.

As mentioned before, faith in "government" is a purely religious belief. As such, the vast majority of those who wear the label "atheist" are not actually atheists, because they believe in the god called "government." They do not recognize it as a religious belief, of course, but their belief in that ethereal, superhuman savior of mankind ("authority") is as deep and faith-based as any other religious belief. Ironically, atheists are often quick to point out the destruction that has been committed throughout history in the name of religion, but fail to notice the gruesome results of the god *they* bow to: "government." The atheists are absolutely right to point out that when churches were the accepted "authority"—the organizations thought to have the right to forcibly control others—many of them committed large-scale, heinous acts of terrorism, torture and murder. But what most modern atheists fail to realize, despite the clear evidence staring them in the face, is that they are members of the most destructive church in history, the church of "government," which has managed to wreak havoc, death and destruction on a level far beyond what even the most vicious churches of the past did. For example, over the span of two hundred years, around one or two million people were killed in the religious wars known as "the Crusades." In comparison, in half that amount of time in the twentieth century, over a *hundred times* as many people were killed by the "progressive policies" of collectivist "governments." Advances in technology no doubt played a large role in the increase in deaths, but the point is, whether the mask of "authority" is worn by a church or a state, the superstition is horribly dangerous, and the results horribly destructive. The fact that so many atheists eagerly condemn one form of the superstition, while vehemently *advocating* it in another form, shows an amazing degree of selective blindness. Often those most critical of oppression via "religion" are some of the most devout "true believers" in the god called "government."

✳ *No Objective Standard*

Again, in the eyes of those who believe in "government," there is a world of difference between acceptable *individual* behavior and acceptable "government" behavior. When an individual steals $100, it is seen as an immoral crime; when those in "government" steal *trillions* of dollars every year, it is seen as acceptable. If the average individual prints his own $100 bill, and goes out and spends it, that is seen as fraud and counterfeiting—an immoral act akin to theft. When "government" gives "legal" permission for the Federal Reserve to do the same thing, but with *trillions* of fiat, out-of-thin-air "dollars," that is seen as acceptable, even useful and necessary. While various "governments" have declared that the average man is not "allowed" to possess firearms, the mercenaries of "government" are allowed to have guns, bombs, fighter jets, tanks, missiles, even nuclear warheads.

Ironically, such weapons—with the exception of nuclear weapons—are routinely put into the hands of the very same people who, *before* they became mercenaries for the state, were prohibited from possessing firearms. In other words, when those individuals use their *own* judgment, some politicians declare them to be too untrustworthy, and too much of a danger to society, to be trusted with a five-shot revolver. But when those same people are blindly following orders, obeying the chain of command, those same politicians declare that they can be trusted to have assault rifles, sniper rifles, grenades, mounted machine guns, tanks, fighter jets, bombers, heavy artillery, and countless other tools of large-scale destruction.

In addition to the huge chasm between what the masses perceive to be acceptable individual behavior and acceptable "government" behavior, the public sense of when "government" has gone "too far" seems almost random. The standards by which average individuals are judged are simple and constant: if they steal, defraud, assault, or murder, that is bad. But the measure of right and wrong for "government" seems largely arbitrary. For example, it is now widely accepted that "outlawing" alcohol would be unjustified, but "outlawing" marijuana—and using wide-spread, constant violence to enforce that prohibition—is legitimate. As an even more bizarre contradiction, most people would be rightfully offended if "government" attempted to coerce everyone into picking up litter in his own neighborhood, but most accept it as legitimate when "government," via the military "draft," coerces people into going to another country to either kill people or die. Bizarrely, this most heinous example of forced labor—forcing people to go to halfway around the world to murder complete strangers—was even committed by a "government" whose own rules (i.e., the Thirteenth Amendment) prohibit "involuntary servitude."

It is clear that the limits of what "government" is allowed to do, as far as the general public is concerned, are not based on any principle whatsoever. One reason people, throughout the world and throughout history have been so slow to resist tyranny is that, as long as the growth of tyranny is slow and steady, the tyrants are never seen as having "crossed the line." This is because, without any underlying principles by which to gauge right and wrong, there can be no line to cross. The belief in "authority" is completely incompatible with *any* moral principles, precisely because the essence of the belief is the idea that those in "authority" are not bound by the same rules of conduct as their subjects. Logically, how could the subjects ever be justified in dictating standards of behavior to their masters? If "taxation" (forced confiscation of wealth) increases from 62% to 63%, how could any statist on principle declare that any line had been crossed, or that "government" had overstepped its bounds? There can be no principled objection to robbery unless it is an objection against any level of robbery, even if "legal." If 1% forced confiscation of wealth by "government" is legitimate in principle, then so is 99%. Either the rulers own the people, and have the right to take as much as they please, or the people own themselves, and the rulers have no right to forcibly take anything from them. There can be no principle anywhere in between. How could there be? What possible rational basis could there be for holding the belief that 46% slavery is good, but that 47% slavery is bad? How could there be any *principled* line anywhere in between 0% and 100%?

When the violence of "government" becomes too widespread, too arbitrary, and too vicious, even devout statists very slowly begin to question it. But there are no real principles guiding how they judge the righteousness of the actions of the ruling class. Once it is accepted that one group of people has the inherent right to commit acts of aggression against others, there is no objective standard for limiting such a right. If "government" can require people to have a "license" to drive to the corner store, why can it not require people to have a "license" to walk down the street? If it is legitimate for "lawmakers" to demand that private firearms be registered and regulated, why is it not also legitimate for them to demand that all forms of speech and expression be registered and regulated? If it is okay for politicians to create an enforced "government" monopoly on delivering letters (as the U.S. Postal Service has), why is it not okay for them to create an enforced "government" monopoly on telephone services?

The reason "government" is always a slippery slope, constantly pushing away from freedom and toward totalitarianism, is that once someone accepts the premise of a ruling class, there is no objective basis whatsoever for applying any limits to the powers of that ruling class. There can be no rational moral standard for saying that a certain person has the right to commit acts of aggression—theft, intimidation, assault and coercion—but that he may commit such acts only to a certain degree, or only if "necessary." For slaves to concede that they are the rightful property of someone else, only to then claim that there are limits on what their owners may do to them, is a logical contradiction. Likewise, for a subject to accept any master (including one called "government"), and to then imagine that he—the subject—will decide the extent of the master's powers, defies logic and reality. Yet that is what all believers in "representative government" seek to do.

In short, those who believe in "authority" have accepted, on the most fundamental level, that they are *owned* by someone else: the people claiming to have "authority." Having accepted that idea, they then proceed to beg their masters for favors. In doing so, however, the people are continually reinforcing the idea that ultimately it is up to the masters what will be done with the subjects. The one constant message that echoes throughout the entire "political process" is this: "Here are the things that we, the people, ask you, the rulers, to *allow* us to do." The implicit message underlying all political action is that the only power the people have is the power to whine and beg, and that, ultimately, it is always up to the masters what will happen. To push for any change in "the law" is to accept that "the law" is legitimate.

In contrast, if an armed driver was accosted by a carjacker with a knife, the driver would feel no need to lobby the aggressor, to beg him to give his *permission* for the driver to keep his own car. If the driver had the means to forcibly repel the attacker, he would have every right to do so. To *ask* for something is to accept that the decision is the other person's to make. To ask those in "government" for a bit more freedom is to admit that it is up to *them* whether the people may be free or not. In other words, to ask for freedom is to not be free, but to accept one's subjugation to someone else. Consider what an oxymoron it is for a person to claim to have an "unalienable right" to do something, and then to ask the politicians for their legislative *permission* to do that thing. The belief in "authority" ultimately leads even those who imagine themselves to be ardent pro-freedom advocates to *condone* their own subjugation. No matter how loudly they "demand" that the politicians change some "law," those who claim to love freedom while still suffering from the "authority" superstition merely reinforce the legitimacy of the ruling class's control over them, by implicitly agreeing that the people need the ruling class's "legislative" *permission* in order to have the right to do anything.

The Effect on Freedom Advocates　✸

"Government" itself does no harm, because it is a fictional entity. But the *belief* in "government" — the notion that some people actually have the moral right to rule over others — has caused immeasurable pain and suffering, injustice and oppression, enslavement and death. The fundamental problem does not reside in any set of buildings, or any group of politicians, or any gang of soldiers or enforcers. The fundamental problem is not an organization that can be voted out, or overthrown, or "reformed." The fundamental problem is the belief itself — the delusion, superstition and myth of "authority" — which resides in the minds of several billion human beings, including those who have suffered the most because of that belief. Ironically, the belief in "authority" dramatically affects the perception and actions even of those who are actively fighting against a particular regime. The superstition drastically alters and limits the ways in which dissenters "fight" oppression, and renders nearly all of their efforts impotent. Furthermore, on the rare occasion that a particular tyrant is toppled, one form of oppression is almost always replaced by another — often one that is even worse than the prior one.

Instead of fighting against a non-existent beast, what "freedom fighters" need to do is to recognize that it is not real, that it does not exist, that it cannot exist, and then act accordingly. Of course, if only a few people overcome the superstition, they will likely be ridiculed, condemned, attacked, imprisoned or murdered by those who are still firm believers in the myth. But when even a significant minority of people outgrow the superstition, and change their behavior accordingly, the world will drastically change. When the people actually *want* true freedom, they will achieve it without the need for any election or revolution.

The trouble is, almost no one actually *wants* humanity to be free, and almost no one opposes oppression in principle. The effects of the myth of "authority" remain intact even in the minds of most people who consider themselves to be rebels, non-conformists and free-thinkers. During their teenage years, many people go through a period of apparent rebelliousness, which consists mostly of doing whatever those in "authority" tell them *not* to do: engaging in smoking, sexual promiscuity, drug use, wearing different clothes or hairstyles, getting tattoos or body piercings, and so on. As such, their actions are still controlled, albeit in a backward way, by the myth of "authority." Instead of obeying for the sake of obeying, they disobey for the sake of disobeying, but still show no signs of being able to think for themselves. They behave like angry children instead of complacent children, but still do not behave like adults. And in most cases, their natural desire to break the chains of "authority" does not last long, they "outgrow" their anti-authoritarian tendencies, and gradually transform back into "model citizens," i.e., obedient subjects.

For example, the supposedly radical, anti-authoritarian hippies of the 1960s more or less *became* the new "government" in the United States with the presidency of Bill Clinton. Even the "peaceniks" whose mantra was "live and let live," when given the opportunity to become the new "authority," chose to forcibly meddle with the lives of others as much as or more than their predecessors did, including via military conquest. Likewise, those in "Generation X," the "MTV" crowd, and so on, have always focused their efforts on putting people who agree with them into power, instead of working to actually achieve freedom. There is a fundamental difference between having complaints about a particular ruling class, and recognizing and opposing the insanity of "authority" in principle. In short, in all the various societal manifestations of so-called rebelliousness and non-conformity, almost none have actually escaped the myth of "authority." Instead, they have merely attempted to make a new "authority," a new ruling class, a new "government," a new centralized machine of coercion through which they could forcibly subjugate and control their neighbors. In short, nearly all so-called "rebels" are phonies, who pretend to be resisting "the man," but who really just want to *be* "the man."

And this should be expected. If one starts with the assumption that there should and must be an "authority," and that a "government" exerting control over a population is a legitimate situation, why would anyone not want to be the one in charge? Each person, by definition, wants the world to be the way he thinks it should be, and what better way could any person accomplish that than by becoming king? If someone accepts the notion that authoritarian power is valid, why would he not want it to be used to try to create the world as he wants it to be? This is why the only people who truly advocate freedom in principle are anarchists and voluntaryists—people who understand that forcibly dominating others is not legitimate, even when it is called "law," and even when it is done in the name of "the people" or "the common good." There is a big difference between striving for a new, wiser, nobler master, and striving for a world of equals, where there are no masters and no slaves.

Likewise, there is a big difference between a slave who believes in the principle of freedom, and a slave whose ultimate goal is to become the new master. And this is true, even if that slave truly intends to be a kind and generous master. Even those who advocate a relatively limited, benign type of "government" are advocating against freedom. As long as the people believe in the myth of "authority," every downfall of one tyrant will be followed by the creation and growth of a new tyrant.

History is replete with examples, such as Fidel Castro and Che Guevera, who portrayed themselves as "freedom fighters" just long enough to become the new oppressors. They were no doubt quite genuine in their vehement opposition to the oppressions which they and their friends suffered from, but they were not opposed to authoritarian oppression in principle, as clearly demonstrated by their behavior once they obtained power themselves. This pattern has been repeated over and over again throughout history, with the resentment of one tyrannical regime becoming the seed of the next tyrannical regime. Even Hitler's rise to power was due in large part to anger at the perceived injustices and oppressions inflicted upon Germany via the Treaty of Versailles. Of course, as long as the rebels suffer from the superstition of "authority," their first priority, once they have overthrown one "government," will be to set up a new one. So even acts of great bravery and heroism, among those who still believe in "government," have accomplished little more than replacing one tyrant with another. Many have been able to recognize and oppose specific acts of tyranny by specific regimes, but very few have recognized that the underlying problem is not who sits on the throne; the problem is that there is a throne to sit on.

The same failure to recognize the real problem occurs in more mundane, relatively peaceful "reform" as well. In the U.S., for example, a large portion of the population is perfectly able to see the injustices resulting from the "war on drugs," global warmongering, and other violations of civil rights committed by Republican tyrants. However, not recognizing the belief in "authority" as the real problem, the solution proposed by those who recognize such injustice is to give the reins of "government" to Democrat tyrants instead. Meanwhile, another large portion of the population is perfectly able to see the injustices resulting from heavy "taxation," "government" micromanaging of industry, wealth-redistribution schemes, citizen disarmament ("gun control"), etc. But, not recognizing the belief in "authority" as the real problem, the solution proposed by those who recognize such injustices is to give the reins of "government" back to Republican tyrants. And so, decade after decade, the machine of oppression changes hands, while individual freedom, in all aspects of life, continues to dwindle. And still, all that most Americans can even contemplate as a solution is yet another election, or another political party, or another lobbying effort, in the hope of begging the ruling class to be more wise or benevolent.

Some people, seeing the disaster caused by the two-party system, blame "extremism" for the negative effects of "government." They surmise that if people would only support a form of coercive control somewhere in between the "far left" and the "far right," things would improve. Such people claim to be independent, openminded and moderate, but in reality are merely general advocates of oppression instead of being advocates of a particular flavor of oppression. The "left" and "right" are merely two masks which the one ruling class wears, and making a new mask which is a compromise between the other two will have no effect whatsoever upon the nature of the beast or the destruction it causes. Taking a position halfway between "left-wing" tyranny and "right-wing" tyranny does not result in freedom; it results in bipartisan tyranny.

Among those who vote Democrat or Republican—or any other party—no one recognizes the underlying problem, and as a result, no one ever gets any closer to a solution. They remain slaves, because their thoughts and discussions are limited to the pointless question of *who* should be their master. They never consider—and dare not consider—the possibility that they should have no master at all. As a result, they focus entirely on political action of one kind or another, which is all founded on the belief in "authority," which is the problem itself. So the efforts of statists are, and always will be, doomed to fail. This is even true of the less mainstream, supposedly more pro-freedom "political movements," including Constitutionalists, the Libertarian party, and others. As long as they think and act within the confines of the "government" game, their efforts are not only completely incapable of solving the problem but actually aggravate the problem by inadvertently legitimizing the system of domination and subjugation which wears the label of "government."

The Rules of the Game ✳

Even most people who claim to love liberty and to believe in "unalienable" rights allow the superstition of "authority" to drastically limit their effectiveness. Most of what such people do, in one way or another, consists of *asking* tyrants to change their "laws." Whether activists campaign for or against a particular candidate, or lobby for or against a particular piece of "legislation," they are merely reinforcing the assumption that obedience to authority is a moral imperative.

When activists try to convince politicians to decrease "taxes," or repeal some "law," those activists are implicitly admitting that they need permission from their masters in order to be free. And the man who "runs for office," promising to fight for the people, is also implying that it is up to those in "government" to decide what the peasants will be allowed to do. As Daniel Webster put it, *"There are men in all ages who mean to govern well, but they mean to govern; they promise to be good masters, but they mean to be masters."* Activists spend huge amounts of time, money and effort begging their masters to change their commands. Many even go out of their way to stress the fact that they are "working within the system," and that they are not advocating anything "illegal." This shows that, regardless of their displeasure with those in power, they still believe in the myth of "authority," and will cooperate with "legal" injustice unless and until they can convince the masters to change the rules—to "legalize" justice. While the intended message of dissenters may be that they disapprove of what the masters are doing, the actual message that all political action sends to those in power is *"We wish you would change your commands, but we will continue to obey whether you do or not."* The truth is, one who seeks to achieve freedom by petitioning those in power to give it to him has already failed, regardless of the response. To beg for the blessing of "authority" is to accept that the choice is the *master's* alone to make, which means that the person is already, by definition, a slave.

One who begs for lower "taxes" is implicitly agreeing that it is up to the politicians how much a man may keep of what he has earned. One who begs the politicians not to disarm him (via "gun control") is, by doing so, conceding that it is up to the master whether to let the man be armed or not. In fact, those who lobby for politicians to respect any of the people's "unalienable rights" do not believe in unalienable rights at all. Rights which require "government" approval are not unalienable, and are not even rights. They are privileges, granted or withheld at the whim of the master. And those who hold positions of power know that they have nothing to fear from people who do nothing but pathetically beg for freedom and justice. However loudly the dissenters talk about "demanding" their rights, the message they actually send is this: "We agree, master, that it is up to *you* what we may and may not do."

That underlying message can be seen in all sorts of activities mistakenly imagined to be forms of resistance. For example, people often engage in protests in front of "government" buildings, carrying signs, chanting slogans, sometimes even engaging in violence, to express their displeasure with what the masters are doing. However, even such "protests," for the most part, do little more than *reinforce* authoritarianism. Marches, sit-ins, protests, and so on, are designed to send a message to the masters, the goal being to convince the masters to change their evil ways. But that message still implies that it is up to the masters what the people may do, which becomes a self-fulfilling prophecy: when the people feel beholden to an "authority," they are beholden to "authority." Those in "government" derive all of their power from the fact that their subjects *imagine* them to have power.

✳ *Legitimizing Oppression*

The harder people try to work within any political system to achieve freedom, the more they will reinforce, in their own minds and the minds of anyone watching, that the "system" is legitimate. Petitioning politicians to change their "laws" implies that those "laws" matter, and should be obeyed. Nothing better shows the power of the belief in "authority" than the spectacle of a hundred million people begging a few hundred politicians for lower "taxes." If the people truly understood that the fruits of a man's labor are his own, they would never engage in such lunacy; they would simply stop surrendering their property to the political parasites. Their trained-in desire to have the approval of "authority" creates in them a mindset not unlike the mindset of a slave: they literally feel bad about keeping their own money and making their own choices without first getting the master's permission to do so. Even when freedom is theirs for the taking, statists continue to grovel at the feet of megalomaniacs, begging for freedom, thus ensuring that they will *never* be free.

The truth is, one cannot believe in "authority" and be free, because accepting the myth of "government" is accepting one's own obligation to obey a master, which means accepting one's own enslavement. Sadly, many people believe that begging the master, via "political action," is all they can do. So they forever engage in rituals which only legitimize the slave-master relationship, instead of simply disobeying the tyrants. The idea of disobeying "authority," "breaking the law," and being "criminals" is more disturbing to them than the idea of being a slave.

Those who want a significantly lower level of authoritarian control and coercion are sometimes accused of being "anti-government," an allegation most vehemently *deny*, saying that they are not against "government" per se, but only want *better* "government." But by their own words they are admitting that they do *not* believe in true freedom, but still believe in the Divine Right of Politicians and the idea that a ruling class can be a good and legitimate thing. Only someone who still feels an abiding obligation to obey the commands of politicians would want to avoid being labeled "anti-government." Since "government" *always* consists of aggression and domination, one cannot be truly pro-freedom *without* being anti-"government." The fact that so many activists reject that label ("anti-government") shows how deeply ingrained the superstition of "authority" remains, even in the minds of those who imagine themselves to be ardent advocates of individual liberty.

(One particularly fascinating phenomenon is worth mentioning here. Outraged by authoritarian injustice, but still unwilling to give up the "authority" superstition in themselves, many in the growing freedom/militia/"patriot" movement continue to seek, or claim to have found, some "legal" remedy which will persuade tyrants to leave them in peace. Over the years, one theory after another has surfaced alleging the existence of some secret "government" form, or some "legal" trick, or some official procedure, which can free an individual from the control of "government." Sadly, this demonstrates only that such people are still doing nothing more than looking for a way to get *permission* to be free. But the road to true freedom has never been, and will never be, a new political ritual, a new "legal" document or argument, or any other form of "political" action. The only road to true freedom is for the individual to let go of his own attachment to the superstition of "authority.")

✳ *The Libertarian Contradiction*

Perhaps the best illustration of how the belief in "authority" warps thinking and gets in the way of achieving freedom is the fact that there is a "Libertarian" political party. The heart and soul of libertarianism is the non-aggression principle: the idea that initiating force or fraud against another is always wrong, and that force is justified only if used in *defense* against aggression. The principle is perfectly sound, but trying to make it a reality via any *political* process is completely self-contradictory, because "government" and non-aggression are utterly incompatible. If the organization called "government" stopped using any threats or violence, except to defend against aggressors, it would cease to be "government." It would have no right to rule, no right to "tax," no right to "legislate," no monopoly on protection, and no right to do anything which any other human being does not have the right to do.

One excuse for libertarian political activism is the claim that society can transform from its current authoritarian arrangement into a truly free society only if it does so slowly and gradually. However, that has never happened, and never will happen, for a very simple reason: either there is such a thing as "authority," or there is not. Either there is a legitimate ruling class with the right to rule everyone, or each individual owns himself and is beholden only to his own conscience. The two are mutually exclusive paradigms. It is impossible for there to be an in-between, because whenever there is a conflict between what "authority" commands and what one's individual judgment dictates, it is impossible to obey both. One must outrank the other. If "authority" outranks conscience, then the common folk are all the rightful property of the ruling class, in which case freedom cannot and should not exist. If, on the other hand, conscience outranks "authority," then each person owns himself, and each must always follow his own judgment of right and wrong, no matter what any self-proclaimed "authority" or "law" may command. There cannot be a "gradual shift" between the two, nor can there be a compromise.

Trying to convert libertarianism into a political movement requires a mangled, perverted hybrid of the two options: the idea that a system of domination ("government") can be used to achieve individual freedom. Whenever a "libertarian" lobbies for legislation or runs for office, he is, by his own actions, conceding that "authority" and man-made "law" is legitimate. But if one actually believed in the non-aggression principle, he would understand that the commands of politicians ("laws") cannot trump that principle, and any "law" that is contrary to the principle is illegitimate. This goes for the idea of "unalienable rights" as well. If an individual has an inherent right to do something, then, by definition, he does not need any permission from tyrants to do it. He does not need to lobby for a change in "legislation," and does not need to try to elect some master who will choose to respect his rights.

Anyone who actually believes in the principle of non-aggression—the underlying premise of libertarianism—must be an anarchist, as it is logically impossible to oppose the initiation of violence while supporting any form of "government," which is nothing but violence. And libertarians cannot be Constitutionalists, as the Constitution quite plainly (in Article I, Section 8) claims to bestow upon some people the right to initiate violence, via "taxation" and "regulation," among other things. The principle of libertarianism logically rules out *all* "government," even a constitutional republic. (Anyone who tries to describe a "government" which commits no acts of aggression will describe, at best, a private security company.) Nonetheless, so many people have been so thoroughly trained into the authoritarian mindset that even when they can see the obvious moral superiority of living by the non-aggression principle (the basis of libertarianism), they still refuse to give up the absurd notion that the right to rule ("authority") can be used as a tool for freedom and justice. There is a fundamental difference between arguing about what the master should do— which is what all "politics" consists of—and declaring that the master has no right to rule at all. To be a Libertarian candidate is to try to do both of these conflicting things. It obviously legitimizes the office the candidate seeks to hold, even while the candidate is claiming to believe in the principles of non-aggression and self-ownership, which completely *rule out* the possibility of any legitimate "public office."

In short, if the goal is individual freedom, "political action" is not only worthless, it is hugely counter-productive, because the main thing it accomplishes is to legitimize the ruling class's power. The only way to achieve freedom is to first achieve mental freedom, by realizing that no one has any right to rule another, which means that "government" is never legitimate, it is never moral, it is never even real. Those who have not yet realized that, and continue to try to petition "the system" to make them free, are playing right into the hands of the tyrants. Even petitioning for lower levels of "taxation" or "government" spending, or asking for things to be "legalized" or "deregulated," or begging for other reductions in "government" control over the people, still does nothing to address the real problem, and in fact adds to the real problem, by unwittingly repeating and reinforcing the idea that if the people want freedom, they need to have freedom "legalized." Political action, by its very nature, always empowers the ruling class and disempowers the people.

If enough people recognize and let go of the "authority" myth, there is no need for any election, any political action, or any revolution. If the people did not imagine themselves to have an obligation to obey the politicians, the politicians would literally be ignored into irrelevance. In fact, the belief in "democracy" dramatically *reduces* the ability of the people to resist tyranny, by limiting the ways in which they resist it. For example, if 49% of the population wanted lower levels of "taxation," but maintained their belief in "authority," they could accomplish exactly nothing via "democracy." On the other hand, if even 10% of the population wanted no "taxation" at all and had escaped the myth of "authority" (including the "democratic" kind), they could achieve their goal easily by simple non-compliance. Using the U.S. as an example, if twenty million people — less than 10% of American "taxpayers" — openly refused to cooperate with attempts by the IRS to extort them, the ruling class would be powerless to do anything about it, and the infamous Internal Revenue Service, along with the massive extortion racket it administers, would grind to a halt. It would be utterly impossible for 100,000 IRS employees to continually rob millions of Americans who felt no obligation to pay. In fact, it would be impossible for any agency to enforce any "law" which even a fraction of the public could disobey with no feeling of shame or guilt. Brute force alone could not achieve compliance.

Any large population of people that did not perceive obedience, in and of itself, to be a virtue, and felt no inherent duty to obey the commands of those claiming the right to rule, would be utterly impossible to oppress. Wars occur because people feel obliged to go into battle when "authority" tells them to. (As the saying goes, "What if they had a war, and nobody came?") As long as the people can be duped into perpetually begging for freedom to be "legalized," they will be easy to subjugate and control. As long as a person's perceived duty to obey "authority" outranks his own individual judgment, his beliefs and values are, practically speaking, irrelevant. Unless and until a freedom advocate is willing to disobey the master — to "break the law" — his supposed love of freedom is a lie, and will accomplish nothing.

Same as the Old Boss ✳

Many have argued that society without rulers is impossible, because the moment one "government" collapses or is overthrown, a new "government" will instantly spring up. In one sense, that is true. If the people continue to adhere to the myth of "authority," after any upheaval of a particular regime they will simply create a new set of masters to replace the old set. But the reason for this is neither the necessity of "government," nor the basic nature of man. What nearly all "freedom fighters" fail to realize, as they rail against tyranny and oppression, is that the underlying problem is never the particular people in power. The underlying problem resides in the minds of the people being oppressed, including the minds of most "freedom fighters." As long as the people accept the myth of "authority," even open revolution will, in the long run, do nothing to reduce oppression. When one group of controllers and exploiters falls, the people will simply set up another. (Though few of those who wave their flags on "Independence Day" may realize it, the level of oppression under King George III, just before the American Revolution, was trivial compared to the current levels of "taxation," "regulation," and other authoritarian intrusion, coercion and harassment which routinely occur in the U.S. today.)

It is easy for people to see specific injustices committed in the name of a particular regime, but far more difficult for those same people to recognize that the root cause of such injustices is the *belief system* of the general public. History books are full of examples of long, bloody reigns of tyrants, followed at last by bloody revolution, followed by the anointing of a new tyrant. The type of tyrant may change — a monarch replaced by a communist regime, a "right wing" tyrant replaced by a "left wing" tyrant, an oppressive theocracy replaced by an oppressive "populist" regime, and so on — but as long as the belief in "authority" remains, so will oppression.

Even the most heinous examples of man's inhumanity to man, committed in the name of "authority," rarely persuade anyone to question the idea of "authority" per se. Instead, it leads them only to oppose a *particular* set of tyrants. As a discouraging example, the main opposition in Germany to the Nazis came from the communists, who themselves advocated a form of oppression just as vicious and destructive as Hitler's regime. Due to their authoritarian mindset, the Germans had no chance to achieve peace or justice, as their entire national debate was concerned only with *which* kind of all-powerful rulers should be in charge, without even a hint at the possibility that *no one* should have such power. The public discourse has been similar throughout most of the world, throughout most of time, focusing on *who* should rule, instead of questioning whether there should be rulers at all.

✳ *A Mix of Wisdom and Insanity*

In the late eighteenth century something very unusual occurred, something that seemed as if it might break the perpetual cycle of serial tyrants. That event was the signing of the Declaration of Independence. What made that event unusual was not that the people were rebelling against a tyrant — which had happened countless times before — but that the rebels expressed some basic philosophical principles, rejecting not just a particular regime but rejecting oppression in principle. Almost.

The American Revolution was the result of a hodge-podge of conflicting ideas, some supporting individual sovereignty, some supporting a ruling class. The Declaration of Independence, and the Constitution which followed some years later, were a combination of profound insight and glaring contradictions. On the bright side, the discussion of the time was not just about who would be in charge, but focused heavily on the concept of individual rights and limiting the power of "government." At the same time, the Declaration of Independence erroneously asserted that "government" can have a legitimate role in society: to protect the rights of individuals. However, this has never been true in practice, and cannot even be true in theory. As explained above, an organization which did nothing more than defend individual rights would not be "government" in any sense of the term. The Declaration also spoke of unalienable rights, and asserted that "all men are created equal" (as far as their rights are concerned). But the authors failed to realize that such concepts completely rule out any possibility of a legitimate ruling class, even a very limited one. The very principles they expressed were then immediately contradicted by their efforts to create a protector "government." One day they were declaring that "*all men are created equal*" (the Declaration of Independence), and the next they were declaring that some men, calling themselves "Congress," had the right to rob ("tax") everyone else (U.S. Const, Art I, Sec 8, Clause 1). Furthermore, the Declaration asserts that when any "government" becomes destructive of individual rights — as *every* "government" always does, the moment it comes into existence — the people have a duty to alter or abolish it. Yet the Constitution claims to give to Congress the power to "suppress insurrections" (U.S. Const, Art I, Sec 8, Clause 15). This implies that the people have a right to resist "government" oppression, but that "government" has a right to violently crush them when they do. In short, the works of the "Founding Fathers" consist of a combination of profound wisdom and utter lunacy. In some places, they described quite well the concept of self-ownership; in others, they sought to create a ruling class. They did not seem to notice that those two agendas are utterly incompatible with each other.

The result of their efforts was, in one sense, a gigantic failure. The regime they created grew far beyond what both the federalists and the anti-federalists said they wanted. The Declaration and the Constitution utterly failed to keep "government" power limited. The promise of a "government" that would be a servant of the people, protecting their rights but otherwise leaving them in peace, grew into the largest, most powerful authoritarian empire the world has ever known, including the largest and most intrusive extortion racket ever known, the largest and most powerful war machine in history, and the most intrusive and invasive bureaucracy in history.

In truth, the idea was doomed from the beginning. Perhaps the most valuable thing the "Great American Experiment" accomplished was to demonstrate that "limited government" is impossible. There cannot be a master who answers to his slaves. There cannot be a lord who serves his subjects. There cannot be a ruler who is both above the people and subordinate to them. Unfortunately, there are still many who refuse to learn this lesson, insisting instead that the Constitution did not fail, the people failed — by not doing it right, by not being vigilant enough, or by some other neglect or corruption. Oddly, this is the same excuse given by communists for why *their* flawed philosophy, when put into practice in the real world, always turns into violent oppression. The truth is that *any* form of authoritarian control — any type of "government," whether constitutional, democratic, socialist, fascist, or anything else—will result in a set of masters forcibly oppressing a group of slaves. That is what "authority" is—all it ever has been, and all it ever could be, no matter how many layers of euphemisms and pleasant rhetoric are used in an attempt to hide it.

✳ *The Contract Myth*

The mythology surrounding the Constitution alleges that it served as a sort of contract between the people and their new "servants" in Congress. But there is not a shred of truth to that. One cannot, by signing a contract, bind someone *else* to an "agreement." The idea that a few dozen white, male, wealthy landowners could enter an agreement on behalf of over two million other people is absurd. Furthermore, no contract can create a right held by none of the participants, which is what all "government" constitutions pretend to do. The form of the document makes it clear that it was not an actual contract, but an attempt to fabricate out of thin air the right to rule, however "limited" it was intended to be. An actual agreement by contract is a fundamentally different thing from any document purporting to create a "government." For example, if a thousand American colonists had signed an agreement saying "We agree to give a tenth of what we produce, in exchange for the protection services of the George Washington Protection Company," they could be morally bound by such an agreement. (Making an agreement and breaching it is a form of theft, akin to going to a store and taking something without paying for it.) But they could not bind anyone else to the agreement, nor could they use such an agreement to give the "George Washington Protection Company" the right to start robbing or otherwise controlling people who had nothing to do with the contract. Also, while the Constitution pretends to authorize "Congress" to do various things, it does not actually *require* Congress to do anything. Who in their right mind would sign a contract which did not bind the other party to do anything? (In *DeShaney v. Winnebago*, 489 U.S. 189, the Supreme Court officially declared that "government" has no actual duty to protect the public.) The result is that the Constitution, rather than being a brilliant, useful, valid contract, was an insane attempt by a handful of men to unilaterally subject millions of other people to the control of a machine of aggression, in exchange for no guarantee of anything. The fact that millions of Constitutionalists are desperately trying to get back to that, in the hopes that it can save their "country" if the people try it again—after it utterly failed the first time—is a testament to the power, and the insanity, of the superstition of "authority."

Part IV

Life Without the Superstition

The Solution ✳

Nearly everyone can see at least some problems with the "government" he lives under, whether it be corruption, war-mongering, socialist redistribution, police state intrusions, or other oppressions. And many are desperate to find a solution to such problems. So they vote for this or that candidate, support this or that political movement or party, lobby for or against this or that legislation, and almost always end up disappointed with the results. They can easily identify and complain about various problems, but an actual solution always eludes them.

The reason they are always disappointed is because the problem does not reside in the people called "government"; it resides in the minds of their victims. Tinkering with "government" cannot fix a problem that does not come from "government." The dissatisfied voter fails to realize that it is his *own* view of reality, his *own* belief in "authority," that is the root cause of most of society's problems. He believes that a ruling class is a natural, necessary, beneficial part of human society, and so all of his efforts focus on bickering over who should be in charge, and on what the power of "government" should be used for. When he thinks of "solutions," he thinks inside the box of statism. As a result, he is powerless from the beginning. Begging masters to be nice, or asking for a new master, never leads to freedom. Instead, such behaviors are clear indicators that the person is not even free inside his own mind. And a man whose mind is not free will never be free in body.

People are so accustomed to engaging in the cult rituals collectively referred to as "politics" (voting, lobbying, petitioning, campaigning, etc.) that any suggestion that they not bother participating in such pointless and impotent endeavors amounts, in their eyes, to suggesting that they "do nothing." Because they view voting, whining and begging as the entire spectrum of possibilities open to them when it comes to "government," they are unable to even comprehend anything that might actually accomplish freedom. So when a voluntaryist or anarchist explains both the problem and the way out of it, but without presenting a new candidate to vote for, a new political party to support, or some new movement or campaign to get behind—in other words, without proposing anything that coincides with the superstition of "government" and "authority"—the average statist will complain that no solutions were offered. From their perspective, anyone who does not play the game of "politics," within the rules set down by the ruling class, is "doing nothing." They enthusiastically declare, "You have to participate!" They fail to realize that participating in the game created and controlled by tyrants *is* "doing nothing"—nothing useful, at least.

In truth, rather than some event needing to occur, or some particular thing needing to be done, the real solution—the only solution to the problems involving "government"—comes from *not* doing certain things, and from certain things *not* happening. In one sense, there is no positive, active solution to "government." The ultimate solution is negative and passive:

Stop advocating aggression against your neighbors. Stop engaging in rituals that condone the initiation of violence and reinforce the notion that some people have the right to rule. Stop thinking and speaking and acting in ways that reinforce the myth that normal people should be, and must be, beholden to some master, and should obey such a master rather than follow their own consciences.

When people stop bowing at the altar of "government," stop playing the games of tyrants, stop respecting arbitrary rules written by megalomaniacs, the problem will go away on its own. Being a mythical entity, "authority" does not need to be overthrown, or voted out, or "reformed." The people need only stop *imagining* something that is not there, and never was. If the people stopped allowing an irrational superstition to warp their perceptions, their *actions* would immediately and dramatically improve. Most aggression, which is now done in the name of "authority," would cease. No one would issue commands, enforce commands, or feel an obligation to obey commands, unless the commands themselves were seen as inherently justified based upon the situation, not based upon the one giving the command, or his supposed "authority." That alone would eliminate the vast majority of theft, extortion, intimidation, harassment, coercion, terrorism, assault and murder which human beings now perpetrate against one another. When the people recognize and accept no master, they will have no master. Ultimately, their bondage, and the means to escape it, exists entirely inside their own minds.

Human society does not need anything added to it to fix most of its problems, nor does it need the institution of some new "system" or the implementation of some new master plan. Instead, it needs to have one thing—one all-pervasive, extremely destructive thing—*removed* from society: the belief in "authority" and "government." What will "make things work" is not any centralized plan, not any authoritarian agenda, but the mutually voluntary interaction of many individuals, each serving his own values and following his own conscience. Of course, this does not fit at all with the way almost everyone was trained to think: that society needs a master plan with "leaders" who will make it happen. In truth, what society needs the most is the complete *lack* of a master plan, and the complete *absence* of authoritarian "leaders" to whom the people must surrender their free will and judgment. The solution is not to add some new thing to society, but simply to understand and dispel the most dangerous superstition.

Reality Is Anarchy ✳

Many people have become anarchists—advocates of a voluntary society without any ruling class—after having come to the conclusion that society would be more prosperous and more peaceful, and would enjoy more justice and security, without any "government" at all. However, that is somewhat akin to an individual deciding, after careful analysis, that Christmas would work better without Santa Claus. If Santa Claus is not real, it is pointless to have a debate about whether he is "needed" in order for Christmas to "work." If Christmas works at all, it already works *without* Santa. And so it is with the usual debate between "government" and "anarchy." "Government" does not exist. It never has and never will, which can be proven, using logic that does not at all depend upon any individual's moral beliefs.

To quickly review, *people cannot delegate rights they do not have*, which makes it impossible for anyone to acquire the right to rule ("authority"). Also, *people cannot alter morality*, which makes the "laws" of "government" devoid of any inherent "authority." Ergo, "authority" — the right to rule — cannot logically exist. The concept itself is self-contradictory, like the concept of a "militant pacifist." A human being cannot have superhuman rights, and therefore no one can have the inherent right to rule. A person cannot be morally obliged to ignore his own moral judgment; therefore, no one can have the inherent obligation to obey another. And those two ingredients — the ruler's right to command and the subject's obligation to obey — are the heart and soul of the concept of "authority," without which it cannot exist.

And without "authority," there is no "government." If the control which the gang called "government" exerts over others is without legitimacy, it is not "government," and its commands are not "laws." Without the *right* to rule, and a simultaneous moral *obligation* to obey on the part of the masses, the organization called "government" is nothing more than a gang of thugs, thieves and murderers. "Government" is an impossibility; it's simply not an option, any more than Santa Claus is an option. And insisting that it is "necessary," when it does not and cannot even exist, or predicting doom and gloom if we do not have the mythical entity, does not change that fact. To argue that human beings *need* to have a rightful ruler, one with the moral right to forcibly control all others, and one whom all others are obligated to obey, does not change the fact that there is no such thing, and can be no such thing.

As such, the purpose of this final chapter is not merely to argue that society would work better without the fiction called "government," but to introduce to the reader the ways in which people will perceive reality differently, think differently, behave differently, and interact differently — very differently, indeed — once they give up the most dangerous superstition: the belief in "authority." Anarchy, meaning an absence of "government," *is what is*. It is what has always been, and will always be. When people accept that truth and stop hallucinating a creature called "authority," they will stop behaving in the irrational and destructive manner they do now.

Almost everyone, at least to begin with, has difficulty thinking clearly about such a concept. Because every politician, and every "government," is constantly proposing "solutions" that deal with how society will be organized, managed and controlled through a centralized, authoritarian "system," most people do not even know how to mentally process the idea of a complete *lack* of any forcibly imposed "system." They instinctively ask things such as "How would the roads work?" or "How would we defend ourselves?" The truth is that no one can know how everything would work or exactly what would happen. Individuals can make suggestions about how things should work, or predictions about how things might work, but no one can possibly know the best way for everything to work. Despite the huge amount of uncertainty this creates, the historical track record of people living in freedom is far better than any centralized, managed "solution" has ever been.

However, statists have been trained to be terrified of this infinitely more complex type of society, where there is not one master plan but billions of individual plans, interacting with each other in innumerable different ways. To them, that means chaos. And in a way, it *is* chaos, in the sense that there is no single guiding idea and no single controlling entity. This does not mean that people cannot make agreements, or work together, or cooperate and find compromises. Instead, it means that each person will view life as an adult instead of throwing away his free will and responsibility to blindly follow someone else's agenda.

As an aside, even without the "authority" superstition, there would still be leaders and followers. But it would usually be actual leadership, where one person leads by example, by demonstrating a level of intelligence, compassion or courage which inspires others to behave similarly. That is a very different phenomenon from what is usually dubbed "leadership" today. When people talk of the "leaders" of countries, they are talking about people coercively controlling millions of others. The term "leader of the free world," when talking about a "government" official, is inaccurate and self-contradictory. Politicians do not lead by example. If anything, they set an example of how to be dishonest, conniving, narcissistic and power-happy. They say what people want to hear, in order to dominate and control them. To call such people "leaders" is as ridiculous as calling thieves "producers," or calling murderers "healers." In the absence of the belief in "government," real leaders could emerge: people who claim no right to rule, no right to force anyone else to follow them, but whose virtues and actions others recognize as being worth emulating.

No one can predict, and no one will control, everything that will happen in a world without the myth of "government." The following is not, therefore, intended to be a complete explanation of how every piece of human society would work once the "authority" myth is gone. Instead, it is an introduction to a few of the ways in which human beings might stop allowing an irrational superstition to distort their thinking and pervert their behavior, and might start behaving as rational, free beings, driven by their own free will and individual judgment, as they ought to be.

✳   *Fear of Freedom*

Most people live their lives surrounded by authoritarian hierarchies, from families, to schools, to businesses, to all levels of "government." As a result, most people have a hard time even beginning to imagine a "leaderless" civilization, a society of equals, an existence devoid of rulers, a world without "legislators" and their "laws." The very thought, in most people's minds, conjures up images of chaos and mayhem.

People are more comfortable with whatever they are accustomed to, and fear the unknown. People are so attached to whatever is familiar to them that even those who live in very high crime areas or war zones rarely leave the world they know to search for something better. Similarly, it is a well-documented fact that some long-term prisoners develop a fear of being released, and when they are, commit further crimes with the *intention* of being sent back to prison. Even slaves can exhibit a dread of being freed. This is because the life of a prisoner or a slave, though not likely fulfilling, is predictable, and imagining a new, drastically changed life, in a strange place, among strangers, with all of the related uncertainties—How will I eat? Where will I live? What will it be like? Will I be safe?—scares almost everyone. So it is when most people contemplate human society without a ruling class. The concept is so foreign to everything they have ever known and ever thought about, and everything they were taught is necessary and good, that they hardly know how to begin to imagine it. Even our very language illustrates our fear of living in society as free equals, because such a state is defined as "anarchy"—a term also used to describe chaos and destruction. We have grown so accustomed to the mental cage which the myth of "authority" has formed around each of us that most of us are terrified of the idea of life *without* that cage. We are literally afraid of our own freedom.

And some people work hard to reinforce that fear. Those who benefit the most from the myth of "authority"—those who crave dominion over others, and the unearned wealth and power it gives them—are constantly pushing the message that life without them in charge would mean constant pain and suffering for everyone. Just about anything people can be afraid of—crime, poverty, disease, invasion, environmental disaster, etc.—has been used by tyrants to scare people into subservience. The details vary, but the template of the message from the tyrants is always the same: "If you do not give us power over you, so that we can protect you, you will suffer horribly." That message, combined with man's inherent fear of the unknown, has allowed for an incomprehensible level of oppression, theft, and outright murder, lasting generation after generation, all around the world. Ironically, it has been the empty promise of protection against suffering and injustice which has duped so many people into accepting the very thing which has *caused* more suffering and injustice than anything else in history: the belief in "government."

It seems strange that any thinking human being would not be naturally open and receptive to the idea that he owns himself and should be in charge of his own life, unhindered by any human "authority." However, the average person who hears such a message often lashes out at the messenger, insists that actual freedom, a world without masters and subjects, would mean chaos and destruction, and then vehemently advocates the continued enslavement of all of mankind, including himself. He does so not based upon any rational thought or any evidence or experience, but based upon his own deep-seated, existential terror of the unknown—the unknown in this case being a society of equals instead of masters and subjects. He has never seen it in action on a large scale and has never thought about it, cannot imagine it, and therefore fears it. And those who desire dominion over others are constantly reinforcing and encouraging that fear in those they seek to subjugate.

Seeing a Different World ✸

When someone who has been indoctrinated into the cult of "authority" finally disentangles himself from the superstition, the first thing that happens is that he *sees* a drastically different reality. When he observes the effects of the "authority" superstition, which infiltrate nearly every aspect of most people's lives, he sees things as they actually are, not as he had formerly imagined them to be. Most of the time, when he sees so-called "law enforcement" in action, he recognizes it as raw, illegitimate and immoral thuggery being used to extort and control the people in order to serve the will of politicians. (The exception to this is when the police use force to stop others who are actually guilty of acts of aggression — ironically, the very acts which the police routinely commit for the ruling class.) When the recovering statist watches various political rituals, whether a presidential election, a legislative debate in Congress, or a local zoning board passing some new "ordinance," he sees it for what it is: the acting out of delusions and hallucinations by people who have been indoctrinated into a completely irrational cult. Any discussions in the media of what "public policy" should be, or which "representatives" should be elected, or what "legislation" should be enacted, appear, to one who has escaped the super-stition, exactly as useful and rational as well-dressed, attractive, respectable-looking people seriously discussing how Santa Claus should handle the next Christmas.

To one who has escaped the myth of "authority," the premise upon which *all* political discussion rests disintegrates, and every bit of the rhetoric which stems from the superstition is recognized as being utterly insane. The un-indoctrinated individual sees every campaign speech, every political argument, every discussion in the news about anything political, every CNN broadcast of another debate on the House floor over some new piece of "legislation," as a display of the symptoms of profound delusions due to the blind acceptance of utterly asinine, cult-like dogma. All voting, campaigning, writing to one's "congressman," signing petitions, suddenly appear no more rational or useful than praying to a volcano god to grant its blessings to the tribe. One who has been deprogrammed sees not only the futility in all "political" action, but sees that such actions, no matter what their intended goals, actually *reinforce* the superstition. Just as everyone in a tribe praying to a volcano god would reinforce the idea that there *is* a volcano god, so begging politicians for favors reinforces the idea that there is a rightful ruling class, that their commands are "law," and that obedience to such "laws" is a moral imperative.

Those whom most people now regard with great respect, and who are often called "honorable," are recognized as delusional, god-complex lunatics by those who have escaped the "authority" myth. The un-indoctrinated would take no more pride in shaking the "President's" hand than he would in shaking the hand of any other psychotic, narcissistic mass murderer. The men who wear black dresses and wield wooden hammers and refer to themselves as "the court" are seen as the madmen they are. Those who wear badges and uniforms, and imagine themselves to be something other than mere human beings, are not seen by the deprogrammed as noble warriors for "law and order" but as confused souls suffering from what is little more than a mental disorder.

Of course, those who have given up the superstition of "authority" can still fear the damage which the megalomaniacs and their mercenaries — soldiers and police — are capable of inflicting, but the mercenaries' actions are no longer seen as being in any way legitimate, or rational, or moral. Those who have escaped the myth begin to see that those whose actions are influenced by their "official" badge are as dangerous as people who are high on PCP, and for the same reason: because they are hallucinating a reality which is not there, which leads them to act out violently, unrestrained by a rational thought process. Those who have escaped the "authority" superstition, when confronted by a "police officer," may still act as they would if confronted by a rabid dog: speaking softly, behaving in a submissive manner, and not making sudden movements. But it is not out of respect for either the "law enforcer" or the rabid dog; it is out of fear of the danger posed by a brain that is malfunctioning because it is infected by a destructive disease, be it rabies or the belief in "authority." When believers in "authority" commit acts of aggression, imagining such acts to be righteous because they are called "law," their targets have few options. When a "tax" collector, or a police officer, or some other enforcer of the will of politicians, attempts to extort, harass, control or assault those who have escaped the myth of "authority," the targets of the "legal" aggression can either go along with what they know to be injustice, or they can try to somehow circumvent or hide from the "legal" aggressors, or they can forcibly resist the aggressors. It is unfortunate that the last option is ever necessary, because, though using defensive force is morally justified (even when "illegal"), it is sad that one good person would ever have to use violence against another *good* person simply because the latter has had his perception of right and wrong twisted and perverted by an irrational superstition. Even the murderous thugs of the most brutal regimes in history, due to their faith in the "authority" myth, thought they were doing their duty; they thought, on some level, that their actions were noble and righteous, or they would not have committed them. Such mindless loyalty to "authority" often leaves the intended victims with only two options:

submit to tyranny or kill the deluded "law enforcers." It would be far better for everyone if, before forcible resistance becomes necessary, the mercenaries of the state could be deprogrammed out of their delusion, so as to avoid the necessity of having to scare, hurt or even kill them to stop them from committing evil.

(Author's personal note: The nicest thing you can do for anyone who has been duped into acting as a pawn of the oppression machine called "government" is to do whatever you can to persuade him to rethink his loyalty to the myth of "authority." If all else fails, give him a copy of this book. As uncomfortable as that might be, you might be doing a lot of his potential future victims a huge favor, and you might even be doing the enforcer himself a huge favor, by negating the need for one of his future intended victims to maim or kill him.)

❋ *A World Without Rulers*

One who has been deprogrammed looks out at the world, and instead of seeing hierarchies of different ruling classes within different jurisdictions, he sees a world of equals—not in talent, ability, or wealth, of course, but in rights. He sees a world in which each person owns himself, and he comes to the realization that he has no rightful master, that there is no one above him, and that that is true of everyone else, as well. He is beholden to no "government," no "country," and no "law." He is a sovereign entity. He is bound by his own conscience, and nothing else.

Such a realization is incredibly freeing, but also can be quite disturbing to those who have always measured their conduct by how well they obeyed others. Obedience not only is easy, as it allows someone else to make all the decisions, but it also allows the one who blindly obeys to imagine that the consequences, whatever they may be, are always someone else's responsibility. To have to *figure out* right and wrong, and to know that you alone are responsible for your decisions and actions, can feel like a huge burden. Essentially, losing the belief in "authority" means growing up, which has advantages and drawbacks. The un-indoctrinated person can no longer face the world as a care-free, irresponsible child, but at the same time, he will possess a level of freedom and empowerment he could not have imagined before.

Statists often have a deep-seated terror of a world in which every person decides for himself what he should do. Unfortunately for them, that is all that has ever existed, and all that ever will exist. Everyone *already* decides for himself what he will do.

That is called "free will." Many assume that if an individual is not bound by any "authority," and has the attitude "I can do whatever I want," he will behave like a selfish animal. Some even imagine that they themselves would become animals if they were not governed by a master. Such a belief implies that people feel a strong moral obligation to do as they are told, but otherwise have no moral compass at all. But most people obey "the law" because they believe that it is *good* to do so. There is no reason to think that, without being subservient to a master, those same people would no longer care about being good. Yet many still imagine human beings to be stupid savages, kept in check only by controllers. So they expect that, if unrestrained by a belief in "authority," most people would become like unchained animals.

Those who have given up the "authority" delusion know better. There are, of course, consequences to actions, with or without "authority." Aside from moral issues, most people usually choose to behave in ways that do not incur the wrath of others. Even if no one believed in right and wrong, being a habitual thief or murderer would be dangerous, and finding ways to peacefully coexist benefits the individual *and* the group. But aside from that, most people try to be good. In fact, that is why they obey "the law": because they were taught that doing so is good. The problem is not that people do not want to be good; it is that their judgment of what is good and what is bad is horribly twisted and perverted by the belief in "authority." They are taught that funding and obeying a gang of thugs is a virtue, and resisting is a sin. They are taught that asking those thugs to rob and control their neighbors (via "legislation") is perfectly moral and legitimate. In short, when it comes to "authority," they are taught that good is evil and that evil is good. Initiating violence via "the law" is seen as good, and resisting such assaults ("breaking the law") is seen as bad.

Without the myth of "authority," people would still have disagreements, and some people would still be malicious or negligent, and would still do stupid or hostile things. The main difference in how human beings would interact without the "authority" superstition is quite simple: <u>If someone did not feel justified in doing something himself, he would not feel justified in asking someone else to do it, nor would he feel justified doing it himself on someone else's behalf.</u> The concept is so simple, almost to the point of sounding trivial, but would lead to a huge change in human behavior. For example, if someone would not feel justified in paying for his children's education by forcibly robbing his neighbors, he also would not feel justified in "voting" for local "government" to impose a "property tax" to pay for "public" schools. And if someone would not feel justified in stealing his neighbor's property to fund a school, he still would not feel justified in doing so even if he was given a badge, and told to do so, in the name of "the law." As another example, if someone would not feel justified in kicking down someone's door and dragging him away and putting him in a cage for years, for having possessed a plant with mind-altering properties, then he would not feel justified in supporting "anti-drug laws" either. Nor would he suddenly feel justified in engaging in such trespassing, assault and kidnapping just because some "authority" gave him a badge and told him to do so, in the name of some "law." As yet another example, if someone would not feel justified using violence to keep a complete stranger from setting foot anywhere in an entire "country," then he would still not feel justified in doing so if someone gave him an I.C.E. badge, nor would he feel justified in supporting "immigration laws" which instruct others to do so.

In a society without the myth of "authority" there would still be thieves, murderers, and other aggressors. The difference is that all of the people who view theft and murder as immoral would not *advocate* and *condone* "legal" theft and murder, which *every* statist now does. Again, to advocate any "law" is to advocate the use of whatever level of authoritarian force is required, up to and including deadly force, to achieve compliance. And the people who perceived theft and murder as immoral would not commit such acts simply because some "authority" or "law" told them to.

How much of what police do on a daily basis would they do on their own, without a "law" or a "government" telling them to? Very little. How much of what "soldiers" routinely do would they do on their own, without an authoritarian military leader telling them to? Very little. How much of what "tax collectors" do now would they do on their own, without any "government" telling them to? None of it. Everything *good* that the people who are called "law enforcers" now do—i.e., trying to stop genuinely hostile, destructive people from harming innocents—they could continue to do without the myth of "authority." And they could do so out of the kindness of their hearts, or as a paid career, in the likely event that other people would want to voluntarily pay them for doing so. At the same time, everything *bad* that "law enforcers" and soldiers now do—e.g., terrorizing or shooting people they know nothing about, aggressing against those who commit victimless "crimes," detaining, interrogating and assaulting complete strangers—most of them would stop doing.

Very few people were assaulted, tortured and murdered by the population of Germany as a whole, or the population of Russia as a whole, or the population of China as a whole, *before* the respective "governments" of those countries, under the regimes of Hitler, Stalin and Mao, enacted "laws" pretending to *legitimize* such atrocities. But how many atrocities were committed *after* "authority" issued commands directing people to commit them? The numbers are staggering: tens of millions murdered, hundreds of millions assaulted, oppressed or tortured. Obviously, the people of those countries (and just about every other country) were far less inclined to commit acts of aggression on their own than they were to commit acts of aggression when commanded to do so by an imagined "authority."

Ironically, when faced with the concept of a purely voluntary society, in which every service, even defense and protection, is funded by willing customers instead of by coercive "taxation," many statists predict that private security firms would evolve into new, abusive, oppressive "governments," or that competing security companies would end up being engaged in perpetual violent conflicts with each other. Such predictions fail to recognize that most people do not *want* to attack and rob their neighbors, and do not want to be attacked and robbed themselves, and it is only through the belief in "authority" that the majority ever feels okay about advocating robbery via "taxation," or ever feels obligated to go along with being attacked and robbed themselves via "obeying the law." Without the notion that "government" has rights that individuals do not, no malicious, aggressive private security firm would ever have popular support. If they were seen merely as private employees of average people, no one involved — neither the customers nor their hired protectors — would imagine the employees to have any right to steal, harass, terrorize, or do anything that anyone else does not have the right to do.

To look at it another way, and to make it more personal, imagine living in a world where none of your neighbors felt justified in advocating that you be "taxed" to fund things which you object to. Imagine if every cause, every plan, every program, every idea, every proposed solution to all sorts of problems, was something you could either *voluntarily* support, or not. Imagine living in a world where none of your neighbors felt that they had the right to forcibly impose their ideas, choices and lifestyles upon you. They would feel justified (as they do already) in using force to stop you if you decided to attack them or rob them, but very few would feel good about committing any sort of aggression against you.

Contrary to what most people assume, this is exactly what a "world without rules" would look like. Each person would be guided by his own conscience — which could be thought of as self-imposed "rules" or "self-government" — and even though some people acting on their own would still make stupid or malicious choices and commit acts of aggression, no longer would anyone imagine that calling something a "law" or a "rule" could make an inherently unjustified act into something good. And if you were to *resist* such an act of aggression, your neighbors would praise you for doing so, instead of condemning you as a "criminal," which nearly all of them would do today if you resisted an act of aggression which happened to be "legal."

✸ *Thinking Differently, Talking Differently*

Many of the terms people use and the discussions they have on a daily basis are based upon the assumption that "authority" can exist. By constantly hearing and repeating the superstition-based dogma, nearly everyone unwittingly reinforces the myth, in their own minds and in the minds of those they talk to. Authoritarian propaganda is so ubiquitous that it does not feel to the masses like a "message" at all; it just feels like "talking about what is."

Most of every history book is about who ruled what area when, which authoritarian regime conquered another authoritarian regime, which individuals or political parties came to power, which forms of "government" and types of "public policy" various empires have had, and so on. They speak about elections, who wielded the power behind the scenes, what "laws" were passed, what "taxes" were imposed, and what the people thought about their "leaders." The underlying premise, which comes through loud and clear even if it is never openly stated, is that it is both inevitable and legitimate for there to be a ruling class — some variety of overlord with the right to forcibly control everyone else.

That message continues to be a constant underlying theme of nearly everything written in the newspapers, or broadcast on the radio or television. The news reports, whether local or national, talk about what "legislation" the "representatives" or "congressmen" have passed, what "law enforcers" did that day, which candidates are running for "public office," what "public policies" they support, and so on. The way every bit of it is reported is heavily tainted by the superstition of "authority." Of

164

course, the way people think affects the way they talk, and each person is constantly expressing his own fundamental beliefs, even in seemingly trivial discussions.

Compare how the same exact situation and events would likely be reported, first by one who believes in "authority," and then by one who does not:

With Superstition: *"Today the local government of Springfield put into place a four percent increase in local building permit fees, the proceeds of which are intended to fund a program to provide certain medical assistance for the elderly."*

Without Superstition: *"Today the local organized crime syndicate issued a formal threat to anyone doing construction or renovation in Springfield, demanding four percent more than the group had previously demanded from such people. The thieves say they intend to give some of the money they seize to the elderly."*

When someone escapes the superstition of "authority," his thought patterns, and therefore his speech patterns, change dramatically. He does not use the euphemistic terms which assign legitimacy to "legal" violence. He describes "tax collectors" as what they actually are: professional extortionists. He describes "law enforcers" as what they actually are: the politicians' hired thugs. He describes "laws" as what they actually are: threats from politicians. He does not proudly describe himself as a "law-abiding taxpayer," because he recognizes what that term actually means: one who allows himself to be robbed and controlled by power-hungry megalomaniacs.

Most statists have a hard time imagining a world in which there is no centralized machine attempting to control everyone else. However, some find it equally difficult imagining a world in which they themselves are not being forcibly controlled. The thought of looking out at the world and feeling beholden to no one, feeling no obligation to obey the "laws" of others, is utterly foreign to anything they have ever contemplated. As sad as it is, many people find it very hard to even imagine a world in which there is no one they must bow to, no legislature they must subjugate themselves to, no "law" or "rule" that can ever outrank their own consciences. Such ideas are worlds away from what nearly everyone has been taught to believe, and accepting such a drastically different view of reality feels like a profound, existential awakening. He who has escaped the myth says to himself something like this:

"Does any person, or any group of people, have the right to demand payment from me for something I did not ask for and do not want to fund? Of course not. If I am not committing

aggression against anyone (via force or fraud), does anyone have the right to force me to make the choices they wish I would make? Of course not. Do I have the right to resist such aggression? Of course I do. Does any person, or any group of people, possess any rights that I do not possess? Of course not. (How and from where would they have gotten such rights?) Do I, at any time or in any place, under any circumstances, ever have an obligation to do anything other than what my own conscience dictates? Is there any situation in which the decrees or 'laws' of any supposed 'authority' could ever obligate me, in any way and to any degree, to abandon my free will, or ignore my own sense of right and wrong? Of course not."

✸ *Teaching Morality vs. Teaching Authority*

It is commonly held that unless children are taught to respect and obey "authority" they will be like wild animals, stealing, assaulting, and so on. But being obedient, in and of itself, merely means that, instead of the individual using his own judgment, he will defer to the judgment of those who seek and acquire positions of power — some of the most immoral, corrupt, callous, malicious, dishonest people on earth. Training people to be merely obedient only prevents animalistic behavior if the supposed "authority" does not itself *condone* and *command* theft and assault, as every "government" in history has done in the name of "taxation" and "law enforcement."

Obviously, teaching obedience does not help civilization if those giving the orders are commanding the very behaviors that harm society: acts of aggression against innocents. The idea that widespread subservience is good for society rests upon the patently false assumption that people in positions of power are morally superior to everyone else. It should be self-evident that having most people disregard their own consciences, instead entrusting politicians to make their choices for them, is not going to make society any safer or more virtuous. Instead, it will simply legitimize the very acts that *interfere* with peaceful human coexistence.

Consider the analogy of a robot which is programmed to do whatever its owner tells it to do, whether productive or destructive, whether civilized or aggressive. This is akin to a child learning to respect "authority." Whether the obedient robot or child ends up being a tool for destruction and oppression depends entirely upon who ends up giving the orders. If, instead, children are taught the principle of self-ownership — the idea that every individual belongs to himself, and should not be robbed, threatened, assaulted, or murdered — then the supposed virtue of obedience is completely unnecessary. Consider which of the following is more likely to lead to a just, peaceful society: billions of people being taught the basics of how to be moral human beings (e.g., the principle of non-aggression), or billions of people being taught merely to obey, in the hopes that the few people who end up in charge will happen to give good orders. If there is any difficulty imagining what would happen in the two scenarios, one need only look to history to see what *has* happened.

Even randomly selected "rulers," when given permission to forcibly control everyone else, will quickly be corrupted, and will become tyrants. But average, decent people are not the ones who desire power over others. The ones who seek and obtain power are usually already narcissists and megalomaniacs, people with a never-ending lust for power, who love the idea of dominating others. And the desire for dominion is never driven by a desire to help those who are being dominated, but always by a desire to empower the controller, at the expense of those whom he controls. Yet people continue to echo the claim that the average person, if guided purely by his own conscience, would be less trustworthy, less civilized and less moral than if he sets aside his own conscience and just blindly does whatever the tyrants of the world tell him to do. If each person relied on his own judgment, that would, by definition, be "anarchy," while widespread obedience to authoritarian tyrants, by definition, constitutes "law and order." Note the drastic contrast between the usual connotations of those terms — "anarchy" sounding scary and violent, "law and order" sounding civilized and just — and the real-world *results* of following conscience versus following rulers. The level of evil committed by individuals acting on their own is completely dwarfed by the level of evil committed by people obeying a perceived "authority."

Though many imagine teaching obedience to "authority" to be synonymous with teaching right and wrong, the two are actually *opposites*. Teaching children to respect the rights of every human being, and teaching them that committing aggression is inherently wrong, is very important. But teaching them that obedience is a virtue, and that "respecting authority" is a moral imperative, will make them grow up to either *advocate* widespread, large-scale aggression, or to *participate* in widespread, large-scale aggression. Every statist does one or the other (or both). In fact, teaching obedience dramatically hinders the social and mental development of children. After having grown up in a situation where they were controlled by others, rewarded for obedience and punished for disobedience, if they ever escape that situation, they will have had little or no training, and little or no experience or practice, in how to think and act from morals and principles. Having never exercised their individual judgment and personal responsibility, knowing only how to do as they are told, they will be like trained monkeys that have escaped, but that have no way to cope with a life of freedom. If their upbringings have been molded mainly by controlling "authority" figures, people become existentially lost if that control vanishes. In short, people trained to obey "authority" do not know how to be independent, sovereign, responsible human beings, because all their lives they have been intentionally and specifically trained *not* to follow their own consciences and *not* to use their own judgment. So the indoctrinated, when they escape one institutionalized control setting ("school"), hallucinate another "authority" to take its place: "government." The escaped monkeys simply build a new cage, and eagerly jump into it, because that is all they know, and all they have ever known.

In a world without the "authority" myth, on the other hand, children could be taught to be moral instead of merely obedient. They could be taught to respect people, instead of respecting the inhuman, violent monster called "government." They could be taught that it is up to them, not only to do the right thing, but to figure out what "the right thing" is. As a result, they could grow up to be responsible, thinking, useful adults, members of a peaceful and productive community, instead of growing up to be little more than cattle on the farms of tyrants.

✳ *No Master Plan*

If tomorrow, by some miracle, everyone in the world let go of the belief in "authority," the vast majority of theft, assault, and murder in society would immediately cease. All wars would end; all robbery in the name of "taxation" would stop; all oppression carried out in the name of "law" would cease. The people as a whole — including the perpetrators, victims, and spectators of oppression — would no longer view such acts of aggression as legitimate.

But there would be another, less immediate change as well. The belief in "authority" is, in essence, a psychological cage. It trains people to believe that they do not need to judge what is right and wrong; that they do not need to take it upon themselves to fix society; that all that is required of them is that they "play by the rules" and do as they are told while looking to "leaders" and "lawmakers" to handle the problems of society. In short, the belief in "authority" trains people to never grow up, to always view the world as children view it: an incomprehensibly complicated place that is, and will always be, someone else's responsibility. Whatever the problem—poverty, crime, disease, economic or environmental trouble—the indoctrinated statists are always on the lookout for some new "leader" to elect, who will promise to fix things. In one way, a world of authoritarians functions exactly the way a kindergarten classroom does: if anything goes wrong—if anything outside of the predictable, pre-planned, centrally-controlled agenda occurs—the "children" call on the "teacher" to fix everything. The entire authoritarian environment of a classroom teaches the children that they are never in charge; it is never up to them to decide what to do. In fact, they are strongly discouraged from ever thinking or acting on their own. After all, if they were allowed to think and make their own decisions, the first decision most of them would make would be to walk out of the classroom.

Likewise, adult authoritarians are constantly told that one should not "take the law into his own hands." The people are trained to call "the authorities" whenever there is a conflict or other problem, and then meekly do whatever the "government" enforcers tell them to do. If there is any dispute between people, the people are told that they should always run to the masters, whether by calling the "police" or by going to authoritarian "courts" to settle disagreements. When discussing societal challenges, the well-trained subjects of the state talk in terms such as: "They should pass a law ..." or "They should make a government program ..." They view their lives as part of a giant, centralized, master plan, so it logically follows that if they want their lives improved, the solution is to petition the planners to change the plan. This view is so ingrained in the masses that many people literally cannot comprehend the idea of individuals living their lives without being part of anyone else's master plan. This is demonstrated by the common response authoritarians have to the idea of a society without rulers. Almost without exception, a statist who ponders a stateless society will begin by asking how things will "work" without a ruling class. He does not ask this simply because he is curious about how roads, defense, trade, dispute resolution, and other things might function without "government." He asks this because he has always been trained to view human existence inside the framework of some centralized, forcibly-imposed master plan, and is literally incapable of thinking outside of that paradigm. And so he will ask how things will work "under anarchy" and will refer to it as a "system," imagining it as a new type of master plan to be inflicted upon the masses, when, of course, it is the exact opposite: a complete *lack* of a centralized, forcibly-imposed plan. But an overall plan for humanity is all that the statist has ever considered, and often it is all that he can comprehend. The idea that *no one* will be "in charge," that *no one* will be making "the rules" for everyone else, that *no one* will be planning or managing mankind as a whole, and that no one will be telling the statist what to do, is simply something most authoritarians have never even imagined. The concept is so unfamiliar that they do not even know how to process it, so they desperately try to fit the idea of "anarchy" (a stateless society) into the mold of a master plan.

(Such contradictory thinking is only reinforced by those who wear the label of "anarcho-communist." The term implies that there would be no ruling class, *and* that society would be organized into a collectivist system. Of course, if some group claims the right to forcibly impose such a system on everyone else, that is authoritarianism, and so the "anarcho" part of the term would not apply. Another option is that those calling themselves "anarcho-communists" are merely *hoping* that, in the absence of a ruling class, every single individual on the planet will freely choose to participate in communes or collectives — which, of course, would not happen. As a final possibility, perhaps the "anarcho-communists" would, for themselves, choose to be part of a commune, but would allow others to choose different arrangements. In the end, the term "anarcho-communist" makes little sense, and is actually a *symptom* of authoritarianism: even when advocating a stateless society, some people automatically imagine that there must be some overarching system or plan, some grand scheme, some form of societal management which must be imposed upon mankind as a whole.)

The truth is, with or without the myth of "authority," no one can guarantee justice or prosperity, or predict everything that might occur, or know every problem that might arise, or how to solve them all. The difference is that those who believe in "authority" continue to pretend, despite constant overwhelming evidence to the contrary, that an authoritarian system of control can guarantee safety, security, prosperity, fairness and justice. Meanwhile, those who have given up the most dangerous superstition no longer pretend that it is possible to control everything and everyone via any "system." Bizarrely, despite the nearly incomprehensible degree of economic disaster, human suffering, and mass oppression which the belief in "government" has repeatedly caused, proponents of authoritarianism still insist that those who oppose statism must be able to describe in minute detail exactly how everything in society would work in the absence of "government," so that nothing bad could possibly happen. And if they cannot — as of course no one can — the statist then proclaims that as proof that "anarchy will never work."

Rather than being a rational conclusion, such an idea is the symptom of deep-seated mental dependency and fear of the unknown. Statists want the promise that some all-knowing, all-powerful entity will take care of them and protect them from all possible misfortune and from all of the bad people in the world. The fact that politicians have been making such promises forever, and have never once actually fulfilled such a promise (because the promise is patently ridiculous), does not stop statists from wanting to *hear* the promise. No matter how many times authoritarian "solutions" fail horrendously, most people still think that some *other* "government" plan is the only answer. What they want is a guarantee that some all-powerful entity outside of themselves will make sure that their lives are comfortable and safe. They do not seem to care, or even notice, that such "guarantees" never come true, and that anyone claiming the power to make such a guarantee is either an amazingly bold liar or a lunatic. Nonetheless, because anarchists and voluntaryists would never make the absurd promise that, without "government," nothing bad will ever happen, most statists remain terrified of the idea of a stateless society.

(Author's personal note: I have found that, whenever the topic of a stateless society comes up in my discussions with statists, almost without fail they begin asking questions in the passive voice: how will this get done, how will that be handled? They speak as if, even when it comes to their own lives, they are little more than spectators, waiting to see what will happen. This is because, for many of their formative years, especially while in "school," they were little more than spectators. The scripts of their lives were written by others; their destiny was determined and decided by "authority," not by themselves. So, in an effort to get them to escape that mindset, when they ask me something like, "Under anarchy, how will this be dealt with?" I respond, "How would you deal with it?" When they ask, "What would be done about this potential problem?" I ask, "What would you do about it?" And they can usually come up with ideas, off the top of their heads, that are better than any authoritarian solution. The problem is not that they are incapable of being in charge of themselves, their futures, and in fact the future of the world; the problem is that it has just never occurred to them that they already are in charge of themselves, their futures, and the future of the world.)

One who understands that "authority" is a myth does not have any obligation to explain how every aspect of a free society would work, any more than someone who says that Santa Claus is not real has some obligation to explain how Christmas will work without him. However, statists often insist, as a condition of even considering the possibility of a stateless society, that someone tell them how every aspect of everyone's life will work without "government." Of course, no one knows—with or without the myth of "government"—everything that might happen, and it is absurd to cling to a provably false, self-contradictory myth, which itself has led to large-scale murder, extortion and oppression, just because someone failed to describe in detail a perfect world without the myth. People can make suggestions or predictions about how different aspects of a free society would work without the involvement of "authority"—and many scholarly treatises do exactly that—but once someone truly understands the insanity inherent in any belief in "authority," he will never go back to accepting the myth regardless of what he thinks might happen without it, any more than an adult would go back to believing in Santa Claus because he does not know whether Christmas would work without him.

✳ *You Rule You, I Rule Me*

By definition, in the absence of "authority," no one would have the power or the right to proclaim, "This is how things will be done." Yet that is the only template of thought which most authoritarians have ever considered. Those who realize that they have neither the ability nor the right to control all of humanity do not think in terms of a master plan for the human race. Instead, they think in terms of the only thing they can truly control: their own actions. They think in terms of, "What should I do about this?" instead of, "What should I ask the masters to do about this?" They are not so arrogant or delusional to think they have the right or the ability to make choices for all of mankind. They make their own choices, and accept the unavoidable reality that other people will make different choices.

On a practical level, it is absurd to expect that a system of centralized control, wherein a handful of politicians, with their limited understanding and experience, come up with a master plan and then force it on everyone else, would work better than comparing and combining the knowledge, ingenuity and expertise of hundreds of millions of individuals, via a network of mutually voluntary trade and cooperation. No matter what the goal is—whether it is food production, road building, protection against aggressors, or anything else—the ideas that come from the "chaos" of millions of people trying different inventions and solutions will always be better than the ideas which a handful of politicians will come up with. This is especially true in light of the fact that, while politicians force their ideas on everyone via "the law," even if they are lousy ideas that no one else likes, free market ideas have to be good enough that others will *voluntarily* support them.

Despite the amazing prosperity already created by relatively free, "anarchistic" trade and mutual cooperation, the thought of people coexisting without all of them being controlled and regulated by some master plan is still incomprehensible to most statists. Most statists have never even begun to contemplate the possibility of truly being in charge of their own lives. Everything about modern authoritarian society trains people to be loyal subjects of a system of control, instead of training people to be what they should be: sovereign entities, figuring things out for themselves, interacting with others as equals, answerable to their own consciences above all else. To most, the idea of a world where *they* are the ones who have to solve problems, settle disputes, help those who need help, protect themselves and others, without being able to run to an all-powerful "authority" instead, is a completely foreign and terrifying concept. They love to advocate authoritarian solutions, but do not really even want to be in charge of themselves, much less to be personally responsible for making society work. And their belief in "authority" is what they use to attempt to evade that responsibility and avoid the realities of life.

The life of a caged animal is, in many ways, easier than life in the wild. Likewise, life as an unthinking human slave can be more predictable and feel safer than a life of responsibility. But, just as living in the wild makes animals stronger, smarter, and far better able to care for themselves, letting go of the "authority" myth will force human beings to be smarter, more creative, more compassionate, and more moral. That is not to say that all people will, without the belief in "government," be wise, kind and generous. But if millions of individuals each understood that it is up to them personally to make the world a better place, instead of merely obediently playing an assigned part in someone else's master plan while crying to "government" to fix everything, it would unleash a level of human creativity, ingenuity, and cooperation beyond what most people could possibly imagine.

✳ _A Different Society_

Today, most people associate the idea of "everyone doing whatever he wants" with chaos and death, and associate everyone being obedient and "law-abiding" with order and civilization. Without the "authority" myth, however, people would have a very different mindset. Without an "authority" to blindly follow and obey, without being able to whine to "the powers that be" to fix everything, people would have to figure out for themselves what is right and wrong, and how to solve problems. Some might claim that human beings are too short-sighted, lazy and irresponsible to run their own lives, but it is precisely the belief in "authority" that has allowed them to become so lazy and helpless. As long as they believed that making things right was not their job, that fixing problems was not their job, and that all they needed to do was to obey their masters, acting as unthinking pawns in someone else's master plan, they had no need to grow up. But shedding the superstition forces one into the position of realizing that there is nothing on earth above him, which means that he is responsible for his own actions (or inaction); he is the one whose job it is to make the world a better place; he is the one who has to make society work.

Clearly, there are statists who are trying to make a positive difference, but more often than not their belief in "authority" converts their good intentions into evil actions, perverts their compassion into violence, and turns their productivity into the fuel of oppression. For example, many people who join the armed forces start with the noble goal of defending their countrymen from hostile foreign powers, and many of those who become "police officers" do so with the intention of helping people, and protecting the good people from the bad people. However, once they become agents of the mythical beast known as "government," they immediately cease to be advocates of their own values and their own perceptions of right and wrong, and instead become enforcers of the arbitrary whims of politicians. In every "government" in history, those purporting to be "defenders" have quickly, if not immediately, transformed into aggressors. The first act of almost every regime is to impose some sort of "taxation," to forcibly rob its subjects, usually under the asinine excuse that it must do so in order to be able to protect the people against robbers. It is, therefore, ironic that so many people accept the idea that "government" is the only entity capable of protecting the good from the wicked. In truth, only in the absence of the superstition of "authority" can the good intentions of would-be protectors and defenders actually serve humanity.

A private militia, for example, formed for the purpose of defending a certain population against foreign invaders—and such a militia is not imagined, by its members or by anyone else, to have any special "authority" whatsoever—will be guided by the personal conscience of each individual member. Such an organization can be an extremely effective means of exerting justified defensive force, while being immune to the usual corruptibility of authoritarian "protection" rackets. A private militia member who did not suffer from the "authority" delusion could not and would not ever use the excuse of "just following orders" to try to deny responsibility for his own actions. If he uses violence, he, and everyone around him, knows that he *personally* made the choice, and that he is personally responsible for it, and should personally be held accountable for his actions. In short, the only time a private, non-authoritarian militia could become oppressive is if every individual in it personally chose to act that way. In contrast, "government" militaries can become oppressive as a result of even *one* genuinely malicious person in the chain of command, if those beneath him have been effectively trained to faithfully follow orders.

Without the myth of "authority," not everyone will act responsibly or charitably. But when each person accepts that he is in charge of himself, it is far less likely that good people will be doing the bidding of evil people, as happens constantly now, by way of the belief in "authority." Statists are often afraid of what some individuals may do if not restrained by "government." What they should fear, however, is what those individuals may do if they *become* "government." The amount of damage which one hostile, malicious individual can do by himself is nothing compared to the damage that one hostile, malicious "authority figure" can do, by way of obedient, but otherwise good people. To put it another way, if evil was only committed by evil people, the world would be a far better place than it is today, with basically *good* people constantly committing evil acts, because a perceived "authority" told them to.

A Different Kind of Rules ✳

Without a belief in "government," communities would almost certainly develop "rules" which, at first glance, might resemble what are now called "laws." But there would be a fundamental difference. It is both legitimate and useful to write down, and publish for all to see, statements about the consequences of doing certain things. People in one town may, for example, make it known that if you get caught stealing in their town, you will be subjected to forced labor until you pay back your victim three-fold for what you stole. Or the people of some neighborhood may make it known that if you are caught driving drunk there, they will take your car and roll it into a lake. But, while such decrees would constitute threats, they would be fundamentally different from what are now called "laws," for several reasons:

1) The ones actually making the threats — the ones who decided what retribution they *personally* would feel justified in inflicting on those who harm or endanger their neighbors — would alone bear the responsibility for making and carrying out such threats.

2) The threats would not require any election or consensus. One person, or a thousand people jointly, could issue a warning in the form of, "If I catch you doing this, I will do *this* to you." The threats would not be seen as "the will of the people," but only as a statement of the intentions of those actually issuing the warning.

3) The legitimacy of such threats would be judged, not by who made the threats, but by whether the threatened consequence is (in the eyes of the observer) appropriate for the crime committed. No one would feel any obligation to agree with, or abide by, such a threat if they deemed it to be unfair or unjustified.

4) Such warnings would not pretend to alter morality, or make up any new "crimes," nor would anyone imagine such warnings to be legitimate simply because they were issued (the way people now view authoritarian "laws"). Instead, such warnings would simply constitute statements about what those making the threats believe to be justified. Therefore, instead of being in the authoritarian formula of, "We hereby *make* the following illegal," the warnings would fit into this template: "I believe that if you do *this*, I have the right to respond in *this* way."

Many people, having been trained into "authority"-worship, would be terrified of such a non-centralized "free for all" method of human interaction. "But what if," the statist will ask, "someone writes a threat that says, if I don't like your religion, or your hair style, or your dietary choices, I'll kill you?" Examining that question, in the context of a society still suffering from the superstition of "authority," and in the context of a society *without* such a belief, shows just how dangerous the "authority" superstition really is. It is true that in the absence of the belief in "government," an individual could still threaten violence in unjustified situations. The point is not that everyone will automatically think and behave properly if there are no rulers, but that such malicious tendencies in human beings would be far less dangerous and destructive *without* the belief in "authority" to legitimize them.

For example, compare what happens when some individuals vehemently oppose alcohol consumption, and when "authority" forbids it. It is possible (if unlikely) that an individual in a stateless society could, on his own, declare, "I consider consuming alcohol to be a sin, and if I find out you've been drinking, I'm coming to your house with a gun to straighten you out." Any person who did so would almost certainly be persuaded, if not by polite reasoning, then by the threat of retaliatory violence, that he should not carry through on his threat, and should stop making such threats.

Obviously one person could not, by himself, inflict oppression upon millions of beer-drinkers. Even among others who also considered drinking alcohol to be a sin, even if it was a majority, few would feel justified in trying to forcibly impose their views onto others. Whether they recognized that such aggression is unjustified, or whether they were simply afraid of what might be done to them if they tried, either way violent conflict would be avoided.

In contrast, suppose a group of people, wearing the label of "government," declared alcohol to be "illegal," and created a heavily armed gang of enforcers to hunt down and imprison any caught possessing alcohol. Since that actually happened, there is no need to theorize about the results. With the promise of fixing most of society's ills, and with public support, the U.S. ruling class enacted alcohol prohibition in 1920. Alcohol consumption continued, slightly reduced, and there immediately sprang up a black market in alcohol production and distribution. A hugely profitable but "illegal" market led to violent conflicts, a jump in organized crime and other crime, and widespread corruption in "government," as well as brutal attempts to crush the alcohol trade. Seeing the actual results of prohibition, a majority of the people soon opposed it, and demanded the repeal of the Eighteenth Amendment, which authorized prohibition at the federal level. And of course, after prohibition ended, *all* of the related violence — "government" violence and private violence — ended.

In this example, and countless others, it can be seen that, left to their own devices, most people will not try to forcibly impose their preferences upon others, but will go out of their way to avoid violent conflicts. However, if there is a "government" that people can use to coercively inflict their values upon others, they will gladly beg it to do so, and feel no shame or guilt for having done so. If every person who made or attempted to enforce a threat (or "rule," as it might be called) had to take personal responsibility for having done so, and had to assume the risk himself, very few people would be so eager to threaten their neighbors. But given the vehicle of "authority," everyone who believes in "government" threatens all of his neighbors on a regular basis, and accepts none of the responsibility and assumes none of the risk for having done so. In short, the belief in "authority" makes everyone who believes in it into a thug *and* a coward.

✳   *Organization Without "Authority"*

Having mentioned the ways in which human society would change absent the "authority" myth, it is equally important to note the things which would *not* change. For some reason, some people seem to think that "anarchy"—a stateless society— equates to "every man for himself," with every person having to grow his own food, build his own house, and so on. The implication of such a belief is that human cooperation and trade occur only because someone is "in charge." Of course this is not the case, and never has been. People trade and cooperate for mutual benefit, as can be seen in the many millions of businesses and transactions which already occur without any "government" involvement.

Supermarkets are examples of highly organized, amazingly efficient means of distributing food, which involve many thousands of individuals, none of whom is coerced into participating, but each of whom does so for his own benefit. Everyone from the farmers, to the truck drivers, to the stock boys, to the checkout clerks, to the store managers, to the owner of entire store chains, does what he does because he receives personal gain for doing so. No one is "legally" required to produce one bite of food for anyone else, and yet hundreds of millions of people are fed, and fed well, with a large variety of food products, of high quality but at a low price, by what is essentially an anarchistic system of food production and distribution.

This is the result of human nature and simple economics. Where there is a need for some product or service, there is money to be made providing it. And where there is money to be made, there will be a number of people—or groups of people—competing for that money, by trying to make products that are better and cheaper. Such a "system"—which is really no system at all—automatically "punishes" those whose products are inferior or too costly, and rewards those who find a way to provide people with what they want at a better price. And giving up the "authority" myth would not hamper that in the slightest.

In fact, the "authority" superstition is constantly interfering with people who attempt to organize for mutual benefit, by throwing "taxes," licensing requirements, regulations, inspectors, and other "legal" obstacles in the way. Even "laws" supposedly intended to protect consumers usually do nothing but *limit* the options available to consumers. The end result is that many businessmen who otherwise would have to focus on making a better product at a better price instead focus on lobbying those in "government" to do things which handicap or destroy competing businesses. Because the mechanism of "government" is always the use of force, it can never help with competition; it can only hinder it. In other words, rather than being essential to an organized society, the myth of "authority" is the biggest *obstacle* to human beings organizing for mutual benefit.

Defense Without "Authority"   ✳

Those who insist that "government" is necessary often raise the issue of defense and protection, claiming that society without "government" would mean that anyone could do anything, there would be no standards of behavior, no rules, no consequences for those who choose to commit theft or murder, and that society would therefore collapse into constant violence and mayhem. Such concerns, however, are based on a profound misunderstanding of human nature, and of what "government" is, and what it is not.

Defending against aggressors requires no special "authority," no "legislation," no "law," and no "law enforcers." Defensive force is inherently justified, regardless of who does it, and regardless of what any "law" says. And having a formal, organized means of providing such defensive force for a community also does not require "government" or "law." Each individual has the right to defend himself, or defend someone else. He may choose to hire someone else to provide defense services, either because he is physically unable to defend himself, or just because he would rather pay someone else to do it. And if a number of people choose to pay to have an organization of trained fighters, with the weapons, vehicles, buildings, and other resources they need to defend an entire town, the people have that right, as well.

At this point, most believers in "government" will protest, saying, "That's all government is." But that is *not* the case. And this is where the difference becomes apparent. What an individual does *not* have the right to do—what no group of people, no matter how large, has any right to do—is to hire someone else (individual or group) to do something which any average individual does *not* have the right to do. They cannot rightfully hire someone to commit robbery, even if they call it "taxation," because the average individual has no right to steal. They cannot rightfully hire someone to spy on and forcibly control the choices and behaviors of their neighbors, even if they call it "regulation." Those in a stateless society would feel justified in hiring someone to use force only in the very limited ways, and in the very limited situations, in which *every* individual has the right to use force: to defend against aggressors. In contrast, most of what the so-called "protectors" in "government" do is *commit* acts of aggression, not defend against them.

Some of what is now classified as "police work"—in fact, all of what the "police" do that is actually legitimate, noble, righteous, and helpful to society—would exist without the "authority" myth. Investigating wrongdoing and apprehending actual criminals—meaning people who harm others, not merely people who disobey politicians—would continue without the "authority" myth, as something that almost everyone would want, and would be willing to pay for. This is demonstrated by the fact that there are already private detectives and private security companies, in addition to the "protection" services of "government" that everyone is forced to fund.

There would be only one difference, though it is a major difference: those doing the job of investigating and protecting, in the absence of the "authority" superstition, would always be viewed as having exactly the same rights as everyone else. While presumably they would be better equipped and better qualified to do their jobs than the average citizen, their actions would be judged by the same standards that the actions of anyone else would be judged, which is not at all the case with so-called "law enforcers." Private protection providers would also judge their *own* actions, not by whether some "authority" had told them to do something, or whether their actions were deemed "legal" by "government," but by whether those actions, in their own personal view, were inherently justified. Not only would an excuse of "just following orders" not convince the general public, but the agents themselves could not, even in their own minds, use such an excuse to evade responsibility for their actions, because no one would be claiming to be an "authority" over them.

Non-authoritarian "police"—if they would even be called that—would be viewed very differently than "government" agents are now. They would not be seen to have the right to do anything that any other person did not have the right to do. They could only go places, question people, use force, or do anything else, in situations where anyone else would be justified in doing the same thing. As a result, the average person would have no reason to feel any nervousness or self-consciousness in their presence, as most people now do when in the presence of "law enforcers." People would feel no more obligation to submit to questioning, or searches, or anything else requested by private protectors, than they would if some stranger on the street made such requests. And if a private protector became abusive, or even violent, his victim would have the right to respond the same way he would if anyone else was behaving that way. More importantly, the individual who resisted aggression from a private protector would have the support of his neighbors if he did so, because his neighbors would not be imagining any obligation to bow to someone because of any badge or any "law."

Ultimately, the best check against a defense organization becoming corrupt or "out of control" is the ability of its customers to simply stop paying. Obviously, no one wants to pay for some gang to oppress him, but most people also do not want to pay a gang to oppress someone else either. As much as the average person wants to see thieves and murderers caught and stopped, he also wants to see to it that the innocent are not harmed. If the customers of some private protection company discovered that their "protectors" were harassing and assaulting innocent people— the type of behavior they were hired to prevent—the customer base would instantly disappear, and the thugs would be out of business. And if, in the absence of any claimed "authority," the thugs decided to try to *force* their former customers to keep paying, the backlash from the people would be swift and severe, as no one would feel any "legal" obligation to allow themselves to be oppressed.

A non-authoritarian protection system would also lack another particularly ludicrous aspect of nearly all "government" forms of "defense." It is standard, not only for "governments" to force people to fund "defense" schemes, but to refuse to even tell the people what all they are funding. The U.S. "government," and in particular the CIA (though many other agencies also engage in secret operations), has spent decades, and *trillions* of dollars, much of which still remains unaccounted for, on operations that its "customers"—the American people—are prohibited from knowing about. Indeed, anyone who tried to tell the American people what all they are funding would be imprisoned—or worse—for causing a breach of "national security."

With nearly unlimited power, nearly unlimited funds, and permission to do all of its deeds in secret, it is utterly absurd to imagine that the military and the CIA would only do useful, righteous things. Indeed, more and more, the American people are learning that the CIA has for decades engaged in drug-running and gun-running, torture, assassination, buying influence with foreign governments, installing puppet dictators, and all sorts of other destructive and evil practices. Even President Harry Truman, who created the CIA, later stated that he never would have done so if he had known it would become the "American Gestapo." Any private company that offered protection or defense services would get no customers at all if its sales pitch was: "If you give us huge sums of money, we will protect you; we just won't tell you what you're paying for, and we won't tell you what we do or how we do it." The only reason "government" gets funding based on such a ridiculous premise is because it gets its money through violent coercion, not voluntary trade. The people are not given a choice of whether to fund it or not.

There is another preposterous aspect of "protection" via "government" which would never occur with private defense and protection providers. Under the guise of "gun control" and other weapons "laws," authoritarian regimes often forcibly prevent the people from being able to defend themselves, while making the ridiculous claim that it is being done for the safety of the very people being disarmed. Those in power know full well that a disarmed public is a helpless public, and that is precisely what tyrants want. The idea that a person who does not mind violating "laws" against theft or murder is going to mind violating weapons "laws" is absurd. Crime statistics and common sense both demonstrate that passing a "law" against private weapon ownership will effect only the "law-abiding," with the result being that the basically good people will end up less able to defend themselves against aggressors. And that is exactly what politicians want, because they have the biggest, most powerful gang of aggressors around. Needless to say, if someone is looking for protection against aggressors, he will not voluntarily pay a company to forcibly take away his own means of self defense.

Furthermore, violent clashes between the police and civilians would obviously be reduced or non-existent if the people could simply stop funding any "protectors" that became aggressors. For example, much of the racial tensions and violence in U.S. history were the result of white "law enforcers" oppressing and abusing black civilians. Rather than "law" acting as a civilizing influence, it was used as the excuse for violent aggression. Given a choice, the inhabitants of a black neighborhood obviously would not have voluntarily paid to have racist, sadistic white thugs intimidating and assaulting them on a regular basis. Many other violent clashes, in the U.S. and elsewhere, have also been the result of people upset with what their ruling class was doing to them. This would include the massacre of thousands of protesters in Tiananmen Square by the Chinese Army in 1989, the killings of several anti-war protesters by the National Guard at Kent State in Ohio in 1970, and so on.

More and more often in the United States, public demonstrations and protests over "government" policies end in authoritarian attacks against protesters, with tear gas, batons, tasers, rubber bullets, and so on. Obviously, no group of people would willingly pay for a gang that forcibly stops those same people from speaking their minds. More importantly, the motivation behind such protests is almost always displeasure with what "government" officials are doing against the will of the people (at least some of the people). If each person was allowed to spend his own money, instead of being forced to fund a centralized, authoritarian agenda, there would be no reason for most of this type of protest, and the resulting clashes, to occur at all.

A non-authoritarian protector would do only things that he *and* his customers viewed as justifiable, which would probably be spelled out in contract form, where the protector agrees to provide specific services for a specific fee. Compare this to the standard "government" version of "protection": "We will forcibly take as much of your money as we want, and we will decide what, if anything, we will do for you."

Most people want aggressors stopped and the innocent protected. In a free market, the way for a company to succeed is by giving the customers what they want. Unlike "government," if a private defense company had to rely on willing customers, it would have a huge incentive not to be careless, wasteful, abusive, or corrupt. If people could take their business elsewhere, there would always be a competition to see who could provide actual justice most effectively. For a private protection company to succeed, it would have to demonstrate to its customers that: 1) it is very good at figuring out who is guilty and who is not; 2) it is very good at making sure that the innocent are not harassed, assaulted, or slandered; 3) it is very good at making sure that the truly dangerous people are caught and prevented from doing further harm; 4) it is very good at making sure that the victims of crimes receive whatever restitution is possible; and 5) it is very good at making it so that those who have done something wrong but do not need to be completely removed from society are put into an environment where their attitude and behavior can actually improve.

In contrast, "government" prosecutors specialize in always demonizing the accused, and always have an incentive to get convictions (or the coerced confessions known as "plea bargains"), regardless of the guilt or innocence of the accused; "government" courts constantly release people who still pose an obvious danger to others, while keeping millions of people locked up who have harmed no one; the "government" prison system, because of how prisoners are degraded, abused, and assaulted, by "guards" as well as other inmates, makes frustrated, angry people into people who are even *more* frustrated and angry, making innocent people into criminals, and making criminals into worse criminals. And the American people are coerced into funding that destructive system, whether they want to or not.

Another important point is that, in the case of a private protection company, if one "protector" becomes abusive, the reputation and career of every other protector depends upon exposing and routing out the thug. In contrast, it is now universally understood that "government" police forces will, first and foremost, protect their own. When one cop is caught doing something corrupt, "illegal," or violent, almost without exception, all of the other cops will help to cover it up or defend it. They function based upon gang mentality, because the people who are forced to pay their salaries are *not* the people they actually have to answer to. Like most "government" employees, they answer to the politicians, and view the general public as cattle, not customers. In contrast, the general public would view private defenders as their friends, their allies, and their employees, and more importantly, as their equals. They would not view them as an "authority" they must grovel before, nor as a constant potential threat to be feared. Everyone, including the hired protector, would recognize that the protector has no more rights than anyone else. Everyone would know that if a hired protector ever committed theft, or assault, or murder, he would be viewed and treated exactly as any other thug would be viewed and treated.

A genuine protector, who defends liberty and property, not only does not require a belief in "authority," he requires an *absence* of that belief. One who imagines himself to have the right to forcibly control everyone else — even if only in a "limited" way — is going to treat people accordingly. The "law enforcer" who hands out tickets for obscure infractions, detains and interrogates people without just cause, and seems always looking for a reason to interfere with people's daily lives, is not a protector, and deserves no respect or cooperation. A non-authoritarian protector, on the other hand, would be nothing more than a normal human being, with the same rights as everyone else, though perhaps more often armed and better trained in physical combat than most. He would be viewed as the neighbor to call if there is trouble, rather than the agent of a gang of thugs which, first and foremost, serves the ruling class. And the job of protector, absent any special "authority," power or status, would mainly attract those who truly want to protect the innocent, but would not attract those who merely want the chance to exercise power and control over others — a human short-coming which the job of modern "law enforcement" feeds. This is not to say that private protectors would never do anything wrong. They would still be human, capable of bad judgment, negligence, and even malicious intent, just like everyone else. However, they would not have "legal" *permission* to do wrong, and would have no "system," no "law," no "authority" which they could blame for their actions or which they could hide behind to avoid the wrath of their victims. If they ever acted as aggressors, retribution against them would be certain and swift. In a population that has given up the superstition of "authority," any group of protectors which decided to become a group of extortionists, thugs and tyrants would not be "voted" against, or sued, or complained about to some "authority." They would be shot. The only thing that allows for the prolonged, widespread oppression of any armed populace is the belief in "authority" among the *victims* of oppression. Without that, it is impossible to subdue or dominate them for long.

✳ *Deterrents and Incentives*

Some assume that, if not for "government," crooks would be free to do as they please without any repercussions. Again, this shows a profound misunderstanding of human nature, and of what "government" is. In truth, the belief in "authority" adds nothing to the effectiveness of any system of defense and protection.

People who use aggression against others, such as assault, theft, and murder, obviously are not restrained by their own morality or respect for the self-ownership of their victims. However, they may choose not to commit a particular crime if they imagine a risk of harm to themselves. That is called "deterrent." And deterrents, by definition, do not depend upon appealing to the conscience of the attacker, but instead make use of the attacker's instinct for self-preservation. To put it bluntly, the message which works on true criminals is not, "Do not do that, because it is wrong"; the message is "Do not do that, or you will get hurt." The supposed moral righteousness or "authority" of the threat against a would-be aggressor is irrelevant to the effectiveness of the deterrent. Whether it is a "police officer," a dog, an angry homeowner, or even another thief, the only question in the attacker's mind is whether he is likely to suffer pain or death if he attempts to rob or attack someone.

Deterrents to other types of bad behavior, which are not so severe or blatant as theft or assault, also do not require "authority." Some assert that without "government" inspectors and regulators, every business would be putting out shoddy, dangerous products. But such a claim is again based upon a profound misunderstanding of human nature and economics. No matter how greedy or selfish a businessman may be, he cannot be successful in the long run if he sells products which do not please his customers. Someone who knowingly sells a defective product, or tainted food, will have few if any customers. The many highly expensive "recalls" which many companies voluntarily carry out, even for relatively trivial defects or problems, attest to this fact. Unlike in the current situation, in which the power of "government" is used to prop up and protect irresponsible and destructive corporations, in a truly free market, with informed consumers and open competition, corruption and crime would not pay, and businesses would be unable to insulate themselves from the consequences of their irresponsibility.

"Government" inspectors and regulators are driven by the incentive to impose fines on people and to enforce "laws" and "regulations," regardless of whether they make any sense. In contrast, a system of private inspectors, which answers only to the people who want to know what is safe, and which has no enforcement power, has no incentive to interfere with business or to make up things to complain about. Businesses could *voluntarily* invite private reviews of their products or facilities, such as is already done by Underwriters Laboratories ("UL"), Consumer Reports and others, in order to be able to show the public an unbiased opinion of how safe and reliable their products are. Many companies do this today, on top of having to jump through all of the bureaucratic hoops which "governments" put in their way.

Many other matters could be handled in similar, non-authoritarian ways. Private building inspectors, already used by many realty companies, would have the job of determining, on behalf of potential buyers, how safe and sound a building is. In addition to private inspectors, restaurants could simply invite potential customers to examine their facilities themselves. All of these actions would be voluntary. A business could choose not to allow any inspections, and potential customers could choose whether or not to patronize that business.

The fact that so many things are assumed to be problems for "authority" to handle is a sign of intellectual laziness. Customers want quality products, and businessmen who want to be successful must provide quality products. It is in the interests of both, therefore, to be able to objectively demonstrate the quality of the products being offered. Contrary to the stereotype of the evil, greedy, profiteering business-man, the way to become rich in a free society is by providing products and services which actually benefit the customer. Almost all of the dishonest schemes that are profitable in the long term are those that are forcibly created or endorsed by "government," such as the "fractional banking" scam, the "legal" counterfeiting scam called "monetary policy," the litigation racket, and so on.

Even without "government" there would occasionally be serious conflicts. For example, suppose a factory was dumping toxic waste into a river, killing all the fish downstream on the property of others, which would constitute a form of trespass and property destruction. The absence of "authority" would not preclude the victims from doing anything about it; in fact, it may make it easier for them to do something about it. Instead of suing in a "government" court, where the judge can be bribed into supporting the billion-dollar business, the response might be something more effective, even if it appears less civilized. The people who live on the river may do something as simple as telling the factory-owner that if he keeps allowing his pollution to flow onto their properties, they will physically destroy his factory.

Obviously, there may be more polite, peaceful ways the problem could be solved, such as boycotts or publicizing the wrongdoing. Either way, the people can create an effective deterrent to improper behavior, *especially* when there is no "government" involved that can be paid off and corrupted. Many campaign contributions now amount to little more than bribes to have "government" regulators "look the other way." Likewise, "government" courts can easily find reasons to dismiss almost any lawsuit, thereby allowing wealthy criminals (the kind with real victims) to prosper.

The cliché of the greedy, evil businessman often omits the fact that large-scale crimes are usually done with the *cooperation* of "government" officials. Without protection from "government," even the most greedy, heartless businessman would have a huge incentive to not anger his customers to the point where they stop buying his products, or to the point where they react violently against him.

Most people, most of the time, would be reluctant to use force, knowing that they alone would bear both the responsibility and the risks of doing so. There would be a huge incentive to settle disputes and disagreements peacefully and by mutual agreement. When the belief in "government" is prevalent, on the other hand, there is *no* incentive to settle things peacefully, because winning the "political" battle poses no risk to those who advocate violence via "government." Without a ruling class to whine to, to legislatively impose some central agenda on everyone, people would be forced to deal with each other as rational adults, instead of as whiny, irresponsible children. People would be far better served by attempts at cooperation and peaceful compromise, than they are by fighting over who can get hold of the sword of "government." When bullying and aggression are no longer recognized as legitimate forms of human interaction, human beings will, out of necessity, learn to "play nice."

✳ *Anarchy in Action*

While many people dread the thought of "anarchy," the truth is that almost everyone experiences "anarchy" on a regular basis. When people go food shopping, or browse at the mall, they are seeing the results of non-authoritarian, mutual cooperation. No one is forced to produce any of the products offered, no one is forced to sell anything, and no one is forced to buy anything. Each person acts in his own best interest, and everyone involved — producer, seller and buyer — profits from the arrangement. All of the individuals benefit, and society in general benefits, without any coercion or rulers involved. There are countless examples of mutually voluntary, cooperative, peaceful, efficient and useful events and organizations that do not involve "government." Nonetheless, though there are a myriad of readily available examples of how efficient, organized and productive "anarchistic" interaction is compared to nearly all "government" endeavors, people still imagine that human beings interacting with each other as equals *all the time* would lead to chaos and mayhem.

When cars meet at a four-way stop, or when people pass on the sidewalk, that is "anarchy" in action. Billions of times every day, people take turns, leave room for others, and so on, without any "authority" commanding them to do so. Sometimes people are inconsiderate, but even then, only very rarely does a serious conflict occur — anything more serious than a rude gesture, or an angry word. Potential conflicts, from very minor things to more serious matters, happen billions of times every day, and in the vast majority of cases, they are resolved without violence, and without the involvement of any "authority." Even regarding more significant problems, people often find ways to reach mutual agreements. While organized, non-governmental methods of dispute resolution — using arbiters, investigations and negotiations — can peacefully solve even major disagreements, most conflicts of interest never get that far. Most people, most of the time, go out of their way to avoid, or quickly settle, potential clashes with others.

Though some people would point to such things as an indicator of the inherent goodness of mankind, there is often another factor at work. Most people simply do not want the hassles and the stress that comes with confrontations, and especially do not want the risks that come with *violent* confrontations. Many people "turn the other cheek" quite often, not necessarily because they are patient and loving, but simply to avoid being bothered with time-wasting, futile bickering. Many, when they encounter someone doing something obnoxious, simply "let it slide," because they have more important things to worry about. There is, in most people, a strong tendency to "get along," even if just for one's own benefit. And if there were no "authority" to run to—no giant mommy or daddy state to cry to—people would handle matters like adults far more often than they do now. This is not to say that every difference of opinion would end peacefully and fairly without "authority," but the *availability* of the giant club of "government" is a constant temptation to anyone who holds a grudge, or wants to hurt someone else, or wants to obtain unearned wealth via "litigation." If it were not there, fewer people would drag out or escalate disagreements or disputes. Whether because of charity, cowardice, or just a desire to avoid the headaches of a prolonged conflict, many people—even those who have a legitimate complaint against someone else—will simply let bygones be bygones, and get on with their lives.

Even without such examples it is utterly irrational to claim that people could not "get along" without "government," when everything "government" does, using violence and the threat of violence to control people, is the precise *opposite* of "getting along." The notion that peaceful coexistence requires aggression and coercion is logically ridiculous. The only thing that bringing "authority" into a situation guarantees is that there will *not* be a non-violent, peaceful resolution to the matter. When someone describes the society he wants to see, he will almost always describe a state of non-violence, of mutual cooperation and tolerance. In other words, what he will describe is the complete antithesis of the violence and coercion of "authority." Yet, having been raised to imagine "authority" to be a vital and positive part of society, people still constantly try to achieve peace by way of war, try to achieve cooperation by way of coercion, try to achieve tolerance by way of intolerance, and try to achieve humanity by way of brutality. Such insanity is the direct result of the people being taught to respect and obey "authority."

✳ *Anti-Authoritarian Parenting*

Parenting is so often based on authoritarianism that many cannot even image what non-authoritarian parenting would look like. It is important to clarify the effect that losing the "authority" superstition would have on parenting. It would not mean that parents would put no restrictions on what their children could do, nor would it rule out parents controlling children against their will in many situations. But it would dramatically change the mindset of both parents and children.

These days, teaching children right and wrong, and teaching them to obey, are seen by most people as the same thing. However, a parent can command a child to do something wrong just as easily as he can command him to do something right. Contrary to what authoritarian parenting teaches, the fact that a parent issued a command does not make it automatically right, and does not make the child obligated to obey. If, for example, a parent commands his child to shoplift, the child has no moral obligation to do so, and disobedience would be perfectly justified (though probably hazardous). Of course, the child might not understand that stealing is wrong, if his parents told him to steal.

On the other hand, a parent may impose a necessary, justified restriction on his child, which the child does not like and does not believe is justified. In either case, the child is only obligated to do whatever he deems right. The alternative would be that he has a moral obligation to do what he deems is wrong, which is impossible. This is where the difference lies: the authoritarian parent teaches the child that obedience, in and of itself, is a moral imperative, regardless of the command (e.g., "*Because I'm your father and I said so!*"). The non-authoritarian parent may also impose restrictions upon the child, but he does not demand that the child *like* it, nor does he pretend that such restrictions are just, simply because the parent imposed them. In other words, the non-authoritarian parent may see the need, because the child does not yet have the knowledge or understanding to be competent enough to make all of his own choices, to force certain restrictions upon a child (regarding bedtime, diet, etc.), but he does not claim that the child has any moral obligation to obey without question. The sooner the child can be taught the *reason* for a "rule," the sooner he can understand why doing what his parent says will benefit him. Of course, that is not always possible, especially when children are very young. The parent who stops the child from eating a box of candy is benefitting the child, who does not yet have enough understanding or self-control to serve his own interests. But to teach the child that he should feel a moral obligation to abide by rules which he sees as unfair, pointless, stupid, or even hurtful, just because "authority" told him to, is to teach that child the most dangerous lesson there can be: that he is morally obligated to put up with unfair, pointless, stupid, hurtful things if they are done by "authority."

To avoid passing on the "authority" superstition, parents should never cite "because I said so" as the reason a child should do something. The parent should express that there are rational reasons for the restrictions, even if the child cannot yet comprehend those reasons. In other words, the justification for the "rules" is not that parents have the right to forcibly impose any rules they want on their children, but that parents (hopefully) have so much more understanding and knowledge than the children that the parents must make many of a child's choices for him, until he becomes competent to make his own choices.

Even more important is how a parent controls his child's behavior toward others. It is extremely important to teach a child that it is inherently wrong to intentionally harm another person (except when necessary to defend an innocent). But if, instead of that principle, the parent teaches "obey me," and then commands the child not to hit others, he has taught the child obedience, but *not* morality. If the child refrains from hitting others, not because he understands that doing so is wrong, but only because he was told not to, then he is functioning in the same manner as an amoral robot, and has learned nothing about being a human being. The short-term practical result may look the same—i.e., the child refrains from hitting others—but the lessons learned are very different. When the child who was merely taught to obey grows up, and some other "authority" tells him that he *should* harm others, he almost certainly will, because he was trained to do as he is told. On the other hand, the child who was taught to respect the rights of others, and was taught the principles of self-ownership and non-aggression, will not lightly abandon those principles just because someone claiming to be "authority" tells him to.

Children learn by example. If a child sees his parents always acting as unquestioning subjects of a ruling class, the child will learn to be a slave. If, instead, the parents demonstrate in their daily lives how to use and to follow one's own heart and mind, the child will learn to do likewise. The child must understand that it is his duty, not merely to follow the rules of being a good person, but to figure out for *himself* what the rules of being a good person are. The standards which a "self-owner" lives by may still be described as "rules," but the worth of such "rules" does not come from the fact that an "authority" issued them, but because the individual believes that such "rules" describe inherently moral behavior. This is not to say that everyone agrees upon what is moral, though there is wide consensus on some basic principles. But even with each person's behavior guided by his own imperfect, incomplete understanding of right and wrong, the overall results would be drastically improved compared to the authoritarian alternative, in which basically good people do things they *know* to be wrong, because they feel compelled to do whatever "authority" tells them to do (as demonstrated by the Milgram experiments).

Again, though many people falsely assume that a society without a centralized, rule-making "authority" would mean "every man for himself," group cooperation and agreements do not require "authority," and those children who spend their formative years learning to interact with different people of all ages on a mutually voluntary basis, instead of learning to blindly do as they are told, are far better equipped to form relationships and enter into joint efforts based upon agreement, compromise and cooperation. Such voluntary interaction can take place between two people, or between two million. Even the limited freedom experienced by Americans has demonstrated that even extremely complex industries can be based entirely upon the willing participation and voluntary cooperation of everyone involved. And history has also demonstrated that the moment a method of organization based upon centralized, coercive control is used, such as occurs in a so-called "planned economy," productivity crashes, and poverty and enslavement appear. Yet most children are still raised in authoritarian environments, with the claim that that will best prepare them for life in the real world. In truth, it prepares them only for a life-time of enslavement.

Halfway There　　　✳

In any group of people that has given up the "authority" myth—whether they are just a small group of friends, or the inhabitants of a town, or the population of an entire continent—the frequency and severity of violent conflicts and acts of aggression *inside* that group will be dramatically lower than it is elsewhere, where most people, by way of "voting" and other "political" actions, advocate and perpetrate aggression on a regular basis. However, though the individuals in such a group would have little to fear from each other, they still would likely have to deal with acts of aggression from those outside of the group who still adhere to the belief in "government." An individual whose mind has been freed, but who still lives in a society plagued by the delusion of "authority," will be at constant risk of being the target of authoritarian aggression. Being free in one's mind—understanding the concept of self-ownership—does not necessarily cause one to be physically free. However, it can make an enormous positive difference, by opening up countless new means through which people can try to cope with, avoid, or even resist authoritarian attempts to control them.

The individual who takes pride in being a "law-abiding citizen" has only one way to even *attempt* to achieve freedom, which is almost never effective: begging his masters to change their "laws." On the other hand, one who understands that he owns himself, owes no allegiance to any supposed master, and needs no "legislative" permission to be free, has many more options. And the more people who have escaped the superstition, the easier avoidance or resistance becomes. For example, even a small number of "self-owners" can create channels of commerce which circumvent the usual controls and extortion schemes imposed by "governments."

Ironically, this entirely legitimate and moral form of voluntary interaction is often referred to as "the black market," or as doing business "under the table," whereas the usual system of aggression, coercion and extortion is viewed as legitimate and righteous by the believers in "government." In reality, the legitimacy of any trade (or any other human interaction) does not depend upon whether some "authority" knows about it and controls it, as the concept of "black market" implies, but depends only upon whether what occurs is mutually consensual. Those who understand this can find many ways in which to circumvent or defeat attempts by "government" to coercively control and exploit them.

Many acts of aggression done in the name of "the law" can be avoided or defeated fairly easily by a relatively small number of people, if they feel no automatic moral obligation to do as they are told. Of course, this is not always the case. If the gang called "government" does anything well, it is exerting brute force, whether in the form of military actions or domestic "law enforcement." However, in almost all cases, most of the power wielded by those in "government" is the result, not of guns and tanks and bombs, but of the *perceptions* of their victims. If 99% of a population obeys the ruling class out of a feeling of obligation or duty to do so, the remaining 1% can usually be controlled by brute force (with the approval of the 99%). But if a more substantial percentage of the population feels no duty to obey, the amount of brute force needed to control them becomes enormous. For example, many of the inhabitants of the United States now surrender about half of what they earn in "taxes" at various levels, and most feel obliged to do so; but if a foreign power somehow invaded and conquered the land, imposing a 50% "tax" would be utterly impossible because the people would feel no moral, legal, or patriotic duty to comply. Two hundred million workers would find two hundred million ways to use evasion, deception, secrecy, or even outright violence, to avoid or defeat such attempts by foreign thieves to enslave them.

Today, there is only one gang capable of oppressing the American people: the U.S. "government." This is because it is the one gang imagined by most people to have the *right* to coerce and control ("regulate"), and rob and extort ("tax") the American people. A common concern among statists is that without a strong "government" to protect them, some foreign power would just come in and take over. But such fears completely overlook how large a role *perception* plays in the ability to oppress. An area of land the size of the U.S., inhabited by a *hundred million* gun owners (in addition to a hundred million other people who would likely *become* gun owners if an invasion occurred) would be impossible to occupy and control by brute force alone. History gives many examples (e.g., the Warsaw Ghetto in World War II, the Vietnam War, the aftermath of the war in Iraq) of how even an enormous, technologically advanced standing army can be indefinitely frustrated by a relatively small number of armed "insurgents." And a land inhabited by "self-owners" has another huge advantage, in that it is literally *impossible* for them to collectively surrender. If there is no "government" pretending to represent the population, and no one who claims to speak on behalf of the people as a whole, there is literally no way for them to "give up," without each and every individual surrendering.

A good way to grasp the reality of the situation is to consider the matter from the perspective of the leader of the invaders. How would one even begin to try to invade and permanently occupy an area in which many millions of the inhabitants, who could be hiding anywhere, can kill anything within at least a hundred yards, as any decent hunter can do? An aspiring tyrant would have a far better chance of gaining power over the people by running for office, thereby obtaining the perceived right, in the minds of his victims, to rule and control them.

Large scale oppression, especially since the advent of firearms, depends a lot more on mind control than it does on body control. Those who crave dominion gain much more power by convincing their victims that it is *wrong* to disobey their commands than by convincing their victims that it is merely *dangerous* (but moral) to disobey.

No matter how much the people complain and protest, as long as the people obey "the law" (the commands of politicians), the tyrants have little to fear. As long as their attempts to control and extort are seen as "legal" acts of "authority," and as long as the people therefore feel an obligation to comply, unless and until the ruling class changes such "laws," the people will remain enslaved in body, because they remain mentally enslaved. Ironically, many people still believe that a strong "government" is the only thing that can protect the people as a whole, when the belief in "government" is actually the only thing which can *oppress* the people as a whole. Brute force alone cannot do it on any large scale, or for any prolonged period of time. Even a gang with tanks, planes, bombs and other weapons has no power to control an armed populace for long unless it first dupes the people into believing that it has the *right* to control them. In other words, only a gang imagined to be "authority" can get away with long-term oppression and enslavement. As a result, "government" (or the belief in it), instead of being essential to the protection of individual rights, is essential only for the prolonged and widespread *violation* of individual rights. Ironically, even most of those who recognize "government" as the biggest threat to liberty today still insist that "government" of some type is necessary for protection. The belief in "authority" is so strong that it can convince otherwise rational people that the very thing which routinely robs, coerces and assaults them is needed to *protect* them from robbery, coercion and assault. The fact that "government" has *always* been an aggressor, and has *never* been purely a protector, anywhere in the world at any time in history, does not shake them of their cult-like belief in the magical powers and virtues of the abstract, mythical entity called "authority."

✸ *The Road to Justice*

Many large-scale injustices in history would have quickly collapsed — or never would have started — if not for "authority" condoning and enforcing such injustices. The evils of slavery, for example, are often blamed on racism and greed, but "authority" played a huge role in making slavery economically feasible. If there was not a huge, organized network of "law enforcers" to capture escaped slaves, and any who helped them escape, how long would slavery have continued? If freeing slaves was not "illegal," and thus immoral in the eyes of authoritarians, how much larger and more effective would the "underground railroad" have been? In fact, it probably would not have been known as an "underground" anything, if it was not "illegal."

The "abolitionist" movement consisted of people who thought slavery was immoral, and who wanted the "laws" changed to officially *declare* slavery to be immoral and "illegal." If, instead of petitioning for a change in "laws," all the abolitionists were actively freeing slaves, the slave trade most likely would have collapsed decades earlier, if it ever happened at all. Shipping slaves halfway around the world would be a very risky business indeed if, the moment you landed, your "cargo" might be forcibly liberated. The problem is that most people believe that even immoral, unjust "laws" should be obeyed until the "law" is changed, showing that such people's loyalty to the myth of "authority" is stronger than their loyalty to morality, and doing what the masters tell them is more important to them than doing what they know is right. And mankind has suffered greatly because of it.

The ability of people to resist tyranny depends largely upon whether they accept the myth of "authority" or not. Those who can see the injustice committed by "government," but who continue to believe that they must "follow the law" and "work within the system," will never achieve justice. On the other hand, those who do not view the political megalomaniacs as rightful rulers, those who do not feel an obligation to obey an immoral "law," those who do not feel the need to treat what is actually a parasite class—a gang of political thieves and thugs—as untouchable, respectable and honorable, have a far better chance of defeating "legal" tyranny. (And most tyranny and oppression which has occurred throughout history was done "legally.")

There are many methods available to those willing to "illegally" resist injustice and tyranny, including everything from passive resistance, to non-violent sabotage, to things such as assassination and other forcible resistance. Depending upon the severity of the oppression, and the individual's own values, conscience, and beliefs about when (if ever) the use of violence is appropriate, one may choose any number of ways to defeat tyranny. Some will simply try to stay "under the radar," avoiding the attention of state enforcers. Some may choose civil disobedience, such as a large group openly smoking marijuana in front of a police station. Some may choose a more active, but non-violent method, such as slashing the tires of police cars, or destroying other property used to commit state aggression. Others may choose the method of openly violent resistance, such as occurred in the American Revolution.

By analogy, the intended victim of a robbery (the non-"governmental" kind) may try to evade the thief, or outsmart him, or even kill him if it comes down to that—

whatever it takes to avoid being victimized. Likewise, those who recognize that "legal" evil is still evil, and resisting it is still justified, would not waste time on elections and lobbying politicians for a change in legislation; they would simply do whatever they could to protect themselves, and possibly others, from being victimized by such "legal" aggression. Beyond a certain point, the more people who resist, the *less* violence is necessary to do so. If a local police force has a dozen "narcotics officers" — people whose main job is to commit acts of aggression against others who have used neither force nor fraud — and several hundred civilians let it be known that they believe that they have the right to use whatever it takes, including deadly force, to stop any attempted kidnappings, home invasions, or similar acts of aggression committed by "narcotics officers," the aggressors (the police), if they did not have any bigger authoritarian gang to appeal to for help, would simply give up to avoid being exterminated. The deterrent effect that works against private criminals can work just as well against "government" criminals.

In India, Mahatma Gandhi and his followers used widespread passive disobedience to undermine British control of that country. Alcohol prohibition in the United States is another example of an immoral "law" that was basically *disobeyed* out of existence. The high levels of disobedience, along with the refusal of most jurors to give their blessing to the "legal" aggression, along with some acts of violent resistance (e.g., tarring and feathering "revenuers") made the immoral "law" unenforceable. The legislatures eventually repealed it in an attempt to save face, because having an unenforceable law on the books goes a long way toward destroying the ruling class's legitimacy in the eyes of its victims. Anywhere the people feel no moral obligation to comply with authoritarian demands, any "legal" acts of aggression can be ignored out of existence. When the number of self-owners is smaller, however, sometimes violence is necessary to defeat "legal" acts of aggression. (And if only a few people recognize the illegitimacy of "legal" oppression, forcible resistance often backfires.)

Where there is oppression, there is always violence. It is usually one-sided, with the agents of "authority" committing most or all of the violence. The man who passively cooperates while claiming to be against violence is in fact *rewarding* the violence of the state. When an act of aggression is committed — whether by "authority" or anyone else — non-violence, by definition, ceases to be an option. The only question is whether the aggressive violence will go unchallenged, or whether defensive force will be used to counter it. Either way, violence will occur.

Of course, the thieves, thugs and murderers who declare their crimes to be "legal"—which every tyrant in history has done—will always brand any who resist them as criminals and terrorists. Only those who feel no shame at being labeled "criminals," because they have shed the myth of "authority" and recognize that the term "law" is often used to try to characterize something evil as something good, have any chance at all of achieving freedom. Again, somewhat ironically, the more people there are who understand self-ownership and the mythical nature of "authority," and who are willing to fight for what is right, and fight against what is "legal" but wrong, the *less* violent the road to true civilization (peaceful coexistence) will be.

Side Effects of the Myth ✳

Looking back in history, there is no shortage of examples of man's inhumanity to man, examples of oppression and suffering, violence and hatred, and situations and events which do not reflect well on the human race in general. And, though many of the most blatant injustices in history were the obvious product of the belief in "government," such as war and overt oppression, many other injustices which are not usually attributed to "government" action would also have been impossible without the involvement of "authority."

In addition to the example of whether slavery could have existed had it not been "legally" enforced (as mentioned above), similar questions could be asked about the treatment of the American Indians. If not for the authoritarian "government" edicts and the state mercenaries to enforce them, would there have been such a large-scale, concerted effort to exterminate or forcibly evict the natives from the lands they had inhabited for generations? No doubt there would still have been smaller conflicts due to the clash of cultures and demands for farming and hunting lands, but would it have been in anyone's personal interest to engage in large-scale violent combat?

After open slavery was ended in the United States (at about the same time that "legal" slavery, the "income tax," first came into being), racial tensions and violent conflicts continued. Many believe that "government" then came along and saved the day. In reality, violent conflict between the races was *encouraged* by "authority." For many years racial segregation was forcibly imposed via "laws." Ironically, racial tensions were later exacerbated further by "government"-mandated *integration*, which sought to coerce people of different races and cultures to mix, whether they wanted to or not. Again, the result was violence. During the entire fiasco, some schools and businesses, if left in freedom, would have chosen segregation and some would have chosen integration. If not for "government" trying to forcibly impose one "official policy" on everyone, parents could simply have chosen which schools to send their children to (segregated or not), and shoppers could simply have chosen which businesses to patronize (segregated or not). Not only was much of the violence committed against blacks done directly by "government" enforcers ("the police"), but even much of the privately committed violence was the result of anger over people being forced by "government" to deal with people of another race and culture. It is silly to think that *forcing* people apart, or *forcing* people together, will make people happier, nicer, or more open-minded and tolerant. In neither case was the peace or security of either race served by authoritarian intervention. While it is impossible to say exactly how widespread or prolonged segregation and racism would have been without "government" involvement, it is common sense that if people of all races and religions are allowed the freedom to choose who to associate with, it is at least *possible* for very different cultures to peacefully coexist. But when "government" gets involved, and the debate is between forcing races to remain separate, or forcing races to mingle, obviously someone will be angered either way.

This is not to say that every point of view is equally valid. The point is that people of vastly different world views—however wise or stupid, open-minded or bigoted, informed or ignorant their views may be—can usually coexist peacefully, even in close proximity, *unless* "government" gets involved. Different people may not like each other, may not approve of each other's beliefs and lifestyles, and in fact may harshly criticize or condemn other cultures. But that does not mean they cannot peaceful coexist, with both sides refraining from violent aggression. But whenever "government" gets involved, the coercion inherent in all "law" makes certain that people will *not* just "get along."

Another example of the indirect, deleterious effects of "government" action is the fact that the violence associated with the "drug trade" (the production and distribution of "illegal" substances) exists only because of "narcotics laws." By "outlawing" a substance, or a behavior, even when all of the participants are willing adults, the politicians create a black market, which not only has a huge profit potential due to limiting the supply, but creates a situation which specifically deprives customers and suppliers of any "legal" protection. For example, if a drug dealer is robbed or assaulted, by the police or by anyone else, he is unlikely to call "law enforcers" to help him. "Outlawing" something consensual—whether it be prostitution, gambling, or drug use—almost guarantees that the market will be controlled by whichever gang is the most violent, or has paid off the most cops and other officials. Again, a perfect "before and after" example of this was alcohol prohibition in the United States. When alcohol became "illegal" it was immediately taken over by organized crime, which was renowned not only for its violence but also for its ability to bribe "government" agents and officials. When alcohol became "legal" again, all of the related violence stopped almost instantly.

Despite that crystal clear example of the horrible results of enacting "laws" to prohibit "vices," most people still support "laws" against behaviors and habits they find distasteful. As a result, the related violence continues. Instead of being recognized as a problem which exists *because* of "government" and its "laws," it is still imagined to be a problem which "government" must fight against. The same could be said of the infamous violence of loan sharks, who deal with "illegal" gambling, and the violence of "pimps" in places where prostitution is "illegal." In such cases, even better than a "before and after" comparison is a side-by-side comparison: does gambling lead to more violence in Atlantic City, where it is "legal," or in places where it is "illegal"? Does prostitution pose a bigger threat to all involved in Amsterdam, where it is "legal," or in all of the places where it is "illegal"? This is not to say that prostitution, gambling and drugs (including alcohol) are good things, but that, good or bad, introducing the coercion of "government" into the situation does not do away with such "vices," but only makes them *more* dangerous for everyone involved, and often for people who are *not* involved.

Lest anyone still imagine that such "vice laws" are the result of good intentions, the politicians are well aware that gambling, prostitution, and "illegal" drug use still occur in "government" *prisons*. The politicians know full well that if even constant captivity, surveillance, random searches and harsh punishments cannot prevent such behaviors in people who are kept in closely monitored cages, "laws" obviously cannot eradicate such behaviors from an entire country. But they can, and do, supply tyrants with a ready excuse for ever-expanding power, and that is exactly why "governments" enact "vice" laws to begin with: to *create* "crime" where there was none, in an attempt to justify the existence of authoritarian power and control.

In a world without the myth of "authority," many people (including this author) would still strongly disapprove of drug use, prostitution, and other "vices," but they would be unlikely to support efforts to have such behaviors violently suppressed. Not only would they usually feel unjustified in advocating violence if they did not have the excuse of "authority" to hide behind, but they would be unlikely to want to provide the billions of dollars necessary to wage a large-scale, violent campaign against such widespread activities. Even the most judgmental person would have both economic and moral incentives to leave others in peace, as well as the fear of retaliation from any he chose to commit acts of aggression against. Of course, open criticism of lifestyles and behaviors, and attempts to persuade people to change their ways, are a perfectly acceptable part of human society. In fact, if people had to try to use reason and verbal persuasion to win people over, instead of using the brute force of "government," perhaps the targets would be more open to listening. At the very least, people would no longer turn an issue of bad habits into an issue of bloodshed and brutality, as happens now with all attempts to "legislate" morality.

The flip side to the notion that, "If it's illegal, it must be bad," is "If it's legal, it must be okay." Perhaps the biggest example of this is the fact that, in 1913, the U.S. "government" not only "legalized" slavery via the "income tax," directly and forcibly confiscating the fruits of people's labor, but also, by way of the Federal Reserve Act, legalized a level of counterfeiting and bank fraud which boggles the mind. In short, the politicians gave bankers "legal" permission to make up money out of thin air, and to loan such fake, fabricated "money" out, at interest, to others, including "governments." Though most people are unaware of the specifics of how such huge frauds and robberies occur via "fiat currencies" and "fractional reserve banking," many people now have a gut instinct that "the banks" are doing something deceptive and corrupt. What they fail to realize is that it was "government" which gave the banks *permission* to defraud and swindle the public out of literally trillions of dollars.

Another particularly controversial example of how a debate of "legality" can trump a debate about facts and morality is the issue of abortion. One side lobbies for "authority" to make or keep abortion "legal," and then defends the practice based upon its "legality." The other side pushes for abortion to be "outlawed," in the hopes of having the violence of "authority" used to prevent the practice. In logical terms, the only relevant question, which is a religious/biological/philosophical question, not a "legal" question, is: At what point does a fetus count as a person? The answer to that question dictates whether abortion amounts to murder, or is the equivalent of having a kidney removed. However, instead of addressing the only question that actually matters — as complex and controversial as it may be — both sides usually focus instead on trying to get the violence of "authority" on their side.

As another example of "legalized" injustice, almost everyone is aware of how outrageous and irrational "lawsuits" have become (e.g., trespassing criminals successfully suing property owners after injuring themselves during a break-in), but they fail to realize that it is the decrees of "government"-appointed "judges" which allow it to happen at all. In addition to "government" being able to "legally" steal from one person to give to another, "government" also creates, via the current system of litigation, a mechanism whereby one person can directly and "legally" rob another.

"Laws" in the name of environmentalism are also used for immoral power-grabs in both directions. With enough money, a company which is actually polluting, and thus infringing on the property rights of others, can trade "campaign contributions" for "legal" *permission* to pollute. At the same time, they can use environmental "laws" to crush competition, by creating and enforcing a maze of environmental "regulations" — many of them unnecessary or counter-productive, sometimes idiotic — to keep smaller companies out of the market. Additionally, politicians can use vague threats of environmental dangers as excuses to gain control of private industry, to control the behavior of millions, or to extort more money for their own purposes.

In many industries, success now depends less upon providing a valuable service at a reasonable price than it does upon obtaining special favors and preferential treatment from "government." This can be in the form of direct handouts (e.g., grants or subsidies), political trading (e.g., no-bid "government" contracts), licensing schemes (such as in the medical industry), tariffs on international trade, regulatory control and favoritism, and many other means. The results of all of these — higher prices, inferior products and services, fewer choices, and so on — is often assumed to be the result of the short-comings of private industry, instead of being recognized for what it is: the adverse consequences of authoritarian control over human interaction.

Another example of a side effect of authoritarianism is the fact that major economic crashes are *always* the result of "government" tampering with commerce, credit and currencies. Short of total physical destruction, the only way to destroy an entire economy is to meddle with the medium of exchange, the "money," through "legalized" counterfeiting, via the issuance of fabricated credit and the issuance of fiat currency. Most people, being ignorant of even basic economics, view inflation and other economic problems as natural, unfortunate but unavoidable occurrences. In truth, they are symptoms of large-scale, "legalized" fraud and theft.

Immigration "laws" give another example of indirect damage and secondary problems caused by "government." Aside from the obvious direct coercion involved, such "laws" cause other problems that would not exist otherwise, including: 1) the lucrative, often vicious racket of smuggling "illegals" into the country; 2) "illegals" being easy targets for human trafficking and other forms of exploitation, because they do not dare to speak out or seek help; 3) "illegals" having trouble finding useful, gainful employment, and therefore resorting to theft, because they cannot "legally" be employed; and 4) people being forced to live under tyrannical regimes, because they cannot physically escape. More generally, because "illegals" are classified as "criminals" and often viewed as "undesirables" simply for being in the country, and receive neither respect nor protection from much of the citizenry, there is less of an incentive for them to try to fit in or otherwise behave in a "law-abiding" manner.

Even many problems that seem to be non-governmental in nature exist because of some "law." Of course, there are, and always will be, instances of fraud and theft committed by unscrupulous individuals acting on their own, but most people are completely unaware of how many seemingly private swindles, schemes and rackets are not only allowed by "authority," but encouraged and *rewarded* by the "laws" of "government," whether intentionally or accidentally. Having no truly free market to compare it to, many continue to assume that state coercion is necessary, when all it actually does is hinder and interfere with human productivity and progress.

✳   *What Society Could Be*

It is impossible to even begin to imagine in how many ways history would have been different if the superstition of "authority" had collapsed long ago. Obviously the atrocities of Nazi Germany, Stalin's Russia, Mao's China, Pol Pot's Cambodia, and many more, would never have happened. Furthermore, while there could still be violent regional cultural or religious clashes, large-scale wars simply could not and would not happen without soldiers blindly obeying a perceived "authority." If the enormous amount of resources, effort and ingenuity that have been poured into mass destruction (war) had been put into something productive, where would we be today? If, instead of spending such a huge amount of time and effort struggling over who should have the reins of power and what that power should be used for, people had spent all those years being inventive and productive, what might the world now look like? What if every person had been allowed to support what he wanted, instead of having "government" robbing everyone and then having a never-ending argument over how those "public funds" should be spent? What if, instead of arguing over which centralized, authoritarian plan should be forcibly imposed on everyone, people lived their own lives, and pursued their own dreams? Who can even imagine how far humanity as a whole could have progressed by now?

This is not to say that without the belief in "authority" personal conflicts would never arise. They would, and they would sometimes end in violence. The difference is that, with the belief in "government," they *always* end in violence (or threats of violence), because coercion is all that "government" ever does. Whereas people, even people of very different viewpoints and backgrounds, can usually find ways to peacefully coexist, any situation which "authority" becomes involved in is automatically "solved" by force.

With the issue of "same-sex marriage," what if, instead of an ongoing argument over what views and choices should be forced upon everyone, every church minister, every employer, and every other individual, could decide for himself how to live, what he wants to call "marriage," and so on? With the issue of "prayer in school," what if, instead of "government" creating a hostile conflict by forcibly confiscating money from all property owners to fund one big, homogeneous "public" school system, each person (Christian, Jewish, Muslim, atheist, etc.) was allowed to choose which schools, if any, he wanted to support? This does not mean that people of different views would like each other, or end up believing the same things. It does mean that *without* believing the same things, they could still peacefully coexist — a situation which "government" does not allow. What if, instead of "government" agencies deciding what drugs and medical treatments it would "legally" allow people to try, and which practitioners would be "licensed" to practice, people could make their own choices? (In such a scenario, the business of providing customers with unbiased information about various products and services would flourish.)

"Government" solutions are always about politicians deciding how to deal with different situations, and then forcibly imposing their ideas on everyone else. But it is neither morally legitimate, nor effective on a practical basis, to have politicians making everyone else's choices for them. And that is true of all sorts of aspects of human society. What would the world look like if, for the past hundred years, instead of arguing over how to forcibly *limit* people's options (which is what every "law" does), people had spent their time and effort trying new ideas, and coming up with new approaches to problems, each person having been allowed to devote his own time, effort and money to whatever he personally chose to support?

What if, instead of a centralized system of forced wealth redistribution ("government welfare"), people had been left in freedom to decide for themselves the best, most compassionate ways to help the needy? Instead of a system that rewards laziness and dishonesty, and breeds dependency, we might have a system that actually helps people. What if, instead of "government" forcing businesses to do whatever the politicians and bureaucrats declared to be "safe," people could come up with new ideas and inventions, set their own priorities, and make their own decisions about how to best protect themselves? What if, instead of having a centralized control machine trying to force people to be "fair," people could choose for themselves who to associate with, what deals to make, and so on?

Everything "government" pays for creates a conflict. Every "public" project—from "grants" given out by the "National Endowment for the Arts," to grants for certain studies or businesses, to schools, to parks, to everything else "public"—amounts to robbing thousands or millions of people, in order to give the money to a few people. Why would anyone expect everyone in an entire country—or even a hundred people—to all exactly agree on how their money should be spent? What if, instead of many *trillions* of dollars in spending power being diverted and hijacked every year to fund the agendas of politicians and their bureaucracies, that wealth had gone into whatever things the people who earned the money actually cared about, and wanted to support?

What if, instead of having an economy constantly dragged down by taxation, regulation, and the inflation caused by fiat currency manipulation, there was truly free exchange, each person investing the fruits of his labors on those things that he values and views as worthwhile? It is impossible to even imagine the levels of technology and prosperity that could be possible, just as people a hundred years ago could not have imagined all of the riches, comforts and conveniences we have today. Just as "the poor" today in the U.S. have many comforts and luxuries which even royalty did not have just a few decades ago, a truly free society could quickly lead to a level of widespread comfort and safety that few can now imagine. Working three hours a day, instead of eight, might become the norm. As the overall wealth increases, people could make very comfortable livings, even doing very menial tasks. With the potential for such abundance, providing the necessities of life for the sick or elderly—those with limited productive abilities—would no longer be a problem. Also, as society as a whole becomes richer, people can then afford to pay more attention to environmental concerns. (In contrast, when people are struggling to find enough food to feed themselves, they will hardly be concerned about the long-term well-being of the local flora and fauna.)

The amount of time, effort and ingenuity that has been hijacked by ruling classes around the world staggers the mind. Trillions upon trillions of dollars have been stolen by various "governments" and spent on conquering, subjugating, killing and destroying—creating not only injustice and suffering, but a gigantic net loss of wealth for humanity. Even state programs supposedly intended to help people are notoriously inefficient, wasteful, fraudulent and susceptible to corruption.

About a *third* of all the wealth produced in the United States every year is taken by the federal ruling class (and more is taken at the state, county and local levels). While some of that comes back to the general public, much of it is simply used up by the bureaucracies and machinery of "government," producing no value in the process. In fact, if a third of everything produced in the U.S. was immediately thrown into a landfill, instead of being given to the federal parasites, the people would be *richer* than they are now. This is because the state does not simply waste and use up productivity and wealth, but actually uses the wealth it steals to pay people to *not* be productive (e.g., Social Security, AFDC, food stamps, and other "welfare"), to pay people to produce things that no one wants (e.g., bureaucracies, "make-work" programs), to pay people to destroy wealth and property (e.g., the military), and to pay people to forcibly interfere with the ability of *other* people to be productive (via taxation, regulation, licensing, permits, zoning, the minimum wage, tariffs and trade restrictions, enforced monopolies, imprisoning non-violent, otherwise productive people, etc.). Add together the amount of productivity directly stolen by the state, *and* the amount of productivity the state forcibly prevents, and one can start to see a glimpse of the level of prosperity the whole world would enjoy if not for the giant economic dead weight known as "government," and the level of prosperity it *will* enjoy once the superstition of "authority" has collapsed.

What humanity could achieve, if not hampered by the myth of "government," staggers the imagination. This would include a drastic jump in material comfort and wealth for billions of people, and would mean an end to poverty and hunger throughout the world. (If not for taxes, regulations, and other "legal" obstacles, we already easily have the means to feed everyone on the planet.) It would also mean an end to debt for almost everyone. Without "legalized" banking fraud (e.g., the Federal Reserve system), and the continual "taxation" of income, property, trade and inheritance, people would be accumulating wealth, instead of barely treading water while enriching politicians and bankers. And an abundance of material wealth would make it so that people could spend most or all of their time and effort on things they love to do, rather than having to work long hours doing things they don't enjoy, just so they can have food and shelter. The lives of average people could be far more enjoyable and fulfilling, where now they are often tedious and stressful.

Ironically, the near utopian visions which many tyrants have promised (but never delivered), can and will eventually be achieved by the exact opposite: a truly free society, absent any rulers or centralized controllers. If not for the superstition of "authority," we would already be there. What if, for the last several thousand years, each person had minded his own business, and not tried to use "government" to force his ideas and priorities on others? What if, instead of a giant, centralized monster violently limiting everyone's choices and options, everyone's creativity and ingenuity, trying to force conformity and sameness, while draining the producers of their ideas and their wealth, different people and different groups had been trying new ideas, and figuring out the best ways to solve problems and create a better world, guided by their own beliefs and values?

Sadly, the idea still terrifies a lot of people, who still imagine that a world forcibly controlled by politicians would be more safe and civilized than a world inhabited by free human beings exercising free will and individual judgment. The fact is that those people who put their faith in "government" to make things work, though they are by far the majority, and though they may mean well, are the problem. As a result of their indoctrination into the cult of "authority," they continue to believe and push the profoundly insane idea that the only road to peace, justice and harmonious civilization comes from constant, widespread coercion and forcible "government" controls, perpetual oppression and enslavement done in the name of "law," and the sacrificing of free will and morality at the altar of domination and blind obedience. As harsh as that may sound, that is the basis of *all* belief in "government."

Accepting Reality ✷

Statists often say, "Show me an example of where anarchy (society without government) has worked." Of course, since they are speaking of societies consisting almost entirely of thoroughly indoctrinated authoritarians, human society without a ruling class is rarely even contemplated, much less attempted. Yet the statists use the fact that they have never tried true freedom — because the concept is completely foreign to their way of thinking — as proof that a stateless society "wouldn't work."

This would be akin to a group of medieval doctors who all use leeches for every ailment, arguing, "Show me one case where a doctor has cured a headache without the use of leeches." Of course, if none of them had ever considered any treatment other than leeches, there would not be an example of alternative methods "working." But this would be a testament to the ignorance of the doctors, not the ineffectiveness of treatments which have never been tried.

But the more important point is that "anarchy" — the absence of "government" — *is what is*. If the alleged "authority" upon which the entire concept of "government" relies is merely an illusion (as has been proven above), then saying that society cannot exist without "government" is exactly as reasonable as saying that Christmas cannot occur without Santa Claus. Society *already* exists without "government," and has from the beginning. It has been the people *imagining* an entity with the right to rule — *hallucinating* the existence of "authority" — which has made the story of mankind consist largely of oppression, violence, suffering, murder and mayhem.

ally, statists often point to the death and suffering which occurs when two or groups are fighting over who should be "in charge," label that as "anarchy" a. cite it as evidence that without "government," there would be chaos and death. But such bloodshed and oppression is the direct, obvious result of the belief in "authority," not the result of a *lack* of "government." It is true that, compared to life under a stable, entrenched authoritarian regime, life in a country where the people are fighting over who the new "authority" should be (via rebellions, civil wars, one nation conquering another, etc.) can be a lot more dangerous and unpredictable. As a result, people living in war-torn areas often wish only for there to be an end to the conflict, for one side to win and become the new "government." To such people, a stable "government" may represent relative peace and security, but the underlying cause of the oppression committed by stable regimes *and* the bloodshed which occurs during struggles for power is the belief in "authority." If no one believed in a legitimate ruling class, no one would fight over who should rule. If there was no throne, no one would fight over it. All civil wars, and nearly all revolutions, rest on the assumption that someone should be in charge. Without the superstition of "authority," there would be no reason for such things to happen at all.

By its very nature, "government" adds nothing positive to society. It creates no wealth and generates no virtue. It adds only immoral violence and the illusion that such violence is legitimate. Allowing some people to forcibly dominate all others— which is all that "government" ever does—does not contribute to society one speck of talent, or ability, or productivity, or resourcefulness, or ingenuity, or creativity, or knowledge, or compassion, or any other positive quality possessed by human beings. Instead, it constantly stifles and limits all of those things through its coercive "laws." It is destructive and insane to accept the notion that civilization requires the forcible limiting of possibilities, and the violent restraint of the human mind and spirit—that civil society can exist only if the power and virtue of every individual is forcibly overcome and suppressed by a gang of masters and exploiters—that the average man cannot be trusted to govern himself, but that politicians can be trusted to govern everyone else—that the only way for the morality and virtue of mankind to shine through is to crush the free will and self-determination of billions of human beings, and to convert them all into unthinking, obedient puppets of a ruling class, and a source of power for tyrants and megalomaniacs—that the path to civilization is the *destruction* of individual free will, judgment, and self-determination.

210

That is the foundation, the heart and soul, of the superstition called "authority." When people are ready to recognize that heinous lie for what it is, and begin to accept personal responsibility for their own actions, and for the state of society — and not one moment before — then true humanity can begin. People can desperately wish for "peace on earth" until they are blue in the face, but they will never see it, unless and until they are willing to pay the price, by giving up one tired, old superstition. The solution to most of society's ills is for you, dear reader, to recognize the myth of "authority" for what it is, give it up in yourself, and then begin efforts to deprogram and wake up all of the people you know who, as a result of their indoctrination into the cult of "authority"-worship, and in spite of their virtues and noble intentions, continue to support and participate in the violent, anti-human, destructive and evil oppression and aggression machine known as "government."

The Punch Line Revisited ✳

Contrary to what nearly everyone has been taught to believe, "government" is not necessary for civilization. It is not conducive to civilization. It is, in fact, the antithesis of civilization. It is not cooperation, or working together, or voluntary interaction. It is not peaceful coexistence. It is coercion; it is force; it is violence. It is animalistic aggression, cloaked by pseudo-religious, cult-like rituals which are designed to make it appear legitimate and righteous. It is brute thuggery, disguised as consent and organization. It is the enslavement of mankind, the subjugation of free will, and the destruction of morality, masquerading as "civilization" and "society." The problem is not just that "authority" *can* be used for evil; the problem is that, at its most basic essence, it *is* evil. In everything it does, it defeats the free will of human beings, controlling them through coercion and fear. It supersedes and destroys moral consciences, replacing them with unthinking blind obedience. It cannot be used for good, any more than a bomb can be used to heal a body. It is always aggression, always the enemy of peace, always the enemy of justice. The moment it ceases to be an attacker, it ceases to fit the definition of "government." It is, by its very nature, a murderer and a thief, the enemy of mankind, a poison to humanity. As dominator and controller, ruler and oppressor, it can be nothing else.

The alleged right to rule, in any degree and in any form, is the *opposite* of humanity. The initiation of violence is the *opposite* of harmonious coexistence. The desire for dominion is the *opposite* of love for mankind. Hiding the violence under layers of complex rituals and self-contradictory rationalizations, and labeling brute thuggery as virtue and compassion, does not change that fact. Claiming noble goals, saying that the violence is "the will of the people," or that it is being committed "for the common good" or "for the children," cannot change evil into good. "Legalizing" wrong does not make it right. One man forcibly subjugating another, no matter how it is described or how it is carried out, is uncivilized and immoral. The destruction it causes, the injustice it creates, the damage it does to every soul that it touches — perpetrators, victims, and spectators alike — cannot be undone by calling it "law," or by claiming that it was necessary. Evil, by any name, is still evil.

The ultimate message here is very simple. All of recorded history screams it, yet very few have, until now, allowed themselves to hear it. That message is this:

If you love death and destruction, oppression and suffering,
injustice and violence, repression and torture,
helplessness and despair, perpetual conflict and bloodshed,
then teach your children to respect "authority,"
and teach them that obedience is a virtue.

If, on the other hand, you value peaceful coexistence,
compassion and cooperation, freedom and justice,
then teach your children the principle of self-ownership,
teach them to respect the rights of every human being,
and teach them to recognize and reject
the belief in "authority" for what it is:
the most irrational, self-contradictory, anti-human,
evil, destructive and dangerous superstition
the world has ever known.